WAR SONGS AND POEMS
OF THE
SOUTHERN CONFEDERACY
1861-1865

GENERAL JOHN B. GORDON

To whose memory this volume is dedicated by the author.

WAR SONGS AND POEMS

OF THE

SOUTHERN CONFEDERACY

1861-1865

A collection of the most popular and impressive songs and poems of war times, dear to every Southern heart. Collected and retold with personal reminiscences of the war.

H. M. Wharton D. D.
Private in General Lee's Army

CASTLE BOOKS

This edition published in 2000 by Castle Books,
A division of Book Sales Inc.
114 Northfield Avenue, Edison, NJ 08837

Printed in the United States of America.

ISBN: 0-7858-1273-3

FORE-WORD

THESE songs and poems belong to
the Nation.

Although our friends at the North
will smile at some, wince at others, and
even have their blood warmed by one
here and there, they must not forget
that they were written by their brothers
and sisters during a family quarrel
when feeling was intense and the fight
hot and fast.

It is all over now; we are more
united than ever and shall never fall
out with each other again.

My object has been to rescue from oblivion, these productions of a people as brave and true as ever lived, and
yet within half a century forgetting the past, they have built
up their shattered fortunes, and side by side with the men
they had once fought, they stood in battle for the defense
of our glorious flag.

No North, no South, no East, no West, but one and
inseparable now and forever.

H. M. Wharton

PHILADELPHIA, March, 1904.

THE AUTHOR'S REMINISCENCES
OF WAR DAYS

STANDING forty years away from the terrible days of the early "sixties", we are able to look back now upon those times with cooler blood and calmer judgment. In all the history of the world there has not been a conflict in which there was greater generalship displayed or more courage, and sacrifice and devotion by the men and women at home or the soldiers in the field.

Never, while memory lasts, shall I forget a scene which transpired early in April, 1861, as our family sat at breakfast in the farm-house home in Culpepper County, Va. My oldest brother suddenly entered the dining-room and exclaimed, "The war has commenced ; Fort Sumter is being bombarded !" I was too young to understand these words, but saw, upon the faces of my father and mother, an expression which filled my heart with anxiety. Little did I know that our own beloved State was to become the battleground of the great struggle, and that our home should be left desolate, while some of the dearest members of that little circle around the breakfast table must soon be taken away forever.

THE COMING OF THE STORM

As to the causes of the War, there can be but little difference of opinion now. When the Union was formed, it was the determination of our forefathers that while many of the rights which would have been held by us as separate colonies should be given up, yet, there were other rights which must ever be held sacred, and among these, the special privilege of conducting our own affairs according to our own will and pleasure. The doctrine of States' Rights was really the beginning of the strife, which commenced years before war was

5

declared. It was well known, however, that the real provoking cause of war was the Negro. While Mr. Lincoln was not nominated or elected upon the platform of Abolition, yet it was a well-known doctrine of his party, and the people knew that the ultimate object of that party was to emancipate the slaves in the Southern States. The platform of the Republican party did claim, however, the privilege of prohibiting slavery in any new States and Territories that might come into the Union, and it was but a step from that position to a further determination to abolish slavery everywhere. Mr. Lincoln could never have been elected but for the fact that there was a remarkable and unprecedented division in the opposing parties. An example of this was found in my own family. My father, and one of my brothers, were for Breckenridge; another brother for Douglas, and still another supported the Bell and Everett ticket. This division and confusion pervaded the country everywhere, and although Mr. Lincoln lacked more than a million to give him the popular vote, he was elected. His election, of course, was the red rag to the Southern bull; it was the fire to the powder; and the very fact that he had to travel in disguise to take his seat at Washington, showed the red-hot condition of popular feeling.

South Carolina, small, impulsive, brave, was the first to take her stand, declaring her right to withdraw from a Union into which she had entered of her own free will and accord. Other States followed in rapid succession and excitement was at high tide.

OLD VIRGINIA'S STAND

All eyes were turned to Virginia, ever regarded the strong, proud, old Commonwealth which had given to the Union its greatest leaders, and whose sons had been first and foremost in peace as well as in war—not only to declare her rights, but to stand to them, and, if necessary, to fight and die for them. A convention was called to meet at Richmond, Virginia, and no sooner had they assembled and the sense of the meeting ascertained, than it was discovered that the great majority were for remaining in the Union, and standing by the Flag of our Country. Mr. Lincoln, at this time, occupied a most unenviable and desperate situation. The people of the South were defiant, and declared their purpose to resist any invasion of their rights. A certain party of the North just as violently declared that the Southern States had no right to secede, and should be forced back into the Union. With these flaming declarations they goaded the new President from day to day. Mr. Lincoln finally yielded, and called for 75,000 troops from the different States to suppress the rebellion. Virginia, being still in the Union, was called upon for her quota. Quick as a flash the sentiment of the great Convention at Richmond changed from a strong determination to remain in the Union, to an immediate decision to withdraw from the United States. See what the Old Commonwealth had to face ! She was called upon to take up arms against her sister States in the South ; nor did she wait or hesitate for one moment but cast in her lot "for weal or woe" with those who were bone of her bone, flesh of her flesh; blood of her blood ; and her most distinguished son and ablest military general of his day, or of any day, who was at that time offered the command of the United States forces, presented his sword to the authorities at Washington, and turned his back upon all that had been dear to him as a citizen and a soldier, and offered his services to his own State and his loved Southland. That man was Robert Edward Lee, whose name grows more precious, not only to the South, but to the North, and to all the world as years roll on.

Events transpired in rapid and bewildering succession. Great trains loaded with soldiers followed in sight of each other along the railways. Armies were established at points where the struggle would likely be the most severe, and of these places, Manassas, a little railway station not far from Alexandria, Virginia, was early chosen. The battle of Bull Run on the 18th of July, and the first battle of Manassas on the 21st, just three days later, have gone forth to the world in the annals of war as the decisive struggles of two great armies. It has been thought, and with much reason, that if the initial victories of the Southern forces on these occasions had been followed up, the war would have ended; but four long weary years must follow, and hundreds and thousands of the best men of the land must die, countless homes be made desolate, and the whole country utterly laid waste and ruined.

MY FATHER'S FAMILY IN THE WAR

Our family remained in the County of Culpepper until about the middle of the war. God took our dear mother from us; the older boys had to go to war and father was alone with his daughters and myself, I being the youngest child. As I was under age, and not large enough to be noticed, I was often in conversation with Federal officers, and also with those from the South. One army or the other seemed almost incessantly passing to and fro through our part of the State. It was my privilege to witness the battle of Cedar Mountain, which was fought two miles from my father's home, and the next day I rode over the field in company with him to see if we might, in any way, minister to the wants of the wounded and suffering. It was my first study of a battle field, and the impression made upon my mind, when I saw hundreds of men lying in every position—the most of them dead, others wounded and dying—can never be removed. It was a matter absolutely incomprehensible to me, that men should kill each other as they had done on the bloody field, and I wonder at it to this day.

I was standing in my father's yard when Pope's army commenced its retreat. Several stragglers came in to get a drink of water, and I inquired of them which way they were going. They answered, " Back where we came from." I asked them who was in command on the other side the day before. The reply was, " That man Jackson; his name is better than

10,000 men any day." Another conversation occurred about this time with reference to General Jackson. Several Federal officers who had been in the fight the day before, were discussing the point whether General Jackson was a Christian. One said, " I do not believe he is a Christian, for if he was he would not be such a devil of a fighter;" the other said, " I do not know whether he is a Christian or not ; but there is one thing certain, if ever he makes up his mind to go to Heaven all hell can't keep him from it." Such was the impression that Stonewall Jackson had made upon the men of the Federal Army. He was a Christian indeed, and when he fell asleep in the arms of victory at Chancellorsville, his last words gave evidence that he had gained another and greater triumph— " Let us cross over the river, and rest under the shade of the trees."

IN THE BREASTWORKS BELOW PETERSBURG

The second day of April, 1865, found me in the breastworks below Petersburg on the Appomattox River,—a boy of sixteen, and a soldier in an army of 40,000 men opposing fully five times that many on the other side. Our attenuated line, which was "long drawn out," extended from beyond Richmond on the one side to miles below Petersburg on the other. These lines were very close together, so close indeed, that we could easily hear the rumbling of wagons within the lines of the Federal Army. Often I have sat at night and witnessed an artillery duel of the batteries, as the flaming messengers of death passed each other in the night air on their mission of destruction. It was Sunday, the second day of April, 1865, when orders came to us to be ready at once to march. It does not take a soldier long to pack his goods and chattels, nor does he have to tarry for many courses at his morning meal. Suffice it to say, we were soon under way, we knew not whither, though the impression on our minds was that it would be to advance, and we should soon be in the thick of the fight.

Our surprise and humiliation may be more easily imagined than described, when our faces were turned away from the enemy's lines, and the firing in the rear told us we were hotly pursued. One solid week of fighting and marching followed. Our soldiers were hungry, sleepless and dispirited. It is no mere war story to say that for days we had nothing to eat, the exception being an ear of hard corn, or, on one occasion, an ox shot down in a pasture, we carved him with our pocket-knives as we passed on the rapid march, and at the first halt broiled on a hastily made fire the raw morsel we had captured. I remember distinctly when nearing Farmville, we crossed a high bridge, one end of which was on fire, and a little beyond as we walked along the road, I went into such a sound sleep, marching with my musket on my shoulder, that I fell, and was only awakened when my tired body struck the earth. Still on we went, with never a thought of anything but victory. The battle of Sailor's Creek is well-known to have been one of the severe fights we had as we went on our way.

GENERALS LEE AND GORDON

General John B. Gordon, of Georgia, a valiant soldier who never knew a fear, and whose splendid patriotism dazzled the eyes of the world; the man who flung himself in front of General Lee's horse, and seizing the bridle turned him back to the rear, then hastening to the front, led the charge himself; the man whose military record was not greater than his record as a follower of Jesus Christ—the now sainted Gordon, I am proud to say, was my commander. Never in all my life, have I known a sweeter spirit, or a nobler character: he has been in my home, held my baby upon his knee, and delighted the household with his words of faith and wisdom, and whether he was delighting a little family circle, or charming and thrilling an immense audience, he was always the same simple-hearted nobleman. To-day, he lives in the hearts of millions of his countrymen, North and South, for be it said to his praise, his great heart was as large as his country, and having fought the battle with uncompromising loyalty, he was as faithful in the hour of surrender, as he was in the day of victory.

A little incident occurred in a fight one day which General Gordon loved to tell. In the course of his splendid lecture— " The Last Days of the Confederacy," he said that one day he discovered a private soldier running to the rear as fast as ever he could go. Calling to him at once General Gordon said, " What are you running for? " " I am running because I can't fly," he answered, and went right on. If ever a man had excuse for running, it surely must have been on occasions like that when trying to escape the storm of shot and shell.

But the end came at last, and on Sunday, the ninth day of April, 1865, as we stood on the battle ground facing the line of the Federal forces, orders came to us to stack arms. It could not have been more thoroughly understood if a book had been written on the subject. Stack arms on the battle field, and in the very face of the enemy! It could mean but one thing, and that was surrender. Many of us felt as General Wise expressed himself when coming out of the camp that morning to the roadside, having washed his face in a mud hole, and could hardly therefore be recognized, he saw General Lee passing, and called to him saying, " General Lee, they tell me you have surrendered. Is it true? O! is it true? " General Lee replied, " General Wise, I am on my way now to arrange the terms of surrender with General Grant." General Wise lifted both hands above his head and said, " O! Lord, what shall I do? What shall I do? " General Lee replied in a quiet tone, " General Wise, I would suggest that you go and wash your face." This little story was given to me one night at a Confederate Veterans' Camp, in the City of Baltimore by Colonel Marshall, the aide and friend of General Lee.

It was a revelation to us (I think there were not more than 8,000 who reached Appomattox) when the salutes began to be fired.   The sound of artillery was all around us, and we discovered for the first time that General Grant's entire army encompassed us.   But the end had come, and we accepted the situation and determined to abide by the decision of our great General.   It is a fact, well-known, that strong influence was brought to bear upon General Lee at that time to prolong the war, as the Boers have since done in South Africa, and there is no telling to what extent it might have been carried on. But with far-seeing wisdom, he determined that the proper course to pursue was for the men to surrender forever the cause for which they had so earnestly fought, and go back to their homes, and to the support of their families, as loyal citizens of the United States.   So deep was the impression of the famous " General Order No. 9 ", that many of us carry much of it in our memories from that day to this.   The first words set forth in full the whole situation : " After four years of arduous service, marked by unsurpassed valor and devotion, the army of Northern Virginia has been compelled to yield to overwhelming numbers and resources."   This, indeed, was the truth of our position, and when we surrendered we ended forever our opposition to the Union.

THE LOYALTY OF THE SOUTHERN PEOPLE

The loyalty of the Southern people has been clearly shown from that day to this, nor have the most skeptical doubted their sincerity since the days of the Spanish-American War, when the men of the South rushed to the defense of our Flag with the same patriotism and courage as the men of any other section of this great country.   So thoroughly was our country cemented together, and so completely were old animosities forgotten, that when William McKinley selected his men to lead our armies, he chose them from the South as well as from the North ; and to-day, if an American is asked for the heroes of that late war he does not hesitate as he mentions Dewey of Vermont, Fitzhugh Lee of Virginia, or Joe Wheeler of Alabama.   The great country is one, and will remain as it is now and forever. Like a fair woman who rests her head upon the snowy pillows of the North and bathes her feet in the placid waters of the Gulf of Mexico, her left hand extended to welcome the nations of the East, while her right unlocks the golden stores of the West, she is destined to lead the world to higher achievements, and more glorious conquest than has ever been known to the sons of men.

THE POETRY AND SONG OF WAR

A popular and characteristic feature of every war is its literature—in poetry and song. " The Marseillaise Hymn " stirred the heart of France as never before ; Cromwell, with his Puritans, went forth to battle singing their hallelujahs of praise ; who that lived amid the days of '61 does not remember the little Irishman, Harry McCarty, who went forth throughout the Southern States singing to the assembled multitudes " The Bonnie Blue Flag " until they went wild with excitement ? What soldier in the Southern States has not had every nerve thrilled as the band would strike up " Dixie ? " It is true that we cannot find much evidence of genius at such times, nor the productions of mature and thoughtful study. Such poems and songs are sparks of flame from the fires of war, and high literary merit must not be expected. But if you wish to find the hearts of the people you will hear it in their songs. It has been a delightful task to me in the past year to collect from all quarters of the South these songs and poems, and so to rescue from oblivion the productions which are dear to every Southern heart and home. Nor is it confined alone to the South, for in the North, and even in other lands, people listen with glad interest to the war songs of those days.

"THE BONNIE BLUE FLAG"

There is an incident of my own adventure connected with this song which brings to my mind some very pleasant associations, and goes to show how very popular the song is wherever it may be sung.

I was crossing the ocean a few summers ago, on the Anchor Line steamer *Furnesia*. It so happened that we found the Fourth of July out in mid-ocean, and determined to celebrate it. There being a great dearth of good speakers, the selection fell upon me to make the address, and I responded the best I could. Of course, I need not say it was eminently patriotic, and loyal to the Stars and Stripes. At the conclusion, however, I announced to my audience that I was the only Southern man on board ship, that I was an Ex-Confederate soldier, and if it pleased them, I would conclude my address by singing a Confederate War Song, thus giving them a piece of unwritten History. This announcement was received with applause, and I proceeded at once to sing with all my might, and the fervor of a true Southern heart, "The Bonnie Blue Flag." The clapping and cheering that followed gave unmistakable evidence that this song of the South was well received.

That day at dinner we had, of course, the usual patriotic meal—Columbia Soup, Star Spangled Banner Pudding, Stars and Stripes Ice Cream, etc.,—and at every plate, save mine, there was a small American flag, about 3 x 4 inches large. At my plate there was a Blue Flag with a White Star in the middle. Several hundred guests, seated at the table, had evidently been informed of the delicate little compliment that had been paid to me, and when I lifted the Flag from its place, a very pleasant greeting came from all who were present, and I proceeded to devour, with unusual delight, the dinner that was set before me.

It has been my purpose to cull from every State the most popular and impressive songs, and to lay them before the world not only for their present use and enjoyment, but to be handed down to generations yet to come. The old veteran will take this book, and with a voice, that may not be as strong or true as of forty years ago, will sing to his grandchild those hymns of the days of battle, while he lives over again the toil and strife for the cause he so truly loved. The walls of our school-houses will resound with declamations from these pages, and generations yet unborn will sing the songs of the great Civil War. I have no word to say in their praise, for none is needed; I have no apology to offer for presenting them to my own people of the South, because I know how gladly they will receive them. I only hope that the sweet spirit which now characterizes our great country will receive this book, and preserve these treasures as a part of the literature of our whole land, and not that of any particular people or section.

God bless our country, and carry us forward to peace and prosperity until the cry of victory over every enemy shall be heard amid the " hosannas " of the redeemed in Heaven,

H. M. WHARTON.

Residence in Richmond, Va., occupied by General Lee while
Commander-in-Chief of the Confederate Armies.

TABLE OF CONTENTS

2

* Also attributed to Wm. K. Randall.

GENERAL ROBERT E. LEE

THE BONNIE BLUE FLAG.

The first flag of the South was of solid blue with one white star.

The " Bonnie Blue Flag " was doubtless the most popular song of the war. The people sang it, the bands played it.

A little Irishman, Harry McCarty, went over the land singing it, and stirred the people as the Frenchman with the "Marseillaise hymn." Often I have heard him sing it when thousands of people went wild with excitement and enthusiasm. See incident described in Introduction.

WE are a band of brothers
  And native to the soil,
Fighting for the property
  We gained by honest toil ;
And when our rights were threatened,
  The cry rose near and far—
" Hurrah for the Bonnie Blue Flag
  That bears the single star ! "

CHORUS.

Hurrah ! hurrah !
  For Southern rights hurrah !
Hurrah for the Bonnie Blue Flag
  That bears the single star.

As long as the Union
  Was faithful to her trust,
Like friends and like brothers
  Both kind were we and just ;
But now, when Northern treachery
  Attempts our rights to mar,
We hoist on high the Bonnie Blue Flag
  That bears the single star.—*Chorus.*

First gallant South Carolina
  Nobly made the stand,
Then came Alabama,
  Who took her by the hand ;

23

Next quickly Mississippi,
  Georgia and Florida
All raised on high the Bonnie Blue Flag,
  That bears the single star.—*Chorus.*

        And here's to old Virginia—
          The Old Dominion State—
        With the young Confed'racy
          At length has linked her fate,
        Impelled by her example,
          Now other states prepare
        To hoist on high the Bonnie Blue Flag
          That bears the single star.—*Chorus.*

Then here's to our Confed'racy,
  Strong are we and brave,
Like patriots of old we'll fight
  Our heritage to save.
And rather than submit to shame,
  To die we would prefer ;
So cheer for the Bonnie Blue Flag
  That bears the single star.—*Chorus.*

        Then cheer, boys, cheer ;
          Raise the joyous shout,
        For Arkansas and North Carolina
          Now have both gone out ;
        And let another rousing cheer
          For Tennessee be given,
        The single star of the Bonnie Blue Flag
          Has grown to be eleven.—*Chorus.*

"The Bonnie Blue Flag."

"MARYLAND! MY MARYLAND!"

These are the familiar airs to which the boys used to sing their favorite songs.
The words are found in their proper places.

THE CONFEDERACY.

By Jane T. H. Cross.

Born in a day, full-grown, our Nation stood,
  The pearly light of heaven was on her face
Life's early joy was coursing in her blood;
  A thing she was of beauty and of grace.

She stood, a stranger on the great broad earth,
  No voice of sympathy was heard to greet
The glory-beaming morning of her birth,
  Or hail the coming of the unsoiled feet.

She stood, derided by her passing foes;
  Her heart beat calmly 'neath their look of scorn;
Their rage in blackening billows round her rose—
  Her brow, meanwhile, as radiant as the morn.

Their poisonous coils about her limbs are cast,
  She shakes them off in pure and holy ire,
As quietly as Paul, in ages past,
  Shook off the serpent in the crackling fire.

She bends not to her foes, nor to the world,
  She bears a heart for glory, or for gloom;
But with her starry cross, her flag unfurled,
  She kneels amid the sweet magnolia bloom.

She kneels to Thee, O God, she claims her birth,
  She lifts to Thee her young and trusting eye,
She asks of Thee her place upon the earth—
  For it is Thine to give or to deny.

Oh, let Thine eye but recognize her right!
  Oh, let Thy voice but justify her claim!
Like grasshoppers are nations in Thy sight,
  And all their power is but an empty name.

Then listen, Father, listen to her prayer!
    Her robes are dripping with her children's blood;
Her foes around "like bulls of Bashan stare,"
    They fain would sweep her off, "as with a flood."

The anguish wraps her close around, like death,
    Her children lie in heaps about her slain;
Before the world she bravely holds her breath,
    Nor gives one utterance to a note of pain.

But 'tis not like Thee to forget the oppressed,
    Thou feel'st within her heart the stifled moan—
Thou Christ! Thou Lamb of God! oh, give her rest!
    For thou hast called her!—is she not Thine own?

"ALL QUIET ALONG THE POTOMAC TO-NIGHT."

By Lamar Fontaine.

There was no poem written during the war that had a wider popularity than this.   It was set to music, and I have often heard it sung, so have many other old veterans.   I know the air, and wish I might be able to give it to you.   Some day when we meet, this will be one of the songs we shall sing.

"All quiet along the Potomac to-night!"
    Except here and there a stray picket
Is shot, as he walks on his beat, to and fro,
    By a rifleman hid in the thicket.

'Tis nothing! a private or two now and then
    Will not count in the news of a battle;
Not an officer lost! only one of the men
    Moaning out, all alone, the death-rattle.

All quiet along the Potomac to-night!
    Where soldiers lie peacefully dreaming;
And their tents in the rays of the clear autumn moon,
    And the light of their camp-fires are gleaming.

A tremulous sigh, as a gentle night-wind
    Through the forest leaves slowly is creeping ;
While the stars up above, with their glittering eyes,
Keep guard o'er the army while sleeping.

There's only the sound of the lone sentry's tread,
    As he tramps from the rock to the fountain,
And thinks of the two on the low trundle bed,
    Far away, in the cot on the mountain.

His musket falls slack, his face, dark and grim,
    Grows gentle with memories tender,
As he mutters a prayer for the children asleep,
    And their mother—" may heaven defend her ! "

The moon seems to shine forth as brightly as then—
    That night, when the love, yet unspoken,
Leaped up to his lips, and when low-murmured vows
    Were pledged to be ever unbroken.

Then drawing his sleeve roughly over his eyes,
    He dashes off tears that are welling ;
And gathers his gun closer up to his breast,
    As if to keep down the heart's swelling.

He passes the fountain, the blasted pine-tree,
    And his footstep is lagging and weary ;
Yet onward he goes, through the broad belt of light,
    Towards the shades of the forest so dreary.

Hark ! was it the night wind that rustled the leaves?
    Was it moonlight so wondrously flashing ?
It looked like a rifle : " Ha ! Mary, good-bye ! "
And his life-blood is ebbing and splashing.

" All quiet along the Potomac to-night ! "
    No sound save the rush of the river ;
While soft falls the dew on the face of the dead,
    And the picket's off duty forever !

DIXIE.

By Albert Pike.

Southrons, hear your Country call you !
    Up ! lest worse than death befall you !
      To arms ! to arms ! to arms ! in Dixie !
Lo ! all the beacon-fires are lighted,
Let all hearts be now united !
      To arms ! to arms ! to arms ! in Dixie !
            Advance the flag of Dixie !
              Hurrah ! hurrah !
        For Dixie's land we'll take our stand,
            To live or die for Dixie !
        To arms ! to arms !
            And conquer peace for Dixie !
        To arms ! to arms !
            And conquer peace for Dixie !

            Hear the Northern thunders mutter !
            Northern flags in South winds flutter !
              To arms ! etc.
            Send them back your fierce defiance !
            Stamp upon the accursed alliance !
              To arms ! etc.
              Advance the flag of Dixie, etc.

Fear no danger ! shun no labor !
Lift up rifle, pike, and sabre !
    To arms ! etc.
Shoulder pressing close to shoulder,
Let the odds make each heart bolder !
    To arms ! etc.
      Advance the flag of Dixie, etc.

            How the South's great heart rejoices
            At your cannon's ringing voices ;
              To arms ! etc.

For faith betrayed and pledges broken,
Wrong inflicted, insults spoken.
>   To arms ! etc.
>   Advance the flag of Dixie, etc.

>   Strong as lions, swift as eagles,
>   Back to their kennels hunt these beagles !
>   To arms ! etc.
>   Cut the unequal bonds asunder !
>   Let them hence each other plunder !
>   To arms ! etc.
>   Advance the flag of Dixie, etc.

Swear upon your country's altar,
Never to submit or falter ;
>   To arms ! etc.
Till the spoilers are defeated,
Till the Lord's work is completed.
>   To arms! etc.
>   Advance the flag of Dixie ! etc.

>   Halt not till our Federation
>   Secures among earth's Powers its station !
>   To arms ! etc.
>   Then at peace, and crowned with glory,
>   Hear your children tell the story !
>   To arms ! etc.
>   Advance the flag of Dixie ! etc.

If the loved ones weep in sadness,
Victory shall bring them gladness ;
>   To arms ! etc.
Exultant pride soon banish sorrow ;
Smiles chase tears away to-morrow.
>   To arms ! etc.
>   Advance the flag of Dixie ! etc.

GEORGIA, MY GEORGIA!

By Carrie Bell Sinclair.

Hark ! 'tis the cannon's deafening roar,
  That sounds along thy sunny shore,
And thou shalt lie in chains no more,
  My wounded, bleeding Georgia !
Then arm each youth and patriot sire,
Light up the patriotic fire,
And bid the zeal of those that ne'er tire,
  Who strike for thee, my Georgia !

    On thee is laid oppression's hand,
    Around thy altars foemen stand,
    To scatter Freedom's gallant band,
      And lay thee low, my Georgia !
    But thou hast noble sons, and brave,
    The Stars and Bars above thee wave,
    And here we'll make oppression's grave,
      Upon the soil of Georgia !

We bow at Liberty's fair shrine,
And kneel in holy love at thine,
And while above our stars still shine,
  We'll strike for them and Georgia !
Thy woods with victory shall resound,
Thy brow shall be with laurels crowned
And peace shall spread her wings around
  My own, my sunny Georgia !

    Yes, these shall teach thy foes to feel
    That Southern hearts, and Southern steel,
    Will make them in submission kneel
      Before the sons of Georgia !

And thou shalt see their daughters, too,
With pride and patriotism true,
Arise with strength to dare and do,
    Ere they shall conquer Georgia!

        Thy name shall be a name of pride—
        Thy heroes all have nobly died,
        That thou mayst be the spotless bride
            Of Liberty, my Georgia!
        Then wave thy sword and banner high,
        And louder raise the battle-cry,
        'Till shouts of victory reach the sky,
            And thou art free, my Georgia!

OUR FAITH IN '61.

By A. J. Requier.

" The governments are instituted among men, deriving their just powers from the consent of the governed; that whenever any form of government becomes destructive of these ends, it is the right of the people to alter or abolish it, and to institute a new government, laying its foundation on such principles, and organizing its powers in such form, as TO THEM SHALL SEEM most likely to effect their safety and happiness."—(Declaration of Independence, July 4, 1776.)

    NOR yet one hundred years have flown
        Since on this very spot,
    The subjects of a sovereign throne—
        Liege-master of their lot—
    This high degree sped o'er the sea,
        From council board and tent,
    " No earthly power can rule the free
        But by their own consent!"

For this, they fought as Saxons fight,
    On bloody fields and long—
Themselves the champions of the right,
    And judges of the wrong ;
For this their stainless knighthood wore
    The branded rebel's name,
Until the starry cross they bore
    Set all the skies aflame !

        And States co-equal and distinct
            Outshone the western sun,
        By one great charter interlinked—
            Not blended into one ;
        Whose graven key that high decree
            The grand inscription lent,
        " No earthly power can rule the free
            But by their own consent ! "

Oh, sordid age, oh, ruthless rage !
    Oh, sacrilegious wrong !
A deed to blast the record page,
    And snap the strings of song ;
In that great charter's name, a band
    By grovelling greed enticed,
Whose warrant is the grasping hand
    Of creeds without a Christ—

        States that have trampled every pledge
            Its crystal code contains,
        Now give their swords a keener edge
            To harness it with chains—
        To make a bond of brotherhood
            The sanction and the seal,
        By which to arm a rabble brood
            With fratricidal steel.

3

Who, conscious that their cause is black,
    In puling prose and rhyme,
Talk hatefully of love, and tack
    Hypocrisy to crime ;
Who smile and smite, engross the gorge
    Or impotently frown ;
And call us " rebels " with King George,
    As if they wore his crown.

        Most venal of a venal race,
           Who think you cheat the sky
        With every pharisaic face
           And stimulated lie ;
        Round Freedom's lair, with weapons bare,
           We greet the light divine
        Of those who throned the goddess there,
           And yet inspire the shrine.

Our loved ones' graves are at our feet,
    Their homesteads at our back—
No belted Southron can retreat
    With woman on his track ;
Peal, bannered host, the proud decree
    Which from your fathers went,
" No earthly power can rule the free
    But by their own consent ! "

VICKSBURG—A BALLAD.

By Paul H. Hayne.

For sixty days and upwards,
　　A storm of shell and shot
Rained 'round us in a flaming shower,
　　But still we faltered not!
" If the noble city perish,"
　　Our brave young leader said,
" Let the only walls the foe shall scale
　　Be the ramparts of the dead!"

　　　　For sixty days and upwards
　　　　　　The eye of heaven waxed dim,
　　　　And even throughout God's holy morn,
　　　　　　O'er Christian prayer and hymn,
　　　　Arose a hissing tumult,
　　　　　　As if the fiends of air
　　　　Strove to ingulf the voice of faith
　　　　　　In the shrieks of their despair.

There was wailing in the houses,
　　There was trembling on the marts,
While the tempest raged and thundered,
　　'Mid the silent thrill of hearts;
But the Lord, our shield, was with us,
　　And ere a month had sped
Our very women walked the streets
　　With scarce one throb of dread.

　　　　And the little children gambolled—
　　　　　　Their faces purely raised,
　　　　Just for a wondering moment,
　　　　　　As the huge bomb whirled and blazed!
　　　　Then turned with silvery laughter
　　　　　　To the sports which children love,
　　　　Thrice mailed in the sweet, instinctive thought,
　　　　　　That the good God watched above.

Yet the hailing bolts fell faster,
    From scores of flame-clad ships,
And about us, denser, darker,
    Grew the conflict's wild eclipse,
Till a solid cloud closed o'er us,
    Like a type of doom and ire,
Whence shot a thousand quivering tongues
    Of forked and vengeful fire.

But the unseen hands of angels
    Those death-shafts turned aside,
And the dove of heavenly mercy
    Ruled o'er the battle tide ;
In the houses ceased the wailing,
    And through the war-scarred marts
The people trod with the step of hope,
    To the music in their hearts.

SONNET—THE AVATAR OF HELL.

Six thousand years of commune, God with man,
    Two thousand years of Christ ; yet from such roots,
Immortal, earth reaps only bitterest fruits !
The fiends rage now as when they first began !
Hate ! Lust ! Greed, Vanity, triumphant still,
Yell, shout, exult, and lord o'er human will !
The sun moves back ! The fond convictions felt.
That, in the progress of the race, we stood,
Two thousand years of height above the flood
Before the day's experience sink and melt,
As frost beneath the fire ! and what remains
Of all our grand ideals and great gains,
With Goth, Hun, Vandal, warring in their pride,
While the meek Christ is hourly crucified !

MONUMENT TO THE CONFEDERATE DEAD IN "HOLLYWOOD"
CEMETERY, RICHMOND, VIRGINIA

Here lie 12,000 Confederate dead, to whose memory Virginia's noble women erected a
monument of rough Virginia granite nearly 100 feet tall in the shape of a pyramid.
From a photograph taken for this work by Edyth Carter Beveridge.

CAPTAIN LATANE.

By John R. Thompson, of Virginia.

This pathetic poem tells its own incident, which appeals to everyone who thinks of stranger hands laying one's friend to rest when death has claimed its own. By the courtesy of Mrs. James T. Halsey, the daughter of the distinguished General Dabney H. Maury, the editor is permitted to reproduce elsewhere for this work a picture in her possession portraying the scene described in this poem.

THE combat raged not long; but ours the day,
    And through the hosts which compassed us around
Our little band rode proudly on its way,
    Leaving one gallant spirit, glory crowned,
Unburied on the field he died to gain;
Single, of all his men, among the hostile slain !

One moment at the battle's edge he stood,
    Hope's halo, like a helmet, round his hair—
The next, beheld him dabbled in his blood,
    Prostrate in death; and yet in death how fair !
And thus he passed, through the red gates of strife,
From earthly crowns and palms, to an eternal life.

A brother bore his body from the field,
    And gave it into strangers' hands, who closed
His calm blue eyes, on earth forever sealed,
    And tenderly the slender limbs composed;
Strangers, but sister, who with Mary's love,
Sat by the open tomb and, weeping, looked above,

A little girl strewed roses on his bier,
    Pale roses—not more stainless than his soul,
Nor yet more fragrant than his life sincere,
    That blossomed with good actions—brief, but whole
The aged matron, with the faithful slave,
Approached with reverent steps the hero's lowly grave.

No man of God might read the burial rite
    Above the rebel—thus declared the foe,
Who blanched before him in the deadly fight ;
But woman's voice, in accents soft and low,
Trembling with pity, touched with pathos, read
Over his hallowed dust, the ritual for the dead !

"'Tis sown in weakness ; it is raised in power."
    Soft the promise floated on the air,
And the sweet breathings of the sunset hour,
    Come back responsive to the mourner's prayer.
Gently they laid him underneath the sod,
And left him with his fame, his country and his God.

We should not weep for him !   His deeds endure ;
    So young, so beautiful, so brave—he died
As he would wish to die.   The past secure,
    Whatever yet of sorrow may betide
Those who still linger by the stormy shore ;
Change cannot hurt him now, nor fortune reach him more.

And when Virginia, leaning on her spear,
    Vitrix et vidua, the conflict done,
Shall raise her mailed hand to wipe the tear
    That starts, as she recalls each martyr son ;
No prouder memory her breast shall sway
Than thine—the early lost—lamented Latane !

Seal of The
Virginia Company.

"THE CONFEDERATE NOTE."

Written by Major S. A. Jones, of Mississippi.

On a Confederate note at the surrender of the Confederate army. See illustration of an old note with endorsement made by a deserving officer.

REPRESENTINING nothing on God's earth now,
    And naught in the water below it—
As a pledge of the nation that's dead and gone,
    Keep it, dear friend, and show it.

Show it to those who will lend an ear
    To the tale that this paper can tell,
Of liberty born, of patriot's dream—
    Of the storm cradled nation that fell.

Too poor to possess the precious ores,
    And too much of a stranger to borrow,
We issued to-day our promise to pay,
    And hope to redeem on the morrow.

The days rolled on and weeks became years,
    But our coffers were empty still,
Coin was so rare that the Treasury quaked,
    If a dollar should drop in the till.

But the faith that was in us was strong indeed,
    And our poverty well discerned ;
And these little checks represented the pay,
    That our volunteers earned.

We know it had hardly value in gold,
    Yet as gold her soldier received it.
It gazed in our eyes with a promise to pay,
    And each patriot soldier believed it.

But our boys thought little of price of pay,
 Or of bills that were ever due ;
We knew if it brought us bread to-day,
 'Twas the best our poor country could do.

   Keep it, for it tells our history o'er,
    From the birth of its dreams to the last,
   Modest and born of the angel Hope,
    Like the hope of success it passed.

EULOGY OF THE DEAD.

By B. F. Porter, of Alabama.

"Weep not for the dead ; neither bemoan him."—Jeremiah.

OH ! weep not for the dead,
 Whose blood for freedom shed,
Is hallowed evermore !
Who on the battle-field
Could die—but never yield !
Oh, bemoan them never more—
They live immortal in their gore !

   Oh, what is it to die
   Midst shouts of victory,
   Our rights and home defending !
   Oh ! what were fame and life
   Gained in that basest strife
   For tyrants' power contending,
   Our country's bosom rending !

Oh ! dead of red Manassas !
Oh ! dead of Shiloh's fray !
Oh ! victors of the Richmond field !
Dead on your mother's breast,

You live in glorious rest!
Each on his honored shield,
Immortal in each bloody field!

Oh ! sons of noble mothers !
Oh ! youth of maiden lovers !
Oh ! husbands of chaste wives !
Though asleep in beds of gore,
You return, oh ! never more ;
Still immortal are your lives !
Immortal mothers ! lovers ! wives !

How blest is he who draws
His sword in freedom's cause !
Though dead on battle-field,
Forever to his tomb
Shall youthful heroes come,
Their hearts for freedom steeled,
And learn to die on battle-field.

As at Thermopylæ,
Grecian child of liberty ;
Swears to despot ne'er to yield—
Here, by our glorious dead,
Let's revenge the blood they've shed,
Or die on bloody field,
By the sons who scorned to yield !

Oh ! mothers ! lovers ! wives !
Oh ! weep no more—our lives
Are our country's evermore !
More glorious in your graves,
Than if living Lincoln's slaves,
Ye will perish never more,
Martyred on our fields of gore !

GENDRON PALMER, OF THE HOLCOMBE LEGION.

By Ina M. Porter, of Alabama.

HE sleeps upon Virginia's strand,
　　While comrades of the Legion stand
With arms reversed—a mournful band—
　　Around his early bier!
His war-horse paws the shaking ground,
The volleys ring—they close around—
And on the white brow, laurel-bound,
　　Falls many a soldier's tear.

　　　　Up, stricken mourners! look on high,
　　　　Loud anthems rend the echoing sky,
　　　　Re-born where heroes never die—
　　　　　　The warrior is at rest!
　　　　Gone is the weary, pain-traced frown;
　　　　Life's march is o'er, his arms cast down,
　　　　His plumes replaced by shining crown,
　　　　　　The red cross on his breast!

Though Gendron's arm is with the dust,
Let not his blood-stained weapon rust,
Bequeathed to one who'll bear the trust,
　　Where Southern banners fly!
Some brave, who followed where he led—
Aye, swear him o'er the martyred dead,
To avenge each drop of blood he shed.
　　Or, like him, bravely die!

　　　　He deemed a death for honor sweet,—
　　　　And thus he fell—'Tis doubly meet,
　　　　Our flag should be his winding-sheet,
　　　　　　Proud banner of the free!
　　　　Oh, let his honored form be laid
　　　　Beneath the loved Palmetto's shade;
　　　　His praises sung by Southern maid,
　　　　　　While flows the broad Santee!

We come around his urn to twine
Sweet clusters of the jasmine vine,
Culled where our tropic sunbeams shine,
  From skies deep-dyed and bright ;
And, kneeling, vow no right to yield !
On, brothers, on ! —Fight ! win the field !
Or dead return on battered shield,
  As martyrs for the right !

  Where camp-fires light the reddened sod,
  The grief-bowed Legion kneel to God,
  In Palmer's name, and by his blood,
    They swell the battle-cry ;
  We'll sheathe no more our dripping steel,
  'Till tyrants Southern vengeance feel,
  And menial hordes as suppliants kneel,
    Or, terror-stricken, fly !

THE SILENT MARCH.

On one occasion during the war in Virginia General Lee lay down by the wayside for a few minutes' rest. Fifteen thousand men passed by with noiseless step, because it was whispered from one to the other all down the line, " Mars Bob's asleep ; don't wake him."

O'ERCOME with weariness and care,
    The war-worn veteran lay
On the green turf of his native land,
    And slumbered by the way ;
The breeze that sighed across his brow,
    And smoothed its deeped lines,
Fresh from his own loved mountain bore
    The murmur of their pines ;
And the glad sound of waters,
    The blue rejoicing streams,
Whose sweet familiar tones were blent
    With the music of his dreams :

They brought no sound of battle's din,
    Shrill fife or clarion,
But only tenderest memories
    Of his own fair Arlington.

While thus the chieftain slumbered,
    Forgetful of his care,
The hollow tramp of thousands
    Came sounding through the air:
With ringing spur and sabre,
    And trampling feet they come,
Gay plume and rustling banner,
    And fife, and trump, and drum;
But soon the foremost column
    Sees where, beneath the shade,
In slumber, calm as childhood,
    Their wearied chief is laid;
And down the line a murmur
    From lip to lip there ran,
Until the stilly whisper
    Had spread to rear from van;
And o'er the host a silence
    As deep and sudden fell,
As though some mighty wizard
    Had hushed them with a spell;
And every sound was muffled,
    And every soldier's tread
Fell lightly as a mother's
    'Round her baby's cradle-bed;
And rank, and file, and column,
    So softly by they swept,
It seemed a ghostly army
    Had passed him as he slept,
But mightier than enchantment
    Was that with magic move—
The spell that hushed their voices—
    Deep reverence and love.

THE BURIAL OF LATANE

From a rare engraving in possession of Mrs. James T. Halsey, President of the "Daughters of the Confederacy," of Philadelphia, loaned for this work. The pathetic story is beautifully described in the poem of the same title.

"THE MARYLAND LINE."

By J. D. M'Cabe, Jr.

The Maryland regiments in the Confederate army adopted the title of
" The Maryland Line," which was so heroically sustained by their patriot
sires of the first Revolution, and which the deeds of Marylanders at Manassas, show that the patriot Marylanders of this second Revolution are worthy
to bear.

By old Potomac's rushing tide,
　　Our bayonets are gleaming;
And o'er the bounding waters wide
　　We gaze, while tears are streaming.
The distant hills of Maryland
Rise sadly up before us—
　　And tyrant bands have chained our land,
　　Our mother proud that bore us.

Our proud old mother's queenly head
　　Is bowed in subjugation ;
With her children's blood her soil is red,
　　And fiends in exultation
Taunt her with shame as they bind her chains,
　　While her heart is torn with anguish ;
Old mother, on famed Manassas' plains
　　Our vengeance did not languish.

We thought of your wrongs as on we rushed,
　　'Mid shot and shell appalling ;
We heard your voice as it upward gush'd,
　　From the Maryland life-blood falling.
No pity we knew ! Did they mercy show
　　When they bound the mother that bore us?
But we scattered death 'mid the dastard foe
　　Till they, shrieking, fled before us.

We mourn for our brothers brave that fell
  On that field so stern and gory;
But their spirits rose with our triumph yell
  To the heavenly realms of glory.
And their bodies rest on the hard-won field—
  By their love so true and tender,
We'll keep the prize they would not yield,
  We'll die, but we'll not surrender.

———

GENERAL ALBERT SIDNEY JOHNSTON.

[Killed at the Battle of Shiloh, Tenn., April 6, 1862,
while leading and directing his troops.]

BY MARY JERVEY, of Charleston.

IN thickest fight triumphantly he fell,
  While into victory's arms he led us on;
A death so glorious our grief should quell:
  We mourn him, yet his battle-crown is won.

No slanderous tongue can vex his spirit now,
  No bitter taunts can stain his blood-bought fame;
Immortal honor rests upon his brow,
  And noble memories cluster round his name.

For hearts shall thrill and eyes grow dim with tears,
  To read the story of his touching fate;
How in his death the gallant soldier wears
  The crown that came for earthly life too late.

Ye people! guard his memory—sacred keep
  The garlands green above his hero-grave;
Yet weep, for praise can never wake his sleep,
To tell him he is shrined among the brave!

"STONEWALL" JACKSON'S WAY.

These verses were found written on a small piece of paper, all stained with blood, in the bosom of a dead soldier of the old Stonewall Brigade, after one of Jackson's battles in the Shenandoah Valley. There had been terrific fighting, and Jackson had encountered three separate armies, defeating each in turn. It is well known that he was a man of prayer. His servant man, a faithful negro, would sometimes go out early in the morning to the officer's camp and say: "Gentlemen, there's gwine to be hard fightin' to-day; Mars Tom was on his knees praying all night long." Jackson's favorite way of sending the news of his victories to Richmond, the headquarters of the Confederacy, was the following telegram: "God has blessed our arms with another glorious victory." No wonder, then, that the spirit of prayer should have been in this wonderful poem. Though the author is unknown, this beautiful production will go down the ages as a classic in the English language. See the air to which this is sung.

COME, stack arms men, pile on the rails—
   Stir up the camp-fire bright;
No matter if the canteen fails,
   We'll make a roaring night.
Here Shenandoah crawls along,
Here burly Blue Ridge echoes strong,
To swell the brigade's rousing song,
   Of "Stonewall Jackson's way."

      We see him now—the old slouched hat
         Couched o'er his eye askew—
      The shrewd, dry smile—the speech so pat,
         So calm, so blunt, so true,
      The "Blue Light Elder" knows 'em well:
      Says he, "That's Bank's, he's fond of shell;
      Lord, save his soul! we'll give him——" well
         That's "Stonewall Jackson's way."

Silence! ground arms! kneel all! caps off!
   Old "Blue Light's" going to pray;
Strangle the fool that dares to scoff!
   Attention! it's his way!

Appealing from his native sod,
    "Hear us, Almighty God!
Lay bare thine arm, stretch forth thy rod,
    "Amen!"   That's Stonewall Jackson's way.

        He's in the saddle now!   Fall in!
            Steady!   The whole brigade!
        Hill's at the ford, cut off; we'll win
            His way out, ball and blade.
        What matter if our shoes are worn?
        What matter if our feet are torn?
        Quick step! we're with him ere the dawn!
            That's Stonewall Jackson's way!

The sun's bright lances rout the mists
    Of morning—and, by George!
Here's Longstreet, struggling in the lists,
    Hemmed in an ugly gorge.
Pope and his Yankees, whipped before;
"Bayonets and grape!" hear Stonewall roar;
"Charge, Stuart! pay off Ashby's score,"
    Is Stonewall Jackson's way!

        Ah! maiden, wait, and watch, and yearn,
            For news of Stonewall's band!
        Ah! widow, read—with eyes that burn—
            That ring upon thy hand!
        Ah! wife, sew on, hope on, and pray!
        Thy life shall not be all forlorn—
        The foe had better ne'er been born,
            That gets in Stonewall's way.

"OH NO, HE'LL NOT NEED THEM AGAIN."

On the morning of the battle of Franklin, Tennessee, Major-General Patrick Cleburne, while riding along the lines encouraging his men, saw an old friend, a Captain of his command, bare-footed, his feet sore and bleeding—a pitiful sight to look upon, indeed. Dismounting at once, he walked up to the Captain and said : " Captain, will you kindly pull off my boots?" The Captain looked up in some surprise, but, always ready to obey his commanding officer, responded at once to the request of the General, and pulled off his boots, holding them in his hands as if asking, " What next? " The General said to him, " Captain, will you try them on and see if they will fit you? " This the Captain did also. The General then turned and mounted his horse, saying, " Captain, I am tired wearing those boots, and can do well without them." The Captain remonstrated, and so did others around him, but he would not listen to them. With a pleasant smile, he saluted the Captain, and saying, " Good-bye, Captain," he rode away. That day he was killed, and was taken from the field in the condition in which he had left the Captain.

OH, no ! he'll not need them again—
    No more will he wake to behold
The splendor and fame of his men,
    The tale of his victories told !
No more will he wake from that sleep
    Which he sleeps in his glory and fame,
While his comrades are left here to weep
    Over Cleburne, his grave and his name.

        Oh, no ! he'll not need them again ;
           No more will his banner be spread
        O'er the field of his gallantry's fame—
           The soldier's proud spirit is fled !
        The soldier who rose 'mid applause,
           From the humblemost place in the van—
        I sing not in praise of the cause
           But rather in praise of the man.

4

Oh, no! he'll not need them again ;
    He has fought his last battle without them,
For barefoot he, too, must go in,
    While barefoot stood comrades about him ;
And barefoot they proudly marched in,
    With blood flowing fast from their feet ;
They thought of the past victories won,
    And the foes that they now were to meet.

        Oh, no! he'll not need them again ;
           He is leading his men to the charge,
        Unheeding the shells, or the slain,
           Or the showers of the bullets at large
        On the right, on the left, on the flanks,
           He dashingly pushes his way,
        While with cheers, double-quick and in ranks,
           His soldiers all followed that day.

Oh, no! he'll not need them again ;
    He falls from his horse to the ground !
Oh, anguish ! oh, sorrow ! oh, pain !
    In the brave hearts that gathered around.
He breathes not of grief, nor a sigh
    On the breast where he pillowed his head,
Ere he fix'd his last gaze upon high—
    " I'm killed, boys, but fight it out," said.

        Oh, no ! he'll not need them again ;
           But treasure them up for his sake ;
        And oh ! should you sing a refrain
           Of the memories they still must awake,
        Sing it soft as the summer-eve breeze,
           Let it sound as refreshing and clear ;
        Tho' grief-born, there's that which can please
           In thoughts that are gemmed with a tear.

"STACK ARMS."

Written in the prison of Fort Delaware, Del., on hearing
of the surrender of General Lee.

By Jos. Blyth Alston.

It makes a great difference as to the circumstances under which the
soldier hears these words of command. Sometimes, upon the drill-ground,
"Stack arms" is a sweet relief; sometimes, after a long and weary march,
"Stack arms" is ordered, and the men know there is rest for their tired
bodies. I stood one day in line with the men of the South when the order
"Stack arms!" was given. It was on Sunday morning, April 9, 1865. We
were in line of battle, and well did we know when this order was given that
it meant the surrender of our army. Two days later we were in line again;
the long blue line of the Federal army confronted us. We stood within ten
feet of each other, face to face. Again the order was given, "Stack arms,"
and we placed our muskets upon the ground, with their muzzles touching
each other in the air, and around the stack we wrapped the tattered, bullet-
torn battle-flag of our loved Confederacy, and came away. Strong men
wept like children as with awkward stride they turned away from the foe
they had never feared to face; and even now, if the command had been
given to "Take arms," the men would have gladly plunged into the fight
until not one should have been left to tell the tale.

" Stack Arms!" I've gladly heard the cry
When, weary with the dusty tread
Of marching troops, as night drew nigh,
I sank upon my soldier bed,
And calmly slept; the starry dome
Of heaven's blue arch my canopy,
And mingled with my dreams of home,
The thoughts of Peace and Liberty.

"Stack Arms!" I've heard it, when the shout
Exulting, rang along our line,
Of foes hurled back in bloody rout,
Captured, dispersed; its tones divine
Then came to mine enraptured ear.
Guerdon of duty nobly done,
And glistening on my cheek the tear
Of grateful joy for victory won.

" Stack Arms ! " In faltering accents, slow
    And sad, it creeps from tongue to tongue.
A broken, murmuring wail of woe,
    From manly hearts by anguish wrung,
Like victims of a midnight dream,
    We move, we know not how nor why,
For life and hope but phantoms seem,
    And it would be relief—to die !

"LORENA."

As the soldier boys went from their homes many of them (not to say every one of them) left their sweethearts behind. Many were the love songs that were written in those days, sung by the lad to his lassie, and then when he was far away at the front he sang them in the camp, and she in the home, with the hope of an early meeting again. As this little song comes to my mind it brings up a thousand associations of the past, as it will do in the minds of others who knew it, and sang it, in the long-ago past.

THE years creep slowly by, Lorena ;
    The snow is on the grass again ;
The sun's low down the sky, Lorena ;
    The frost gleams where the flowers have been.
But the heart throbs on as warmly now
    As when the summer days were nigh ;
Oh ! the sun can never dip so low
    Adown affection's cloudless sky.

A hundred months have passed, Lorena,
    Since last I held that hand in mine,
And felt the pulse beat fast, Lorena,
    Though mine beat faster far than thine,
A hundred months—'twas flowery May,
    When up the hilly slope we climbed,
To watch the dying of the day
    And hear the distant church bells chimed.

HOUSE IN WHICH "STONEWALL" JACKSON DIED

We loved each other then, Lorena,
    More than we ever dared to tell;
And what we might have been, Lorena,
    Had but our loving prospered well!
But then, 'tis past; the years have gone,
    I'll not call up their shadowy forms;
I'll say to them, Lost years, sleep on,
    Sleep on, nor heed life's pelting storms.

    The story of the past, Lorena,
        Alas! I care not to repeat;
    The hopes that could not last, Lorena,
        They lived, but only lived to cheat.
    I would not cause e'en one regret
        To rankle in your bosom now—
    " For if we try we may forget,"
        Were words of thine long years ago.

Yes, these were words of thine, Lorena—
    They are within my memory yet—
They touched some tender chords, Lorena,
    Which thrill and tremble with regret.
'Twas not the woman's heart which spoke—
    Thy heart was always true to me;
A duty stern and piercing broke
    The tie which linked my soul with thee.

    It matters little now, Lorena,
        The past is in the eternal past;
    Our hearts will soon lie low, Lorena,
        Life's tide is ebbing out so fast.
    There is a future, oh, thank God!
        Of life this is so small a part—
    'Tis dust to dust beneath the sod,
        But there, up there, 'tis heart to heart.

"NELLIE GRAY."

The sweetest singers in all the world are the " darkeys" of the South. You may call their songs "Plantation ditties," or "Coon songs," or whatever you will, but to me there is more of pathos and power in one of the old-fashioned " darkey " songs of the South than in many of the magnificent oratorios and operas of the present day. This charming little song is one of them. It comes along down the years like a bird to entertain us with its sweet and charming music. This song is sung to-day both North and South, and like most popular songs it may be printed in several forms. We believe the following version is as it should appear. The authorship of the poem is in doubt. It is suggested by Mrs. A. T. Smythe, President of the "Daughters of the Confederacy," Charleston, South Carolina, that the author is Stephen D. Foster, who composed it to be sung at a public entertainment.

There's a low green valley on the old Kentucky shore,
    There I've whiled many happy hours away;
Sitting and singing in my little cabin door,
    Where lived my darling Nellie Gray.

CHORUS:

Oh, my poor Nellie Gray,
    They have taken you away
And I'll never see my darling any more,
    I'm sitting by the river,
And I'm watching all the day,
    For you've gone from my old Kentucky shore.

When the moon had climbed the mountains,
    And the stars were shining too,
Then I'd take my darling Nellie Gray,
    And we'd float down the river
In our little red canoe
    While my banjo sweetly I would play.—*Chorus.*

My canoe is under water,
    And my banjo is unstrung,
I'm tired of living any more.
    My eyes shall look downward,
And my song shall be unsung
    If she's gone from my old Kentucky shore.—*Chorus.*

My eyes are getting blinded
    And I cannot see my way.
Hark! there is someone knocking at the door.
    Oh, I hear the angels calling,
And I see my Nellie Gray.
    Farewell, to the old Kentucky shore.—*Chorus.*

"YE MEN OF ALABAMA!"

By JOHN D. PHELAN, of Montgomery, Alabama.

It is well known that the first Capital of the Confederacy was established at Montgomery, Alabama. The men of that noble State responded to the call of their country from every town, and hamlet, and home, nor did they ever, in all the four years, lack courage and devotion to her cause. The name Alabama is an Indian name, and means "Here we rest." It was a misnomer in those days, for it was "Here we hustle, and here we fight," "*Usque ad finem.*"

Ye men of Alabama,
    Awake, arise, awake!
And rend the coils asunder
    Of this Abolition snake.
If another fold he fastens—
    If this final coil he plies—
In the cold clasp of hate and power
    Fair Alabama dies.

        Though round your lower limbs and waist
            His deadly coils I see,
        Yet, yet, thank Heaven! your head and arms,
            And good right hand are free;

And in that hand there glistens—
　　O God ! what joy to feel !—
A polished blade, full sharp and keen,
　　Of tempered State Rights steel.

　　　　Now, by the free-born sires
　　　　　　From whose brave loins ye sprung !
　　　　And by the noble mothers
　　　　　　At whose fond breasts ye hung !
　　　　And by your wives and daughters,
　　　　　　And by the ills they dread,
　　　　Drive deep that good Secession steel
　　　　　　Right through the Monster's head.

This serpent Abolition
　　Has been coiling on for years ;
We have reasoned, we have threatened,
　　We have begged almost with tears :
Now, away, away with Union,
　　Since on our Southern soil
The only union left us
　　Is an anaconda's coil.

　　　　Brave, little South Carolina
　　　　　　Will strike the self-same blow,
　　　　And Florida, and Georgia,
　　　　　　And Mississippi, too ;
　　　　And Arkansas, and Texas ;
　　　　　　And at her death, I ween,
　　　　The head will fall beneath the blows
　　　　　　Of all the brave Fifteen.

In this our day of trial,
　　Let feuds and factions cease,
Until above this howling storm
　　We see the sign of Peace.

Let Southern men, like brothers,
 In solid phalanx stand,
And poise their spears, and lock their shields,
 To guard their native land.

The love that for the Union
 Once in our bosoms beat,
From insult and from injury
 Has turned to scorn and hate;
And the banner of Secession
 To-day we lift on high,
Resolved, beneath that sacred flag,
 To conquer, or TO DIE!

"STONEWALL" JACKSON.

Mortally wounded—"The Brigade must not know, sir."

It is a well known fact that Stonewall Jackson was killed by his own men. He rode through the picket lines at Chancellorsville, and gave orders that they must fire on any who came along their road, not expecting to return that way himself; but changing his mind afterward, his men, obedient to orders, poured a volley of shot into the little group of officers and men, and we all know with what deadly effect. As they bore General Jackson to the rear, mortally wounded, he said to the officer who had him in charge, "The brigade must not know, sir, that I am wounded."

"WHO'VE ye got there?"—"Only a dying brother,
 Hurt in the front just now."
"Good boy! he'll do. Somebody tell his mother
 Where he was killed, and how."

"Whom have you there?"—"A crippled courier, major,
 Shot by mistake, we hear.
He was with Stonewall." "Cruel work they've made here:
 Quick with him to the rear!"

" Well, who comes next ? "—Doctor, speak low, speak low, sir;
    Don't let the men find out.
"It's *Stonewall !* "   "God !"   " The brigade must not know, sir,
    While there's a foe about."

Whom have we *here*—shrouded in martial manner,
    Crowned with a martyr's charm ?
A grand dead hero in a living banner,
    Born of his heart and arm.

The heart whereon his cause hung—see how clingeth
    That banner to his bier !
The arm wherewith his cause struck—hark ! how ringeth
    His trumpet in their rear !

What have we left ?   His glorious inspiration,
    His prayers in council met.
Living, he laid the first stones of a nation ;
    And dead, he builds it yet.

CAROLINA.   April 14, 1861.

CAROLINA !   Carolina !
    Noble name in State and story,
    How I love thy truthful glory,
    As I love the blue sky o'er ye,
        Carolina evermore !

        Carolina !   Carolina !
            Land of chivalry unfearing,
            Daughters fair beyond comparing,
            Sons of worth and noble daring,
                Carolina evermore !

Carolina !   Carolina !
    Soft thy clasp in loving greeting,
    Plenteous board and kindly meeting,
    All thy pulses nobly beating,
        Carolina evermore !

Carolina !   Carolina !
> Green thy valleys, bright thy heaven,
> Bold thy streams through forest riven,
> Bright thy laurels, hero-given,
>> Carolina evermore !

Carolina !   Carolina !
> Holy name, and dear forever,
> Never shall thy children, never,
> Fail to strike with grand endeavor,
>> Carolina evermore !

> JOHN A WAGNER, of S. C.

THE ORIGINAL "DIXIE."

The song of "Dixie" is indelibly connected with the South. We all know the air, but how few have seen the original song ! There have been many versions, but we give here the original one, from which they all sprang.

I WISH I was in the land of cotton,
   Old times dar am not forgotten ;
Look away, look away, look away, Dixie Land,
In Dixie Land, whar I was born in
Early on one frosty mornin',
Look away, look away, look away, Dixie Land.

CHORUS :
> Den I wish I was in Dixie,
> Hooray ! hooray !
> In Dixie Land I'll took my stand,
> To lib and die in Dixie.
> Away, away, away down South in Dixie;
> Away, away, away down South in Dixie.

Old missus marry " Will de weaber? "
William was a gay deceaber,
Look away, look away, look away, Dixie Land.

But when he put his arm around 'er,
He smiled as fierce as a forty-pounder,
Look away, look away, look away, Dixie Land.

His face was as sharp as a butcher's cleaber,
But dat did not seem to greabe 'er,
Look away, look away, look away, Dixie Land.
Old missus acted the foolish part,   .
And died for the man dat broke her heart,
Look away, look away, look away, Dixie Land.

Now here's a health to the next old missus,
And all the gals dat want to kiss us.
Look away, look away, look away, Dixie Land.
But if you want to drive away sorroe,
Come and hear dis nig to-morrow ;
Look away, look away, look away, Dixie Land.

Der buckwheat cakes and ingen batter
Makes you fat, or a little fatter.
Look away, look away, look away, Dixie Land.
Den hoe it down and scratch your grabble
To Dixie Land I'm bound to trabble.
Look away, look away, look away, Dixie Land.

The Old Bell House, Capitol Square, Richmond, Va.

GENERAL JAMES LONGSTREET

GENERAL RICHARD S. EWELL

"DIXIE'S LAND."

"STONEWALL JACKSON'S WAY."

These are the well-known airs of war days for songs, then so popular with the soldier boys.

"OUR CONFEDERATE DEAD."
What the Heart of a Young Girl Said to a Dead Soldier.
BY A LADY OF AUGUSTA, GEORGIA.

One of the most beautiful customs that exist in the South is the habit of the people once a year to go forth and scatter flowers upon the graves of our dead.

Not long since a friend of mine was standing in the cemetery at Nashville, on Decoration Day, and seeing a cart pass through the gates, loaded with a heavy marble slab, he followed it, and soon came to a grave where preparations were being made to plant this stone. A gentleman was standing near, and my friend asked him if it was the grave of his son. "No," said he, "I was a member of the Tennessee Company; my wife was at the point of death, our company was ordered to the front, and this young man, though under the prescribed age, came to me and insisted upon taking my place. He was killed at the battle of Missionary Ridge, near Chattanooga." Upon the stone was the inscription of the name of the young man who had been killed, then of the name of the man who was having the stone placed at the grave, and underneath it all these simple words: "He died for me." What a book could be written of such incidents of splendid heroism as characterized the true warm-hearted men of those days.

UNKNOWN to me, brave boy, but still I wreathe
        For you the tenderest of wildwood flowers;
And o'er your tomb a virgin's prayer I breathe,
        To greet the pure moon and the April showers.

        I only know, I only care to know,
                You died for me—for me and country bled;
        A thousand Springs and wild December snow
                Will weep for one of all the *Southern dead.*

Perhaps some mother gazes up the skies,
        Wailing, like Rachel, for her martyred brave—
Oh, for her darling sake, my dewy eyes
        Moisten the turf above your lowly grave.

                The cause is sacred, when our maidens stand
                        Linked with sad matrons and heroic sires,
                Above relics of a vanquished land
                        And light the torch of sanctifying fire

Your bed of honor has a rosy cope
    To shimmer back the tributary stars;
And every petal glistens with a hope
    Where Love hath blossomed in the disk of Mars.

Sleep! On your couch of glory slumber comes
    Bosomed amid the archangelic choir;
Not with the grumble of impetuous drums
    Deep'ning the chorus of embattled ire.

Above you shall the oak and cedar fling
    Their giant plumage and protecting shade;
For you the song-bird pause upon his wing
    And warble requiems ever undismayed.

Farewell! And if your spirit wander near
    To kiss this plant of unaspiring art—
Translate it, even in the heavenly sphere,
    As the libretto of a maiden's heart.

THE SOUTHERN REPUBLIC.

By Miss Thomas, of Mississippi.

In the galaxy of nations,
    A nation's flag's unfurled,
Transcending in its martial pride
    The nations of the world.
Though born of war, baptized in blood,
    Yet mighty from the time,
Like fabled phœnix, forth she stood—
    Dismembered, yet sublime.

        And braver heart, and bolder hand,
           Ne'er formed a fabric fair
        As Southern wisdom can command,
           And Southern valor rear.

Though kingdoms scorn to own her sway,
    Or recognize her birth,
The land blood-bought for Liberty
    Will reign supreme on earth.

        Clime of the Sun !   Home of the Brave !
           Thy sons are bold and free,
        And pour life's crimson tide to save
           Their birthright, Liberty !
        Their fertile fields and sunny plains
           That yield the wealth alone,
        That's coveted for greedy gains
           By despots—and a throne !

Proud country ! battling, bleeding, torn,
    Thy altars desolate ;
Thy lovely dark-eyed daughters mourn
    At war's relentless fate ;
And widows' prayers, and orphans' tears,
    Her homes will consecrate,
While more than brass or marble rears
    The trophy of her great.

        Oh ! land that boasts each gallant name
           Of Jackson, Johnson, Lee,
        And hosts of valiant sons, whose fame
           Extends beyond the sea ;
        Far rather let thy plains become,
           From gulf to mountain cave,
        One honored sepulchre and tomb,
           Than we the tyrant's slave !

Fair, favored land ! thou mayst be free;
    Redeemed by blood and war ;
Through agony and gloom we see
    Thy hope—a glimmering star ;

Thy banner, too, may proudly float,
  A herald on the seas—
Thy deeds of daring worlds remote
  Will emulate and praise!

  But who can paint the impulse pure,
    That thrills and nerves thy brave
  To deeds of valor, that secure
    The rights their fathers gave?
  Oh! grieve not, hearts; her matchless slain,
    Crowned with the warrior's wreath.
  From beds of fame their proud refrain
    Was "Liberty or Death!"

"TELL THE BOYS THE WAR IS ENDED."

By EMILY J. MOORE.

Our brave Fitzhugh Lee, of Virginia, relates an interesting anecdote concerning himself and an old farmer: After the surrender at Appomattox, General Lee was on his way home. He met an old farmer on the road on his way to mill, who of course inquired of the soldier the latest news. "General Lee has surrendered," he answered, "and you can tell your neighbors that the war is over." "What," said the old farmer, "General Lee?" "Yes," he replied." "Oh, no," said he, "You cannot mean Robert Lee?" "Yes, sir," replied the General, "Robert Lee has surrendered." "I don't believe it," said the old farmer, and he rode on, saying as he went, "That fool, Fitz Lee, may have surrendered, but not old Robert." The General concluded his account of the incident by saying that he thought it best, under the circumstances, not to make himself known.

"TELL the boys the war is ended,"
    These were all the words he said;
"Tell the boys the war is ended,"
    In an instant more was dead.
Strangely bright, serene, and cheerful
    Was the smile upon his face,
While the pain, of late so fearful,
    Had not left the slightest trace.

5

" Tell the boys the war is ended,"
   And with heavenly visions bright
Thoughts of comrades loved were blended,
   As his spirit took its flight.
" Tell the boys the war is ended,"
    " Grant, O God, it may be so,"
Was the prayer which then ascended,
   In a whisper deep, though low.

        " Tell the boys the war is ended,"
           And his warfare then was o'er,
        As, by angel bands attended,
           He departed from earth's shore.
        Bursting shells and cannon roaring
           Could not rouse him by their din ;
        He to better worlds was soaring,
           Far from war, and pain, and sin.

PRESIDENT DAVIS.

By Jane T. H. Cross.

THE cell is lonely, and the night
   Has filled it with a darker gloom;
The little rays of friendly light,
   Which through each crack and chink found room
To press in with their noiseless feet,
All merciful and fleet,
And bring, like Noah's trembling dove,
God's silent messages of love—
   These, too, are gone, shut out and gone,
And that great heart is left alone.

Alone, with darkness and with woe,
   Around him Freedom's temple lies,
Its arches crushed, its columns low,
   The night-wind through its ruin sighs ·
Rash, cruel hands that temple razed,
Then stood the world amazed !
And now those hands—ah, ruthless deeds !
Their captive pierce—his brave heart bleeds ;
   And yet no groan
   Is heard, no groan !
He suffers silently, alone.

     For all his bright and happy home,
       He has that cell, so drear and dark,
     The narrow walls, for heaven's blue dome,
       The clank of chains, for song of lark ;
     And for the grateful voice of friends—
     That voice which ever lends
     Its charm where human hearts are found—
     He hears the key's dull, grating sound ;
       No heart is near,
       No kind heart near,
     No sigh of sympathy, no tear !

Oh, dream not thus, though true and good !
   Unnumbered hearts on thee await,
By thee invisibly have stood,
   Have crowded through thy prison-gate ;
Nor dungeon bolts, nor dungeon bars,
   Nor floating "stripes and stars,"
Nor glittering gun or bayonet,
Can ever cause us to forget
   Our faith to thee,
   Our love to thee,
Thou glourious soul ! thou strong ! thou free !

THE IRREPRESSIBLE CONFLICT.

It is a well-known fact that during the War many people spoke and sang more bravely than they fought. I remember a fiery speech that I heard in the early days of the War on the great green in our County. The speech was made in a frenzied manner by a prominent and wealthy farmer. One expression I shall not forget—" If those Yankees come down to this sacred soil, I will take my negroes, and my neighbors, and drive them out of the country with corn stalks." The truth is, before the gentlemen referred to appeared in sight, this farmer was seen with his slaves, and his cattle (but not his neighbors) making his way to the South, and he never caught the smell of powder during the whole War.

THEN welcome be it, if indeed it be
    The Irrepressible Conflict! Let it come;
There will be mitigation of the doom,
If, battling to the last, our sires shall see
Their sons contending for the homes made free
    In ancient conflict with the foreign foe!
    If those who call us brethren strike the blow;
    No common conflict shall the invader know!
War to the knife, and to the last, until
    The sacred land we keep shall overflow
With blood as sacred—valley, wave, and hill,
Or the last enemy finds his bloody grave!
Aye! welcome to your graves—or ours! The brave
    May perish, but ye shall not bind one slave.

THE FIRST WHITE HOUSE OF THE CONFEDERACY

This was the residence of President Jefferson Davis at Montgomery, Alabama. It is now known as the home of the Ladies' Memorial Association.

MONUMENT TO THE CONFEDERATE SOLDIERS

Erected on the Capitol Grounds, Montgomery, Alabama, by the Ladies' Memorial Association.

SOUTH CAROLINA.

1719. Colonial Revolution.
1763. Colonial History—Progress.
1776. American Revolution.
1812-15. Second War with Great Britain.
1830-32. Nullification for State Rights.
1835-40. Florida War.
1847. Mexican War—Palmetto Regiment.
1860-61. Secession, and Third War for Independence.

MY brave old Country! I have watched thee long
    Still ever first to rise against the wrong;
To check the usurper in his giant stride,
And brave his terrors and abase his pride;
Forsee the insidious danger ere it rise,
And warn the heedless and inform the wise;
Scorning the lure, the bribe, the selfish game,
Which, through the office, still becomes the shame;
Thou stood'st aloof—superior to the fate
That would have wrecked thy freedom as a State.
In vain the despot's threat, his cunning lure;
Too proud thy spirit, and thy heart too pure;
Thou hadst no quest but freedom, and to be
In conscience well-assured, and people free.
The statesman's lore was thine, the patriot's aim,
These kept thee virtuous, and preserved thy fame;
The wisdom still for council, the brave voice,
That thrills a people till they all rejoice.
These were thy birthrights; and two centuries pass'd,
As, at the first, still find thee at the last;
Supreme in council, resolute in will,
Pure in thy purpose—independent still!

The great good counsels, the examples brave,
Won from the past, not buried in its grave,
Still warm your soul with courage—still impart

Wisdom to virtue, valor to the heart!
Still first to check th' encroachment—to declare
" Thus far! no further, shall the assailant dare ; "
Thou keep'st thy ermine white, thy State secure,
Thy fortunes prosperous, and thy freedom sure ;
No glozing art deceives thee to thy bane ;
The tempter and the usurper strive in vain !
Thy spear's first touch unfolds the fiendish form,
And first, with fearless breast, thou meet'st the storm ;
Though hosts assail thee, thou thyself a host,
Prepar'st to meet the invader on the coast :
Thy generous sons contending which shall be
First in the phalanx, gathering by the sea ;
No dastard fear appals them, as they teach
How best to hurl the bolt, or man the breech !

Great Soul in little frame !   the hope of man
Exults, when such as thou art in the van!
Unshaken, unbeguiled, unslaved, unbought,
Thy fame shall brighten with each battle fought;
True to the examples of the past, thou'lt be,
For the long future, best security.

A BALLAD OF THE WAR.

By George Herbert Sass, of Charleston, South Carolina.

Watchman, what of the night?
    Through the city's darkening street,
Silent and slow the guardsmen go
    On their long and lonely beat.

Darkly, drearily down
    Falleth the wintry rain ;
And the cold, gray mist hath the roof-tops kissed,
    As it glides o'er town and plain.

Beating against the windows,
    The sleet falls heavy and chill,
And the children draw nigher 'round hearth and fire,
    As the blast shrieks loud and shrill.

        Silent is all without,
           Save the sentry's challenge grim,
        And a hush sinks down o'er the weary town,
           And the sleeper's eyes are dim.

Watchman, what of the night?
    Hark! from the old church-tower
Rings loud and clear on the misty air,
    The chime of the midnight hour.

        But another sound breaks in,
           A summons deep and rude,
        The roll of the drum, and the rush and hum
           Of a gathering multitude.

And the dim and flickering torch
    Sheds a red and lurid glare,
O'er the long dark line, whose bayonets shine
    Faintly, yet sternly there.

        A low, deep voice is heard:
           " Rest on your arms, my men."
        Then the muskets clank through each serried rank,
           And all is still again.

Pale faces and tearful eyes
    Gaze down on that grim array,
For a rumor hath spread that that column dread
    Marcheth ere break of day.

Marcheth against " the rebels,"
    Whose camp lies heavy and still,
Where the driving sleet and cold rain beat
    On the brow of a distant hill.

        And the mother's heart grows faint,
            As she thinks of her darling one,
        Who perchance may lie 'neath that wintry sky,
            Ere the long, dark night be done.

Pallid and haggard, too,
    Is the cheek of the fair young wife ;
And her eyes grow dim as she thinks of him
    She loveth more than life.

        For fathers, husbands, sons,
            Are the " rebels " the foe would smite,
        And earnest the prayer for those lives so dear,
            And a bleeding country's right.

And where their treasure is,
    There is each loving heart ;
And sadly they gaze by the torches' blaze,
    And the tears unbidden start.

        Is there none to warn the camp,
            None from that anxious throng?
        Ah, the rain beats down o'er plain and town—
            The way is dark and long.

No man is left behind,
    None that is brave and true,
And the bayonets, bright in the lurid light
    With menace stern shine through.

Guarded is every street,
    Brutal the hireling foe;
Is there one heart here will boldly dare
    So brave a deed to do?

        Look! in her still, dark room,
           Alone a woman kneels,
        With Care's deep trace on her pale, worn face,
           And Sorrow's ruthless seals.

Wrinkling her placid brow,
    A matron, she, and fair,
Though wan her cheek, and the silver streak
    Gemming her glossy hair.

        A moment in silent prayer
           Her pale lips move, and then,
        Through the dreary night, like an angel bright,
           On her mission of love to men.

She glideth upon her way,
    Through the lonely, misty street,
Shrinking with dread as she hears the tread
    Of the watchman on his beat.

        Onward, aye, onward still,
           Far past the weary town,
        Till languor doth seize on her feeble knees,
           And the heavy hands hang down.

But bravely she struggles on,
    Breasting the cold, dank rain,
And, heavy and chill, the mist from the hill
    Sweeps down upon the plain.

Hark ! far behind she hears
    A dull and muffled tramp,
But before her the gleam of the watch-fire's beam
    Shines out from the Southern camp.

      She hears the sentry's challenge,
        Her work of love is done ;
      She has fought a good fight, and on Fame's proud height
        Hath a crown of glory won.

Oh, they tell of a Tyrol maiden,
    Who saved from a ruthless foe
Her own fair town, 'mid its mountains brown,
    Three hundred years ago.

      And I've read in tales heroic
        How a noble Scottish maid
      Her own life gave, her king to save
        From the foul assassin's blade.

But if these, on the rolls of honor,
    Shall live in lasting fame,
Oh, close beside, in grateful pride,
    We'll write this matron's name.

      And when our fair-haired children
        Shall cluster round our knee,
      With wondering gaze, as we tell of the days
        When we swore that we would be free.

We'll tell them the thrillling story,
    And we'll say to each childish heart,
"By this gallant deed, at thy country's need,
    Be ready to do thy part."

MANASSAS.

By Catherine M. Warfield.

One of the most distinguished men in our county in Virginia was the Honorable James Barbour, a prominent lawyer and Member of Congress. Before ever the first gun was fired in our State, I heard him say in a brief speech: "You men who want to fight, go to Manassas, for there the armies will meet, and there the struggle will begin." It was a true prophecy, for the thundering guns of Manassas were heard soon after all around the world.

They have met at last—as storm-clouds meet in heaven ;
    And the Northmen, back and bleeding, have been driven ;
        And their thunders have been stilled,
        And their leaders crushed or killed,
And their ranks, with terror thrilled, rent and riven !

Like the leaves of Vallambrosa they are lying ;
In the moonlight, in the midnight, dead and dying ;
        Like those leaves before the gale,
        Swept their legions, wild and pale :
While the host that made them quail stood, defying.

When aloft in morning sunlight flags were flaunted,
And "swift vengeance on the rebel" proudly vaunted
        Little did they think that night
        Should close upon their shameful flight,
And rebels, victors in the fight, stand undaunted.

But peace to those who perished in our passes !
Light be the earth above them ! green the grasses !
        Long shall Northmen rue the day,
        When they met our stern array,
And shrunk from battle's wild affray at Manassas !

CHARLESTON.

By Paul H. Hayne.

WHAT! still does the Mother of Treason uprear
    Her crest 'gainst the Furies that darken her sea?
Unquelled by mistrust, and unblanched by a Fear,
    Unbowed her proud head, and unbending her knee,
        Calm, steadfast, and free?

Aye! launch your red lightnings, blaspheme in your wrath,
    Shock earth, wave, and heaven with the blasts of your ire;—
But she seizes your death-bolts, yet hot from their path,
    And hurls back your lightnings, and mocks at the fire
        Of your fruitless desire.

Ringed round by her Brave, a fierce circlet of flame,
    Flashes up from the sword-points that cover her breast
She is guarded by Love, and enhaloed by Fame,
    And never, we swear, shall your footsteps be pressed
        Where her dead heroes rest!

Her voice shook the Tyrant—sublime from her tongue
    Fell the accents of warning,—a Prophetess grand,—
On her soil the first life-notes of Liberty rung,
    And the first stalwart blow of her gauntleted hand
        Broke the sleep of her land!

What more! she hath grasped with her iron-bound will
    The Fate that would trample her honor to earth,—
The light in those deep eyes is luminous still
    With the warmth of her valor, the glow of her worth,
        Which illumine the Earth!

FIRST BATTLE OF BULL RUN, 1861

On July 21, 1861, occurred the first great battle of the War, resulting in the
complete defeat of the Union army, which fled in panic from the field.

And beside her a Knight the great Bayard had loved,
    "Without fear or reproach," lifts her Banner on high;
He stands in the vanguard, majestic unmoved,
      And a thousand firm souls, when that Chieftain is nigh
        Vow, "'tis easy to die!"

Their swords have gone forth on the fetterless air!
    The world's breath is hushed at the conflict! before
Gleams the bright form of Freedom with wreaths in her hair—
      And what though the chaplet be crimsoned with gore,
        We shall prize her the more!

And while Freedom lures on with her passionate eyes
    To the height of her promise, the voices of yore,
From the storied Profound of past ages arise,
      And the pomps of their magical music outpour
        O'er the war-beaten shore.

Then gird your brave Empress, O! Heroes, with flame
    Flashed up from the sword-points that cover her breast.
She is guarded by Love, and enhaloed by Fame,
      And never, base Foe! shall your footsteps be pressed
        Where her dead Martyrs rest!

THE LONE SENTRY

By James R. Randall.

Previous to the first battle of Manassas, when the troops under Stonewall Jackson had made a forced march, on halting at night, they fell on the ground, exhausted and faint. The hour arrived for setting the watch for the night. The officer of the day went to the general's tent, and said:

" General, the men are all wearied, and there is not one but is asleep. Shall I wake them ? "

"No," said the noble Jackson ; let them sleep. and I will watch the camp to-night."

And all night long he rode round that lonely camp, the one lone sentinel for that brave, but weary and silent body of Virginia heroes. And when glorious morning broke, the soldiers awoke fresh and ready for action, all unconscious of the noble vigils kept over their slumbers.

'Twas in the dying of the day,
  The darkness grew so still ;
The drowsy pipe of evening birds
  Was hushed upon the hill ;
Athwart the shadows of the vale
  Slumbered the men of might,
And one lone sentry paced his rounds,
  To watch the camp that night.

A grave and solemn man was he,
  With deep and sombre brow ;
The dreamful eyes seemed hoarding up
  Some unaccomplished vow.
The wistful glance peered o'er the plains
  Beneath the starry light,
And with the murmured name of God,
  He watched the camp that night.

The Future opened unto him
  Its grand and awful scroll :
Manassas and the Valley march
  Came heaving o'er his soul ;

Richmond and Sharpsburg thundered by
    With that tremendous fight
Which gave him to the angel hosts
    Who watched the camp that night.

        We mourn for him who died for us
            With one resistless moan ;
        While up the Valley of the Lord
            He marches to the Throne !
        He kept the faith of men and saints
            Sublime, and pure, and bright—
        He sleeps—and all is well with him
            Who watched the camp that night.

Brothers ! the Midnight of the Cause
    Is shrouded in our fate ;
The demon Goths pollute our halls
    With fire, and lust, and hate.
Be strong—be valiant—be assured—
    Strike home for Heaven and Right !
The soul of Jackson stalks abroad,
    And guards the camp to-night.

THE SWORD OF ROBERT LEE.

By Father Ryan.

Forth from its scabbard, pure and bright,
    Flashed the sword of Lee !
Far in the front of the deadly fight,
High o'er the brave, in the cause of right,
Its stainlees sheen, like a beacon-light,
    Led us to victory.

Out of its scabbard, where full long—
    It slumbered peacefully—
Roused from its rest by the battle-song,
Shielding the feeble, smiting the strong,
Guarding the right, and avenging the wrong—
    Gleamed that sword of Lee !

        Forth from its scabbard, high in air,
            Beneath Virginia's sky—
        And they who saw it gleaming there,
        And knew who bore it, knelt to swear,
        That where the sword led they would dare
            To follow and to die.

Out of its scabbard !   Never hand
    Waved sword from stain as free,
Nor purer sword led braver band,
Nor braver bled for a brighter land,
Nor brighter land had a cause as grand,
    Nor cause, a chief like Lee !

        Forth from its scabbard ! how we prayed
            That sword might victor be !
        And when our triumph was delayed,
        And many a heart grew sore afraid,
        We still hoped on, while gleamed the blade
            Of noble Robert Lee !

Forth from its scabbard ! all in vain !
    Forth flashed the sword of Lee !
'Tis shrouded now in its sheath again,
It sleeps the sleep of our noble slain,
Defeated, yet without a stain,
    Proudly and peacefully.

A PRAYER FOR PEACE.

By S. Teacle Wallis, of Maryland.

One of the most distinguished lawyers and citizens of Baltimore, Maryland, was the Honorable S. Teacle Wallis. His " Prayer for Peace " will be read with deep interest by all. There were many other prayers for peace, and though it may provoke a smile, I will tell you of one which occurred a little farther South than Maryland. It was not long before the close of the War. The old man was a farmer, loyal and true. A little prayer meeting of a small remnant of citizens was being held, and one after another was praying for the Southern cause. Finally, this old man was called upon. His first sentence, it seems to me, covered the whole ground. He said, " O Lord ! have mercy on our Southern Confederacy, for her affairs are in a very bad shape, we do assure Thee."

PEACE ! Peace ! God of our fathers grant us Peace !
Unto our cry of anguish and despair
Give ear and pity ! From the lonely homes,
Where widowed beggary and orphaned woe
Fill their poor urns with tears ; from trampled plains,
Where the bright harvest Thou hast sent us rots—
The blood of them who should have garnered it
Calling to Thee—from fields of carnage, where
The foul-beaked vultures, sated, flap their wings
O'er crowded corpses, that but yesterday
Bore hearts of brother, beating high with love
And common hopes and pride, all blasted now—
Father of Mercies ! not alone from these
Our prayer and wail are lifted. Not alone
Upon the battle's seared and desolate track !
Nor with the sword and flame, is it, O God,
That thou hast smitten us. Around our hearths,
And in the crowded streets and busy marts,
Where echo whispers not the far-off strife
That slays our loved ones ; in the solemn halls
Of safe and quiet counsel—nay, beneath
The temple-roofs that we have reared to Thee,
And 'mid their rising incense—God of Peace !

6

The curse of war is on us.   Greed and hate
Hungering for gold and blood ; Ambition, bred
Of passionate vanity and sordid lusts,
Mad with the base desire of tyrannous sway
Over men's souls and thoughts, have set their price
On human hecatombs, and sell and buy
Their sons and brothers for the shambles. Priests,
With white, anointed, supplicating hands,
From Sabbath unto Sabbath clasped to Thee,
Burn in their tingling pulses, to fling down
Thy censers and Thy cross, to clutch the throats
Of kinsmen, by whose cradles they were born,
Or grasp the hand of Herod, and go forth
Till Rachel hath no children left to slay.
The very name of Jesus, writ upon
Thy shrines beneath the spotless, outstretched wings
Of Thine Almighty Dove, is wrapt and hid
With bloody battle-flags, and from the spires
That rise above them angry banners flout
The skies to which they point, amid the clang
Of rolling war-songs tuned to mock Thy praise.

All things once prized and honored are forgot ;
The freedom that we worshipped next to Thee ;
The manhood that was freedom's spear and shield ;
The proud, true heart ; the brave, outspoken word,
Which might be stifled, but could never wear
The guise, whate'er the profit, of a lie ;
All these are gone, and in their stead have come
The vices of the miser and the slave—
Scorning no shame that bringeth gold or power,
Knowing no love, or faith, or reverence,
Or sympathy, or tie, or aim, or hope,
Save as begun in self, and ending there.
With vipers like to these, oh ! blessed God !
Scourge us no longer ! Send us down, once more,

Some shining seraph in Thy glory clad,
To wake the midnight of our sorrowing
With tidings of good-will and peace to men;
And if that star, that through the darkness led
Earth's wisdom the guide, not our folly now,
Oh, be the lightning Thine Evangelist,
With all its fiery, forked tongues, to speak
The unanswerable message of Thy will.

Peace ! Peace ! God of our fathers, grant us peace !
Peace to our hearts, and at Thine altars ; peace
On the red waters and their blighted shores ;
Peace for the 'leaguered cities, and the hosts
That watch and bleed around them and within,
Peace for the homeless and the fatherless ;
Peace for the captive on his weary way,
And the mad crowds who jeer his helplessness ;
For them that suffer, them that do the wrong
Sinning and sinned against.   O God ! for all ;
For a distracted, torn, and bleeding land—
Speed the glad tidings !   Give us, give us Peace !

"THE SOUTHERN CROSS."

By St. George Tucker, of Virginia.

Oh ! say can you see, through the gloom and the storm,
    More bright for the darkness, that pure constellation!
Like the symbol of love and redemption its form,
As it points to the haven of hope for the nation.
Now radiant each star, as the beacon afar,
Giving promise of peace, or assurance in war,
'Tis the Cross of the South, which shall ever remain
To light us to freedom and glory again !

How peaceful and blest was America's soil,
'Till betrayed by the guile of the Puritan demon,
Which lurks under virtue, and springs from its coil
To fasten its fangs in the life-blood of freemen.
Then boldly appeal to each heart that can feel,
And crush the foul viper 'neath Liberty's heel !
And the Cross of the South shall in triumph remain,
To light us to freedom and glory again !

'Tis the emblem of peace, 'tis the day-star of hope,
Like the sacred Labarum that guided the Roman ;
From the shores of the Gulf to the Delaware's slope,
'Tis the trust of the free, and the terror of foemen.
Fling its folds to the air, while we boldly declare
The rights we demand or the deeds that we dare !
While the Cross of the South shall in triumph remain,
To light us to freedom and glory again !

And if peace should be hopeless and justice denied,
And war's bloody vulture should flap its black pinions,
Then gladly " to arms," while we hurl, in our pride,
Defiance to tyrants and death to their minions !
With our front in the field, swearing never to yield,
On return, like the Spartan, in death on our shield !
And the Cross of the South shall triumphantly wave,
As the flag of the free, or the pall of the brave !

GENERAL LEE'S INVASION OF THE NORTH

" THE BALTIMORE GRAYS."

It is a well-known fact that some of the first blood that was shed during the war was upon the streets of Baltimore when the Sixth Massachusetts Regiment undertook to march from one station to another. Although Maryland remained in the Union, some of her finest fighters were on the Confederate side. But it is a significant evidence of the splendid feeling later existing throughout the country, that early in the days of the Spanish-American War, when the Sixth Massachusetts Regiment was again to pass through Baltimore, although railways have been constructed now through the State and city, and it was not necessary for them to walk, the city, through its Mayor, requested the Commanding General of the United States Armies to permit the Sixth Massachusetts Regiment to leave the train at one station in that city, and march through the streets to another station, so that Baltimore might show her true loyalty to the United States, and her hospitality to its soldiers. I was on the street side when the regiment passed along through a living wall of enthusiastic citizens on each side. We threw them flowers, we deafened them with cheers, we filled their stomachs full, and sent them on their way rejoicing. " Hurrah for America!" rang from ten thousand throats.

A<small>H</small>, well I remember that long summer's day
    When, round about Richmond our broken ranks lay.
Week in and week out they had been at the front,
And bore without flinching the battle's fierce brunt.
Till, shattered and weary, we needed repose
Ere we met in death-struggle our numberless foes.
Our knapsacks were empty, our uniforms worn,
Our feet, from long marching, were naked and torn ;
But not a man grumbled in the rank or the file,
We bore all our hardships with a joke and a smile,
For Jackson was with us, and under his eye,
Each soldier determined to do or to die.

That evening old Jack had us out on review,
When a glance down the line showed us all something new—
Eighty-seven young boys from old Baltimore,
Who had run the blockade and that day joined the corps.
Their clothes were resplendent, all new, spick and span—
'Twas plain that a tailor had measured each man.

When we learned who they were what a shout we did raise!
How we cheered our new allies, the " Baltimore Grays!"
There were Lightfoots and Carters, and Howards and Kanes,
The grandsons of Carroll, the nephews of Gaines,
And in each of the brave boys dressed up in a row,
You could see the pure blood of the proud Huguenot.

But we were old vets of Stonewall's brigade;
We'd been fighting so long that war seemed a trade;
And some of us laughed at the youngsters so gay
Who had come to the battle as if coming to play;
And all through the camp you could hear the rough wits
Cry, " Hullo, young roosters!" and " Dandified cits!"
But the boys took it bravely, and heartily laughed
At the hungry " Confeds" by whom they were chaffed,
Till one ragged soldier, more bold than the rest,
Fired off this rough joke, which we all thought the best:
" Boys, you'd better go home; 'tis getting quite late."
Then the girlish-faced captain spoke up and said, " Wait!"

They didn't wait long, for the very next day
We were ordered right off to the thick of the fray;
For early that morning we'd heard the dull roar
Of the guns of our foeman on Rapidan's shore,
And all of us knew, with old Jack in command,
If fighting was near him, he'd at once take a hand.
And, sure enough, soon marching orders we got,
And we swung down the road in " foot-cavalry " trot.
The boys were behind us.   I fell to the rear,
To see how the youngsters on march would appear.
Their files were close up, their marching was true,
I reported to Stonewall, " Yes, General, they'll do."

In a few minutes more the action began.
We met the first shock, for we were the van;
But we stood to our ranks like oaks of the field,

For Stonewall's brigade never knew how to yield.
Upon us, however, a battery played,
And huge gaps in our ranks were now and then made,
Till Jackson commanded a charge up the hill.
We charged—in a moment the cannon were still.
Jackson said to the Grays, "Such valor you've shown,
You'll veterans be ere your beards are full grown;
In this, your first action, you've proved yourself bold;
I'll station you here, these guns you must hold."

Then the girlish-faced captain, so straight and so tall,
Saluted, and said, "You'll here find us all,
For, wherever stationed, this company stays."
How we laughed, how we cheered the bold Baltimore Grays!
But the red tide of battle around us still flowed,
And we followed our leader, as onward he rode;
Cried "Good-by" to the boys; "take care of the guns—
We'll relieve you as soon as the enemy runs."
Ah, yes, indeed! soon the brave boys were relieved,
But not in the manner we all had believed;
Alas, the sisters who weep and the mothers who pine
For the loved and the lost of the Maryland line!

By some fatal blunder our left was exposed,
And by thousands of Federals the boys were enclosed;
They asked for no quarter, their Maryland blood
Never dreamed of surrender, they fell where they stood.
We heard in the distance the firing and noise,
And double-quicked back to the help of the boys.
The guns were soon ours; but oh, what a sight!
Every Baltimore boy had been killed in the fight,
Save the girlish-faced captain, and he scarce alive.
When he saw us around him he seemed to revive,
And smiled when we told him the field had been won,
And the Baltimore Grays had saved every gun.

The Stonewall rode up and endeavored to speak,
But his utterance was choked, and down his bronzed cheek
The hot tears flowed, as he gazed on the dead,
"God pity their mothers and sisters!" he said.
Then, dismounting, he knelt on the blood-sodden sand,
And prayed while he held the dying boy's hand;
The gallant young hero said, "General, I knew
That the Grays to your orders would always be true;
You'll miss not a Gray from our final call;
Look around you, my General—you'll here find us all."
The blood gushed from his mouth, his head sunk on his breast,
And the girlish-faced captain lay dead with the rest.

THE RIFLEMAN'S FANCY SHOT.

"RIFLEMAN, shoot me a fancy shot,
    Straight at that heart of yon prowling vedette;
Ring me a ball on the glittering spot
    That shines on his breast like an amulet."

"Ah, captain! here goes for a fine-drawn bead;
    There's music around when my barrel's in tune."
Crack! went the rifle; the messenger sped,
    And dead from his horse fell the ringing dragoon.

"Now, rifleman, steal through the bushes, and snatch
    From yon victim some trinket to handsel first blood:
A button, a loop, or that luminous patch
    That gleams in the moon like a diamond stud."

"Oh, captain! I staggered, and sank in my track,
    When I gazed on the face of the fallen vedette;
For he looked so like you, as he lay on his back,
    That my heart rose upon me, and masters me yet.

" But I snatched off the trinket—this locket of gold ;
    An inch from the centre my lead broke its way,
Scarce grazing the picture, so fair to behold,
    Of a beautiful lady in bridal array."

" Ha ! rifleman ! fling me the locket—'tis she !
    My brother's young bride ; and the fallen dragoon
Was her husband.   Hush, soldier !—'twas heaven's decree ;
    We must bury him there, by the light of the moon.

" But hark ! the far bugles their warning unite ;
    War is a virtue, and weakness a sin;
There's a lurking and lopping around us to-night :
    Load again, rifleman, keep your hand in !"

JOE JOHNSTON.

By John R. Thompson.

ONCE more to the breach for the land of the West !
    And a leader we give of our bravest and best,
    Of his State and his army the pride ;
Hope shines like the plume of Navarre on his crest,
    And gleams in the glaive at his side.

For his courage is keen, and his honor is bright
As the trusty Toledo he wears to the fight,
    Newly wrought in the forges of Spain ;
And this weapon, like all he has brandished for right,
    Will never be dimmed by a stain.

He leaves the loved soil of Virginia behind,
Where the dust of his fathers is fitly enshrined,
    Where lie the fresh fields of his fame ;
Where the murmurous pines, as they sway in the wind,
    Seem ever to whisper his name.

The Johnstons have always borne wings on their spurs,
And their motto a noble distinction confers—
    " Ever ready ! " for friend or for foe—
With a patriot's fervor the sentiment stirs
    The large, manly heart of our JOE.

We read that a former bold chief of the clan,
Fell, bravely defending the West, in the van,
    On Shiloh's illustrious day ;
And with reason we reckon our Johnston's the man
    The dark, bloody debt to repay.

There is much to be done ; if not glory to seek,
There's a just and a terrible vengeance to wreak
    For crimes of a terrible dye ;
While the plaint of the helpless, the wail of the weak,
    In a chorus rise up to the sky.

For the Wolf of the North we once drove to his den,
That quailed with affright 'neath the stern glance of men,
    With his pack has returned to the spoil ;
Then come from the mountain, the hamlet, the glen,
    And drive him again from your soil.

Brave-born Tennesseeans, so loyal, so true,
Who have hunted the beast in your highlands, of you
    Our leader had never a doubt ;
You will troop by the thousand the chase to renew,
    The day that his bugles ring out.

But ye " Hunters," so famed, " of Kentucky " of yore,
Where now are the rifles that kept from your door
    The wolf and the robber as well ?
Of a truth, you have never been laggard before
    To deal with a savage so fell.

Has the love you once bore to your country grown cold ?
Has the fire on the altar died out ?   Do you hold
    Your lives than your freedom more dear ?

Can you shamefully barter your birthright for gold,
    Or basely take counsel of fear?

We will not believe it; Kentucky, the land
Of a Clay, will not tamely submit to the brand
    That disgraces the dastard, the slave;
The hour of redemption draws nigh, is at hand,
    Her own sons her own honor shall save!

Mighty men of Missouri, come forth to the call,
When the rush of your rivers, when tempests appal,
    And the torrents their sources unseal;
And this be the watchword of one and of all—
    " Remember the butcher, McNeil!"

Then once more to the breach for the land of the West;
Strike home for your hearths—for the lips you love best;
    Follow on where your leader you see;
One flash of his sword, when the foe is hard pressed,
    And the land of the West shall be free!

The Memorial Tablet to Major-General Forrest,
C. S. A., Erected on Forrest Avenue, Atlanta, Ga.

THE DENOMINATIONAL TEAM.

BY MORTON BRYAN WHARTON, D. D.

My brother, M. B. Wharton, as I have already said, is given to poetry. He is a Baptist preacher, and was such during the war, but he served his country also, and did double duty in that service. I hardly think his own patriotism ever rose to such a fervent heat, as did another minister's, who was pastor of a church in Alabama. He was a man of the back country, but he knew what loyalty was, and did not fail to express his feelings. The first soldier who was killed and brought back home was buried from the church of which this aged minister was pastor. There was no building large enough to hold the crowd present on that occasion, so the funeral services were conducted out of doors, and the old man stood on a box under a tree, as he read the hymns, commented upon the Scriptures, and delivered his sermon. In concluding his earnest remarks, he cried out, " Ah, my brethren, our young friend has gone from us, but we shall meet again, for the Scriptures tell us that many shall come from the East, and many shall come from the West, and many shall come from the South," and then pausing, his gray hair floating in the breeze, his cheeks wet with tears, he lifted both hands to Heaven, and closing his eyes said, in a low, hardly audible voice, and " perhaps a very few may come from the North."

A RUSTIC teamster on the street
    Of a Texas town appears,
He brings the people to their feet,
They stand in wonderment complete,
    For the names he called his steers.

    " Get up, get up there, Methodist ;
      Whoa, Baptist ! " loud he cries.
    He gives his whip a lightning twist,
    Old Presbyterian's barely missed,
      To " Campbellite " it flies.

" Pray tell us what your names may mean ? "
    Exclaimed a wag who passed ;
The man replied, " Each steer, I ween,
Does to some sect of Christians lean,
    And so I've got them classed."

NEARING APPOMATTOX

"Just look at Methodist," he said ;
 "He goes at a rapid pace,
He bellows till he splits your head;
But once neglected to be fed
 He's sure to fall from grace.

  "Episcopalian's kind and bright,
   But gay and giddy ever,
  While the reverse is Campbellite ;
  He's always spoiling for a fight,
   And lies down in the river.

"There's Presbyterian, strict new school,
 Has hydrophobia sorter ;
He's true and faithful as a rule,
But when he strikes a stream or pool
 He leaps clean o'er the water.

  "There's Baptist, good, but very queer,
   On charity he's off ;
  He's willing and obedient e'er,
  But won't permit another steer
   To eat from out his trough.

"That big fat ox is Catholic ;
 He's of most ancient birth ;
He's up to many a crafty trick,
 Against all other steers will kick,
  And always wants the earth.

  "But though these steers are different quite,
   At one great end they aim ;
  'Tis true they sometimes skulk and fight,
  But still they keep the goal in sight,
   And get there all the same."

OVER THE RIVER.

By Jane T. Cross.

We hail your " Stripes " and lessened " stars,"
    As one may hail a neighbor ;
Now forward move ! no fear of jars,
    With nothing but free labor ;
And we will mind our slaves and farm,
And never wish you any harm,
    But greet you—over the river.

The self-same language do we speak,
    The same dear words we utter ;
Then let's not make each other weak,
    Nor 'gainst each other mutter ;
But let each go his separate way,
And each will doff his hat, and say :
    " I greet you—over the river ! "

Our flags, almost the same, unfurl,
    And nod across the border ;
Ohio's waves between them curl—
    Our stripe's a little broader ;
May yours float out on every breeze,
And, in our wake, traverse all seas—
    We greet you—over the river !

We part as friends of years should part,
    With pleasant words and wishes,
And no desire is in our heart
    For Lincoln's loaves and fishes :
" Farewell," we wave you from afar,
We like you best—just where you are—
    And greet you—over the river !

KENTUCKY REQUIRED TO YIELD HER ARMS.

Boone.

It will be observed that the name of Boone stands here as the author of this song. It puts me in mind of the following story: Many years ago there lived upon the frontier a man and his family, struggling in the depths of the forest to make a living, and to establish himself upon what was then the Western Territory. Indians and wild animals were around him everywhere, and when the farmer went to the forests, he went with axe in one hand, and gun in the other. One day he heard the screams of his wife, and rushing out of the woods to his little cabin he saw an Indian running away with his baby boy. He lifted his rifle, took the best aim he could, and fired. The Indian only turned and laughed at him, and went on. Just then he heard a voice behind him, saying, " A little too low; you aimed too low." And with that he heard the crack of a rifle and saw the Indian fall, as the little boy, released from his grasp, came running back to his father and mother. The glad-hearted father turned to the man who had killed the Indian, and said to him, "Tell me who you are; give me your name that I may teach it to my child, and ever remember it with a grateful heart." The man smiled, and, extending his hand, said, " Daniel Boone, with my best wishes," and turned away to the forest. He had aimed exactly right, and so did the Kentucky soldiers during the war. No wonder they were called upon to give up their arms.

Ho ! will the despot trifle,
　　In dwellings of the free ;
Kentuckians yield the rifle,
　　Kentuckians bend the knee !
With dastard fear of danger,
　　And trembling at the strife ;
Kentucky, to the stranger,
　　Yield liberty for life !
Up ! up ! each gallant ranger,
　　With rifle and with knife !

　　　　The bastard and the traitor,
　　　　　　The wolfcub and the snake,
　　　　The robber, swindler, hater,
　　　　　　Are in your homes—awake !

Nor let the cunning foeman
 Despoil your liberty ;
Yield weapon up to no man,
 While ye can strike and see,
Awake, each gallant yoeman,
 If still ye would be free !

  Ay, see to sight the rifle,
   And smite with spear and knife,
  Let no base cunning stifle
   Each lesson of your life :
  How won your gallant sires
   The country which ye keep ?
  By soul, which still inspires
   The soil on which ye weep !
  Leap up ! their spirit fires,
   And rouse ye from your sleep !

" What ! " cry the sires so famous,
 In Orleans' ancient field,
" Will ye, our children, shame us,
 And to the despot yield ?
What ! each brave lesson stifle
 We left to give you life ?
Let apish despots trifle
 With home and child and wife?
And yield, O shame ! the rifle,
 And sheathe, O shame ! the knife ? "

"THERE'S LIFE IN THE OLD LAND YET."

B<small>Y</small> blue Patapsco's billowy dash
 The tyrant's war-shout comes,
Along with the cymbal's fitful clash
 And the growl of his sullen drums ;

We hear it, we heed it, with vengeful thrills,
    And we shall not forgive or forget—
There's faith in the streams, there's hope in the hills,
    " There's life in the Old Land yet ! "

        Minions ! we sleep, but we are not dead,
            We are crushed, we are scourged, we are scarred—
        We crouch—'tis to welcome the triumph-tread
            Of the peerless Beauregard.
        Then woe to your vile, polluting horde,
            When the Southern braves are met ;
        There's faith in the victor's stainless sword,
            " There's life in the Old Land yet ! "

Bigots ! ye quell not the valiant mind
    With the clank of an iron chain ;
The spirit of Freedom sings in the wind
    O'er Merryman, Thomas, and Kane ;
And we—though we smite not—are not thralls,
    We are piling a gory debt ;
While down by McHenry's dungeon walls
    " There's life in the Old Land yet ! "

        Our women have hung their harps away,
            And they scowl on your brutal bands,
        While the nimble poignard dares the day
            In their dear defiant hands ;
        They will strip their tresses to string our bows
            Ere the Northern sun is set—
        There's faith in their unrelenting woes—
            " There's life in the Old Land yet ! "

There's life, though it throbbeth in silent veins,
    " 'Tis vocal without noise ;
It gushed o'er Manassas' solemn plains
    From the blood of the Maryland boys.

7

That blood shall cry aloud and rise
　　With an everlasting threat—
By the death of the brave, by the God in the skies,
" There's life in the Old Land yet ! "

THE BATTLE OF RICHMOND.

By George Herbert Sass, Charleston, South Carolina.

Now blessed be the Lord of Hosts through all our Southern
　　land,
And blessed be His holy name, in whose great might we
　　stand ;
For He who loves the voice of prayer hath heard His people's
　　cry,
And with His own almighty arm hath won the victory ;
Oh, tell it out through hearth and home, from blue Potomac's
　　wave
To those far waters of the West which hide De Soto's grave.

Now let there be through all the land one grand triumphant
　　cry,
Wherever beats a Southern heart, or glows a Southern sky ;
For He who ruleth every fight hath been with us to-day,
And the great God of battles hath led the glorious fray ;
Oh, then unto His holy name ring out the joyful song,
The race hath not been to the swift, the battle to the strong.

　*　　*　　*　　*　　*　　*　　*

From royal Hudson's cliff-crowned banks, from proud Ohio's
　　flood,
From that dark rock in Plymouth's bay where erst the
　　Pilgrims stood,
From East and North, from far and near, went forth the
　　gathering cry,

And the countless hordes came swarming on with fierce and
      lustful eye.
In the great name of Liberty each thirsty sword is drawn;
In the great name of Liberty each tyrant presseth on.

Alas, alas! her sacred name is all dishonored now,
And blood-stained hands are tearing off each laurel from her
      brow,
But ever yet rings out the cry, in loud and mocking tone,
Still in her holy shrine they strive to rear a despot's throne;
And pressing on with eager tread, they sweep across the land,
To burn, and havoc, and destroy—a fierce and ruthless band.

I looked on fair Potomac's shore, and at my feet the while
The sparkling waves leaped gayly up to meet glad summer's
      smile;
And pennons gay were floating there, and banners fair to see,
A mighty host arrayed, I ween, in war's proud panoply;
And as I gazed a cry arose, a low, deep-swelling hum,
And loud and stern along the line broke in the sullen drum.

Onward, o'er fair Virginia's fields, through ranks of nodding
      grain,
With shout and song they sweep along, a gay and gallant
      train.
Oh, ne'er, I ween, had those broad plains beheld a fairer sight,
And clear and glad those skies of June shed forth their glorious
      light.
Onwards, yea, ever onwards, that mighty host hath passed,
And "On to Richmond" is the cry which echoes on the
      blast.

I looked again, the rising sun shines down upon the moors,
And 'neath his beams rise ramparts high and frowning
      embrasures,
And on each proud abattis yawn, with menace stern and
      dread,

Grim-visaged messengers of death; the watchful sentry's
　　tread
In measured cadence slowly falls; all Nature seems at ease,
And over all the Stars and Stripes are floating in the breeze.

But far away another line is stretching dark and long,
Another flag is floating free where armed legions throng;
Another war-cry's on the air, as wakes the martial drum,
And onward still, in serried ranks, the Southern soldiers
　　come,
And up to that abattis high the charging columns tread,
And bold and free the Stars and Bars are waving at their
　　head.

They are on it! they are o'er it! who can stay that living
　　flood?
Lo, ever swelling, rolleth on the weltering tide of blood.
Yet another and another is full boldly stormed and won,
And forward to the spoiler's camp the column presseth on.
Hurrah! hurrah! the field is won! we've met them man to
　　man,
And ever still the Stars and Bars are riding in the van.

They are flying! they are flying! and close upon their track
Comes our glorious "Stonewall" Jackson, with ten thousand
　　at his back;
And Longstreet, too, and gallant Hill, and Rhodes, and brave
　　Hugee,
And he whose name is worth a host, our bold, devoted Lee;
And back to where the lordly James his scornful billows rolls,
The recreant foe is fleeing fast—those men of dastard souls.

They are flying! they are flying! horse and foot, and bold
　　dragoon,
In one refluent mass are mingled, 'neath the slowly waning
　　moon;

THE WASHINGTON MONUMENT IN RICHMOND, VIRGINIA
From photograph made for this work by Edyth Carter Beveridge.

And louder still the cry is heard, as borne upon the blast,
The shouts of the pursuing host are rising full and fast;
"On, on unto the river, 'tis our only chance for life!
We needs must reach the gunboats, or we perish in the
      strife!"

'Tis done! the gory field is ours; we've conquered in the
      fight!
And yet once more our tongues can tell the triumph of the
      right;
And humbled is the haughty foe, who our destruction sought,
For God's right hand and holy arm have great deliverance
      wrought.
Oh, then, unto His holy name ring out the joyful song—
The race has not been to the swift, the battle to the strong.

THE GUERRILLAS: A SOUTHERN WAR SONG.

Composed in the Yankee Bastille.

BY S. TEACLE WALLIS, of Maryland.

Mr. Wallis died in Baltimore a few years ago. He was an eminent
lawyer and a valued citizen.

"AWAKE! and to horse, my brother!
    For the dawn is glimmering gray;
And hark! in the crackling brushwood
    There are feet that tread this way.
Who cometh?" "A friend." "What tidings?"
    "O God! I sicken to tell,
For the earth seems earth no longer,
    And its sights are sights of hell!

" From far-off conquered cities
    Comes a voice of stifled wail,
And the shrieks and moans of the houseless
    Ring out like a dirge on the gale.
I've seen, from the smoking village,
    Our mothers and daughters fly ;
I've seen where the little children
    Sank down in the furrows to die.

" On the banks of the battle-stained river
    I stood, as the moonlight shone,
And it glared on the face of my brother,
    As the sad wave swept him on !
Where my home was glad are ashes ;
    And horrors and shame had been there—
For I found, on the fallen lintel,
    This tress of my wife's torn hair.

" They are turning the slaves upon us,
    And, with more than the fiend's worst art,
Have uncovered the fire of the savage,
    That slept in his untaught heart.
The ties to our heart that bound him,
    They have rent with curses away,
And maddened him with their madness,
    To be almost as brutal as they.

" With halter, and torch, and Bible,
    And hymns to the sound of the drum,
They preach the gospel of Murder,
    And pray for Lust's kingdom to come.
To saddle ! to saddle ! my brothers !
    Look up to the rising sun,
And ask the God who shines there,
    Whether deeds like these shall be done !

" Whenever the vandal cometh,
 Press home to his heart with your steel,
And when at his bosom you cannot,
 Like a serpent, go strike at his heel.
Through thicket and wood go hunt him,
 Creep up to his camp fireside,
And let ten of his corpses blacken,
Where one of our brothers hath died.

  In his fainting, footsore marches,
   In his flight from the stricken fray,
  In the snare of the lonely ambush,
   The debts we owe him pay.
  In God's hand, alone, is vengeance!
   But He strikes with the hands of men,
  And His blight would wither our manhood,
   If we smite not the smiter again.

" By the graves where our fathers slumbered !
 By the shrines where our mothers prayed !
By our homes, and hopes, and freedom !
 Let every man swear on his blade,
That he will not sheath nor stay it,
 Till from point to hilt it will glow,
With the flush of almighty vengeance,
 In the blood of the felon foe."

  They swore—and the answering sunlight
   Leapt red from their lifted swords,
  And the hate of their hearts made echo
   To the wrath in their burning words.
  There's weeping in all New England,
   And by Schuylkill's banks a knell,
  And the widows there, and the orphans,
   How the oath was kept can tell.

OUR DEAD HEROES.

(Introduction by MORTON BRYAN WHARTON, D. D.

THE angels above us hover,
     And the breezes a requiem sing,
As we meet this day to cover,
     Our dead with the flowers of Spring.
They were brave, they were true, devoted,
     They died for their country's laws,
And Montgomery will e'er be noted
     As the cradle of their cause.

          The waves of the Alabama
               Will no longer be seen to roll,
          Ere the men of that mighty drama
               Shall fade from memory's scroll.
          The names of Lee and Davis
               Shall gild the wing of time,
          Their armies and their navies,
               Be praised for deeds sublime !

Since then long years have vanished,
     Their forms have gone to dust,
Their flags have all been banished,
     Their swords have gone to rust.
But their souls are up in glory,
     And now like angels gleam ;
Last night their mystic story,
     Came to me in a dream.

THE PHANTOM HOST.

By Father Ryan.

MY form was wrapped in the slumber
    Which steals from the heart its cares,
For my life was weary
    With its barren waste of years;
But my soul, with rapid pinions,
    Fled swift to the light which seems
From a phantom's sun and planets
    For the dreamer in his dreams.

    I stood in a wondrous woodland,
        Where the sunlight nestled sweet
    In the cups of snowy lilies
        Which grew about my feet;
    And while the Gothic forest arches
        Stirred gently with the air
    The lilies underneath them
        Swung their censors pale in prayer.

I stood amazed and wondering,
    And a grand memoriam strain
Came sweeping through the forest,
    And died; then rose again.
It swelled in solemn measure,
    Till my soul, with comfort blessed,
Sank down among the lilies
    With folded wings to rest.

    Then to that mystic music
        Through the forest's twilight aisle
    Passed a host with muffled footsteps
        In martial rank and file;

And I knew those gray-clad figures,
 Thus slowly passing by,
Were the souls of Southern soldiers
 Who for freedom dared to die.

    In front rode Sidney Johnston,
     With a brow no longer wrung
    By the vile and senseless slanders
     Of a prurient rabble tongue;
    And near him mighty Jackson,
     With a placid front, as one
    Whose warfare was accomplished,
     Whose crown of glory won.

There Hill, too, pure and noble,
 Passed in the spirit train,
For he joined the martyred army
 From the South's last battle plain.
The next in order followed
 The warrior-priest, great Polk,
With joy to meet his Master,
 For he had nobly borne the yoke.

    There Stuart, the bold, the daring,
     With matchless Pelham rode;
    With earnest, chastened faces,
     They were looking up to God.
    And Jenkins, glorious Jenkins,
     With his patient, fearless eyes,
    And the brave devoted Garnett,
     Journeyed on to Paradise.

Before a shadowy squadron
 Rode Morgan, keen and strong,
And I knew by his tranquil forehead
 He'd forgotten every wrong.

There peerless Pegram marching
    With a dauntless, martial tread,
And I breathed a sigh for the hero,
    The young, the early dead.

        'Mid spectral black-horse troopers
            Passed Ashby's stalwart form,
        With that proud, defiant bearing
            Which so spurned the battle storm;
        But his glance was mild and tender,
            For in that Phantom Host
        He dwelt with lingering fondness
            On the brother he had lost.

Then strode the brave Maloney,
    Kind, genial adjutant;
And next him walked the truthful,
    The lion-hearted Gantt.
There to that solemn music
    Passed a triad of the brave :
Lomax, Phelan, Alfred Pinckney—
    All had found a soldier's grave.

        They were young and gentle spirits,
            But they quaffed the bitter cup,
        For their country's flag was falling,
            And they fell to lift it up.
        And then passed in countless thousands
            In that mighty phantom host
        True hearts and noble patriots
            Whose names on earth are lost.

There " the missing " found their places—
    Those who vanished from our gaze,
Like brilliant, flashing meteors,
    And were lost in glory's blaze.

Yes, they passed, that noble army—
They passed to meet their Lord:
And a voice within me whispered:
"They but march to their reward."

YE CAVALIERS OF DIXIE.

By Benj. F. Porter, of Alabama.

Ye Cavaliers of Dixie
  That guard our Southern shores,
Whose standards brave the battle-storm
That round the border roars;
Your glorious sabres draw again,
And charge the invading foe;
Reap the columns deep
Where the battle tempests blow,
Where the iron hail in floods descends
And the bloody torrents flow.

Ye Cavaliers of Dixie!
Though dark the tempest lower,
No arms will wear a tyrant's chains!
No dastard heart will cower!
Bright o'er the cloud the sign will rise,
To lead to victory;
While your swords reap his hordes,
Where the battle-tempests blow,
And the iron hail in floods descends,
And the bloody torrents flow.

Ye Cavaliers of Dixie!
Though Vicksburg's towers fall,
Here still are sacred rights to shield!
Your wives, your homes, your all!

CONFEDERATE MONUMENT IN "OAKWOOD," RICHMOND, VIRGINIA

From photograph made for this work by Edyth Carter Beveridge.

The inscriptions read: "The epitaph of the soldier, who falls with his country, is written in the hearts of those who love the right, and honor the brave." "In memory of 16,000 Confederate soldiers from thirteen States, erected by the Ladies' Oakwood Memorial Association, organized May 10th, 1866."

With gleaming arms advance again,
Drive the raging foe,
Nor yield your native field,
While the battle-tempests blow,
And the iron hail in floods descends,
And the bloody torrents flow.

> Our country needs no ramparts,
> No batteries to shield!
> Your bosoms are her bulwarks strong,
> Breastworks that cannot yield!
> The thunders of your battle-blades
> Shall sweep the hated foe,
> While their gore stains the shore,
> Where the battle-tempests blow,
> And the iron hail in floods descends,
> And the bloody torrents flow.

The spirits of your fathers
Shall rise from every grave!
Our country is their field of fame,
They nobly died to save!
Where Johnson, Jackson, Tilghman fell,
Your patriot hearts shall glow ;
While you reap columns deep,
Through the armies of the foe,
Where the battle storm is raging loud,
And the bloody torrents flow.

> The battle-flag of Dixie
> On crimson field shall flame,
> With azure cross, and silver stars,
> To light her sons to fame!
> When peace with olive-branch returns,
> That flag's white folds shall glow,
> Still bright on every height,

Where the storm has ceased to blow,
Where the battle tempests rage no more,
Nor bloody torrents flow.

The battle-flag of Dixie
Shall long triumphant wave,
Where'er the storms of battle roar,
And victory crowns the brave!
The Cavaliers of Dixie!
In woman's songs shall glow
The fame of your name,
When the storm has ceased to blow,
When the battle tempests rage no more,
Nor the bloody torrents flow.

"NOT DOUBTFUL OF YOUR FATHERLAND.

Not doubtful of your fatherland,
    Or of the God who gave it;
On, Southrons! 'gainst the hireling band
    That struggle to enslave it;
        Ring boldly out
        Your battle-shout,
Charge fiercely 'gainst these felon hordes:
        One hour of strife
        Is freedom's life,
And glory hangs upon your swords!

A thousand mothers' matron eyes,
    Wives, sisters, daughters weeping,
Watch, where your virgin banner flies,
    To battle fiercely sweeping:
        Though science fails,
        The steel prevails,

When hands that wield, own hearts of oak:
　　These, though the wall
　　Of stone may fall,
Grow stronger with each hostile stroke.

　　　The faith that feels its cause as true,
　　　　The virtue to maintain it;
　　　The soul to brave, the will to do,—
　　　　These seek the fight, and gain it!
　　　　　The precious prize
　　　　　Before your eyes,
　　　The all that life conceives of charm,
　　　　　Home, freedom, life,
　　　　　Child, sister, wife,
　　　All rest upon your soul and arm!

And what the foe, the felon race,
　　That seek your subjugation?
The scum of Europe, her disgrace,
　　The lepers of the nation.
　　　And what the spoil
　　　That tempts their toil,
The bait that goads them on to fight?
　　　Lust, crime, and blood,
　　　Each fiendish mood
That prompts and follows appetite.

　　　Shall such prevail, and shall you fail,
　　　　Asserting cause so holy?
　　　With souls of might, go, seek the fight,
　　　　And crush these wretches lowly.
　　　　　On, with the cry,
　　　　　To do or die,
　　　As did, in darker days, your sires,
　　　　　Nor stay the blow,
　　　　　Till every foe,
　　　Down stricken, in your path, expires!
　　　　　　　—Charleston Mercury.

"THE VOLUNTEER."

"IMOGEN."

GRAVE OF ALBERT SIDNEY JOHNSTON.

By J. B. Synnott.

The Lone Star State secretes the clay
   Of him who led on Shiloh's field,
Where mourning wives will stop to pray,
   And maids a weeping tribute yield.

     In after time, when spleen and strife
        Their madd'ning flame shall have expired,
     The noble deeds that gemm'd this life
        By Age and Youth will be admired.

As o'er the stream the boatmen rove
   By Pittsburg Bend at early Spring,
They'll show with moist'ning eye the grave
   Where havoc spread her sable wing.

     There, 'neath the budding foliage green,
        Ere Night evolved her dewy breath,
     While Vict'ry smiled upon the scene,
        Our Chieftan met the blow of death.

Great men to come will bless the brave ;
   The soldier, bronzed in War's career,
Shall weave a chaplet o'er his grave,
   While Mem'ry drops the glist'ning tear.

     Though envy wag her scorpion tongue,
        The march of Time shall find his fame ;
     Where Bravery's loved and Glory's sung,
        There children's lips shall lisp his name.

8

SONNET.

Written in 1864.

WHAT right to freedom when we are not free?
    When all the passions goad us into lust;
    When, for the worthless spoil we lick the dust,
And while one-half our people die, that we
May sit with peace and freedom 'neath our tree,
The other gloats for plunder and for spoil:
Bustles through daylight, vexes night with toil,
Cheats, swindles, lies and steals!—Shall such things be
Endowed with such grand boons as Liberty
    Brings in her train of blessings?   Should we pray
    That such as these should still maintain the sway—
These soulless, senseless, heartless enemies
Of all that's good and great, of all that's wise,
Worthy on earth, or in the Eternal Eyes!

CLEBURNE.

By M. A. Jennings, of Alabama.

" Another Star now Shines on High."

ANOTHER ray of light hath fled, another Southern brave
    Hath fallen in his country's cause and found a laureled
        grave—
Hath fallen, but his deathless name shall live when stars shall
        set,
For, noble Cleburne, thou art one this world will ne'er forget.

'Tis true, thy warm heart beats no more, that on thy noble head
Azrael place his icy hand, and thou art with the dead;
The glancing of thine eyes are dim; no more will they be bright
Until they ope in Paradise, with clearer, heavenlier light.

No battle news disturbs thy rest upon the sun-bright shore,
No clarion voice awakens thee on earth to wrestle more,
No tramping steed, no wary foe bids thee awake, arise,
For thou art in the angel world, beyond the starry skies.

Brave Cleburne, dream in thy low bed, with pulseless, deadened
      heart;
Calm, calm and sweet, O warrior rest! thou well hast borne
      thy part,
And now a glory wreath for thee the angels singing twine,
A glory wreath, not of the earth, but made by hands divine.

A long farewell—we give thee up, with all thy bright renown,
A chieftain here on earth is lost, in heaven an angel found.
Above thy grave a wail is heard—a nation mourns her dead;
A nobler for the South ne'er died, a braver never bled.

A last farewell—how can we speak the bitter word farewell!
The anguish of our bleeding hearts vain words may never tell.
Sleep on, sleep on, to God we give our chieftain in his might;
And weeping, feel he lives on high, where comes no sorrow's
      night.

                 —*Selma Despatch, 1864.*

THE BATTLE RAINBOW.

By John R. Thompson, of Virginia.

The poem which follows was written just after the Seven Days of Battle,
near Richmond, in 1862. It was suggested by the appearance of a rainbow
the evening before the grand trial of strength between the contending
armies. This rainbow overspread the eastern sky, and exactly defined the
position of the Confederate army, as seen from the Capitol at Richmond.

THE warm, weary day, was departing—the smile
    Of the sunset gave token the tempest had ceased;
And the lightning yet fitfully gleamed for a while
    On the cloud that sank sullen and dark in the east.

There our army—awaiting the terrible fight
   Of the morrow—lay hopeful and watching, and still;
Where their tents all the region had sprinkled with white,
   From river to river, o'er meadow and hill.

While above them the fierce cannonade of the sky
   Blazed and burst from the vapors that muffled the sun,
Their " counterfeit clamors " gave forth no reply;
   And slept till the battle, the charge in each gun.

When, lo! on the cloud, a miraculous thing!
   Broke in beauty the rainbow our host to enfold!
The centre o'erspread by its arch, and each wing
   Suffused with its azure and crimson and gold.

Blest omen of victory, symbol divine
   Of peace after tumult, repose after pain;
How sweet and how glowing with promise the sign,
   To eyes that should never behold it again!

For the fierce flame of war on the morrow flashed out,
   And its thunder-peals filled all the tremulous air:
Over slippery intrenchment and reddened redoubt,
   Rang the wild cheer of triumph, the cry of despair.

Then a long week of glory and agony came—
   Of mute supplication, and yearning, and dread;
When day unto day gave the record of fame,
   And night unto night gave the list of its dead.

We had triumphed—the foe had fled back to his ships—
   His standard in rags and his legions a wreck—
But alas! the stark faces and colorless lips
   Of our loved ones, gave triumph's rejoicing a check.

Not yet, oh, not yet, as a sign of release,
   Had the Lord set in mercy His bow in the cloud;
Not yet had the Comforter whispered of peace
   To the hearts that around us lay bleeding and bowed.

THE FATAL WOUNDING OF "STONEWALL" JACKSON

But the promise was given—the beautiful arc,
  With its brilliant profusion of colors, that spanned
The sky on that exquisite eve, was the mark
  Of the Infinite Love overarching the land.

And that Love, shining richly and full as the day,
  Through the tear-drops that moisten each martyr's proud
    pall,
On the gloom of the past the bright bow shall display
  Of Freedom, Peace, Victory, bent over all.

SOUTHERN WAR HYMN.

By JOHN A. WAGENER, of South Carolina.

A RISE! arise! with arm of might,
    Sons of our sunny home!
Gird on the sword for the sacred fight,
    For the battle-hour hath come!
Arise! for the felon foe draws nigh
    In battle's dread array;
To the front, ye brave! let the coward fly,
    'Tis the hero that bides the fray!

Strike hot and hard, my noble band,
    With the arm of fight and fire;
Strike fast for God and Fatherland,
    For mother, and wife, and sire.
Though thunders roar and lightnings flash,
    Oh! Southrons, never fear,
Ye shall turn the bolt with the sabre's clash,
    And the shaft with the steely spear.

Bright blooms shall wave o'er the hero's grave,
    While the craven finds no rest;
Thrice cursed the traitor, the slave, the knave,
    While thrice is the hero blessed.

To the front in the fight, ye Southrons, stand.
  Brave spirits, with eagle eye,
And standing for God and for Fatherland,
  Ye will gallantly do or die.

THE TREE, THE SERPENT, AND THE STAR.

By A. P. GRAY, of South Carolina.

FROM the silver sands of a gleaming shore,
    Where the wild sea-waves were breaking,
A lofty shoot from a twining root
    Sprang forth as the dawn was waking;
And the crest, though fed by the sultry beam,
    (And the shaft by the salt wave only)
Spread green to the breeze of the curling seas,
    And rose like a column lonely.
        Then hail to the tree, the Palmetto tree,
        Ensign of the noble, the brave, and the free.

As the sea-winds rustled the bladed crest,
    And the sun to the noon rose higher
A serpent came, with an eye of flame,
    And coiled by the leafy pyre;
His ward he would keep by the lonely tree,
    To guard it with constant devotion;
Oh, sharp was the fang, and the armed clang,
    That pierced through the roar of the ocean,
        And guarded the tree, the Palmetto tree,
        Ensign of the noble, the brave, and the free.

And the day wore down to the twilight close,
    The breeze died away from the billow;
Yet the wakeful clang of the rattles rang
    Anon from the serpent's pillow;

When I saw through the night a gleaming star
　　O'er the branching summit growing,
Till the foliage green and the serpent's sheen
　　In the golden light were glowing,
　　　　That hung o'er the tree, the Palmetto tree,
　　　　Ensign of the noble, the brave, and the free.

By the standard cleave every loyal son,
　　When the drums' long roar shall rattle;
Let the folds stream high to the victor's eye
　　Or sink in the shock of the battle.
Should triumph rest on the red field won,
　　With a victor's song let us hail it;
If the battle fail and the star grow pale,
　　Yet never in shame will we veil it,
　　　　But cherish the tree, the Palmetto tree,
　　　　Ensign of the noble, the brave, and the free.

"WHAT THE VILLAGE BELL SAID."

By JOHN G. M'LEMORE, of South Carolina.*

FULL many a year in the village church,
　　Above the world have I made my home;
And happier there, than if I had hung
　　High up in the air in a golden dome;
　　　　For I have tolled
　　　　When the slow hearse rolled
　　Its burden sad to my door;
　　　　And each echo that woke,
　　　　With the solemn stroke,
　　Was a sigh from the heart of the poor.

*Mortally wounded at the Battle of Seven Pines.

I know the great bell of the city spire
   Is a far prouder one than such as I;
And its deafening stroke, compared with mine,
   Is thunder compared with a sigh:
      But the shattering note
      Of his brazen throat,
   As it swells on the Sabbath air,
      Far oftener rings
      For other things
Than a call to the house of prayer.

Brave boy, I tolled when your father died,
   And you wept while my tones pealed loud;
And more gently I rung when the lily-white dame,
   Your mother dear, lay in her shroud:
      And I sang in sweet tone
      The angels might own,
When your sister you gave to your friend;
      Oh! I rang with delight,
      On that sweet summer night,
When they vowed they would love to the end!

But a base foe comes from the regions of crime,
   With a heart all hot with the flames of hell;
And the tones of the bell you have loved so long
   No more on the air shall swell:
      For the people's chief,
      With his proud belief
That his country's cause is God's own,
      Would change the song,
      The hills have rung,
To the thunder's harsher tone.

Then take me down from the village church,
   Where in peace so long I have hung;
But I charge you, by all the loved and lost,
   Remember the songs I have sung.

Remember the mound
Of holy ground,
Where your father and mother lie;
And swear by the love
For the dead above
To beat your foul foe or die.

Then take me; but when (I charge you this)
You have come to the bloody field,
That the bell of God, to a cannon grown,
You will ne'er to the foeman yield.
By the love of the past,
Be that hour your last,
When the foe has reached this trust;
And make him a bed
Of patriot dead,
And let him sleep in this holy dust.

SONG OF SPRING (1864).

By John A. Wagener, of South Carolina.

Spring has come! Spring has come!
The brightening earth, the sparkling dew,
The bursting buds, the sky of blue,
The mocker's carol in tree and hedge,
Proclaim anew Jehovah's pledge—
"So long as man shall earth retain,
The seasons gone shall come again."

Spring has come! Spring has come!
We have her here, in the balmy air,
In the blossoms that bourgeon without a care;
The violet bounds from her lowly bed,
And the jasmine flaunts with a lofty head;
All nature, in her baptismal dress,
Is abroad—to win, to soothe, and bless.

Spring has come!   Spring has come!
    Yes, and eternal as the Lord,
    Who spells her being at a word;
    All blest but man, whose passions proud
    Wrap Nature in her bloody shroud—
His heart is winter to the core,
    His spring, alas! shall come no more!

"STONEWALL" JACKSON.

By H. L. Flash.

Not 'midst the lightning of the stormy fight
    Not in the rush upon the vandal foe,
Did kingly death, with his resistless might,
    Lay the great leader low!

His warrior soul its earthly shackles bore
    In the full sunshine of a peaceful town;
When all the storm was hushed, the trusty oak
    That propped our cause, went down.

Though his alone the blood that flecks the ground,
    Recording all his grand heroic deeds,
Freedom herself is writhing with his wound,
    And all the country bleeds.

He entered not the nation's "Promised Land,"
    At the red belching of the cannon's mouth;
But broke the "House of Bondage" with his hand—
    The Moses of the South!

Oh, gracious God i not gainless is our loss;
    A glorious sunbeam gilds Thy sternest frown;
And while his country staggers with the cross—
    He rises with the crown!

"STONEWALL" JACKSON.

A DIRGE.

Go to thy rest, great chieftain!
  In the zenith of thy fame;
With the proud heart stilled and frozen,
  No foeman e'er could tame;
With the eye that met the battle
  As the eagle's meets the sun,
Rayless—beneath its marble lid,
  Repose—thou mighty one!

Yet ill our cause could spare thee;
  And harsh the blow of fate
That struck its staunchest pillar
  From 'neath our dome of State.
Of thee, as of the Douglas,
  We say with Scotland's king,
"There is not one to take *his* place
  In all the knightly ring."

Thou wert the noblest captain
  Of all that martial host
That front the haughty Northman,
  And put to shame his boast.
Thou wert the strongest bulwark
  To stay the tide of fight;
The name thy soldiers gave thee
  Bore witness of thy might!

But we may not weep above thee;
  This is no time for tears!
Thou wouldst not brook their shedding,
  Oh! saint among thy peers!

Couldst thou speak from yonder heaven,
　　Above us smiling spread,
Thou wouldst not have us pause for grief,
　　On the blood-stained path we tread !

　　　Not—while our homes in ashes
　　　　　Lie smouldering on the sod !
　　　Not—while our houseless women
　　　　　Send up wild wails to God !
　　　Not—while the mad fanatic
　　　　　Strews ruin on his track !
　　　Dare any Southron give the rein
　　　　　To feeling, and look back ;

No !　Still the cry is " onward ! "
　　This is no time for tears ;
No !　Still the word is " vengeance ! "
　　Leave ruth for coming years.
We will snatch thy glorious banner
　　From thy dead and stiffening hand,
And high, 'mid battle's deadly storm,
　　We'll bear it through the land,

　　　And all who mark it streaming—
　　　　　Oh ! soldier of the cross !—
　　　Shall gird them with a fresh resolve
　　　　　Sternly to avenge our loss ;
　　　Whilst thou, enrolled a martyr,
　　　　　Thy sacred mission shown,
　　　Shalt lay the record of our wrongs
　　　　　Before the Eternal throne !

THE SCOUTS

"LITTLE GIFFIN."

By Dr. Francis O. Ticknor.

Mr. P. H. Hayne said of this little poem : "A ballad of such unique and really transcendent merit that, in my judgment, it ought to rank with the rarest gems of modern martial poetry."

It is a fact that in all wars boys have taken part, and often showed the greatest endurance and bravery. It was so with the boys of the South. The battle of New Market, one of the hardest fought fights in the Valley of Virginia, was won by a lot of boys from the Virginia Military Institute. People said of them that their behavior on the field was so perfect that they moved like machinery, nor did they ever falter or waver in any part of the conflict.

OUT of the focal and foremost fire,
Out of the hospital walls as dire,
Smitten of grapeshot and gangrene
(Eighteenth battle, and he sixteen),
Specter such as we seldom see,
Little Giffin of Tennessee.

"Take him and welcome!" the surgeon said ;
"Much your doctor can help the dead!"
And so we took him and brought him where
The balm was sweet on the summer air ;
And we laid him down on a wholesome bed
Utter Lazarus, heel to head !

Weary War with the bated breath,
Skeleton boy against skeleton Death,
Months of torture, how many such !
Weary weeks of the stick and crutch !
Still a glint of the steel-blue eye
Spoke of the spirit that wouldn't die—

And didn't ; nay, more ! in death's despite,
The crippled skeleton learned to write !
" Dear Mother," at first, of course, and then,

" Dear Captain," inquiring about the " men."
Captain's answer : " Of eight and five,
Giffin and I are left alive."

" Johnston's pressed at the front, they say ! "
Little Giffin was up and away ;
A tear, his first, as he bade good-bye,
Dimmed the glint of his steel-blue eye.
" I'll write, if spared."   There was news of a fight,
But none of Giffin ! he did not write !

I sometimes fancy that were I king
Of the princely Knights of the Golden Ring,
With the song of the minstrel in mine ear,
And the tender legend that trembles here,
I'd give the best on his bended knee,
The whitest soul of chivalry,
For little Giffin of Tennessee.

Monument marking spot where General J. E. B. Stuart fell,
seven miles from Richmond.

BEAUFORT.

By W. J. GRAYSON, OF SOUTH CAROLINA.

OLD home! what blessings late were yours;
    The gifts of peace, the songs of joy!
No, hostile squadrons seek our shores,
    To ravage and destroy.

    The Northman comes no longer there
        With soft address and measured phrase,
    With bated breath, and sainted air,
        And simulated praise.

He comes a vulture to his prey;
    A wolf to raven in your streets;
Around on shining stream and bay
    Gather his bandit fleets.

    They steal the pittance of the poor;
        Pollute the precincts of the dead;
    Despoil the widow of her store,—
        The orphan of his bread.

Crimes like their crimes—of lust and blood,
    No Christian land has known before;
Oh, for some scourge of fire and flood,
    To sweep them from the shore!

    Exiles from home, your people fly,
        In adverse fortune's hardest school;
    With swelling breast and flashing eye—
        They scorn the tyrant's rule!

Away, from all their joys away,
    The sports that active youth engage;
The scenes where childhood loves to play,
    The resting-place of age.

Away, from fertile field and farm ;
   The oak-fringed island-homes that seem
To sit like swans, with matchless charm,
   On sea-born sound and stream.

     Away, from palm-environed coast,
       The beach that ocean beats in vain ;
     The Royal Port, your pride and boast,
       The loud-resounding main.

Away, from orange groves that glow
   With golden fruit or snowy flowers,
Roses that never cease to blow,
   Myrtle and jasmine bowers.

     From these afar, the hoary head
       Of feeble age, the timid maid,
     Mothers and nurslings, all have fled,
       Of ruthless foes afraid.

But ready, with avenging hand,
   By wood and fen, in ambush lie
Your sons, a stern, determined band,
   Intent to do or die.

     Whene'er the foe advance to dare
       The onset, urged by hate and wrath,
     Still have they found, aghast with fear,
       A Lion in the path.

Scourged, to their ships they wildly rush,
   Their shattered ranks to shield and save,
And learn how hard a task to crush
   The spirit of the brave.

     O, God ! Protector of the right,
       The widows' stay, the orphans' friend,
     Restrain the rage of lawless might,
       The wronged and crushed defend !

Be guide and helper, sword and shield !
From hill and vale, where'er they roam,
Bring back the yeoman to his field,
The exile to his home !

Pastors and scattered flocks restore ;
Their fanes rebuild, their altars raise ;
And let their quivering lips once more
Rejoice in songs of praise !

OLD MOULTRIE.

By Catherine Gendron Poyas, of Charleston.

THE splendor falls on bannered walls
Of ancient Moultrie, great in story ;
And flushes now his scar-seamed brow,
With rays of golden glory !
Great in his old renown,
Great in the honor thrown
Around him by the foe,
Had sworn to lay him low !

The glory falls—historic walls
Too weak to cover foes insulting,
Become a tower—a sheltering bower—
A theme of joy exulting ;
God, merciful and great,
Preserved the high estate
Of Moultrie, by His power
Through the fierce battle-hour !

The splendor fell—his banners swell
Majestic forth to catch the shower ;
Our own loved *blue* receives anew
A rich immortal dower !
Adown the triple bars
Of its companion, spars
Of golden glory stream ;
On seven-rayed circlet beam !

9

The glory falls—but not on walls
    Of Sumter deemed *the post of duty;*
A brilliant sphere, it circles clear
    The harbor in its beauty;
        Holding in its embrace
        The city's queenly grace;
        Stern battery and tower,
        Of manly strength and power.

But brightest falls on Moultrie's walls,
    Forever there to rest in glory,
A hallowed light—on buttress height—
    Oh, fort, beloved and hoary!
        Rest *there* and tell that *faith*
        Shall never suffer scaith;
        Rest there—and glow afar—
        Hope's ever-burning star!

St. Paul's Church, Richmond, Va., where President Jefferson Davis and General Lee had pews during the war.

ONLY ONE KILLED.

By Julia L. Keyes, Montgomery, Alabama.

Only one killed—in company B,
　　’Twas a trifling loss—one man !
A charge of the bold and dashing Lee—
While merry enough it was to see
　　The enemy, as he ran.

　　　Only one killed upon our side—
　　　　　Once more to the field they turn.
　　　Quietly now the horsemen ride—
　　　And pause by the form of the one who died,
　　　　　So bravely, as now we learn.

Their grief for the comrade loved and true
　　For a time was unconcealed ;
They saw the bullet had pierced him through,
That his pain was brief—ah ! very few
　　Die thus, on the battle-field.

　　　The news has gone to his home, afar—
　　　　　Of the short and gallant fight,
　　　Of the noble deeds of the young La Var
　　　Whose life went out as a falling star
　　　　　In the skirmish of that night.

“ Only one killed !　It was my son,”
　　The widowed mother cried.
She turned but to clasp the sinking one,
Who heard not the words of the victory won,
　　But of him who had bravely died.

　　　Ah ! death to her were a sweet relief,
　　　　　The bride of a single year.
　　　Oh ! would she might, with her weight of grief,
　　　Lie down in the dust, with the autumn leaf
　　　　　Now trodden and brown and sere !

But no, she must bear through coming life
    Her burden of silent woe,
The aged mother and youthful wife
Must live through a nation's bloody strife,
    Sighing and waiting to go

Where the loved are meeting beyond the stars,
    Are meeting no more to part.
They can smile once more through the crystal bars—
Where never more will the woe of wars
    O'ershadow the loving heart.

"THE LAND OF KING COTTON."

Air—"Red, White, and Blue."

By J. Augustine Signaigo.

[From the *Memphis Appeal*, December 18, 1861.]

This was a favorite song of the Tennessee troops, and especially of the Thirteenth and One Hundred and Fifty-fourth Regiments. There were no braver men than those from Tennessee, as I had occasion to know more than once. At the close of the war, Ex-Governor Isham G. Harris, of Tennessee, upon whose head Governor Brownlow, of war fame, set a price, went away with General Price and General Shelby and others to Mexico. I was one of the party. We lived there for a while under the care of the Emperor Maximilian, but found our way back to our own land before long. Governor Harris became a United States Senator, General Price occupied prominent positions in Missouri, and General Shelby held a high office under the Government. Governor Harris, the distinguished Tennesseean, was fond of martial music, and delighted in the old Southern songs.

Oh! Dixie, dear land of King Cotton,
    "The home of the brave and the free,"
A nation by freedom begotten,
    The terror of despots to be ;
Wherever thy banner is streaming,
    Base tyranny quails at thy feet,
And liberty's sunlight is beaming,
    In splendor of majesty sweet.

THE FIRST CAPITOL OF THE CONFEDERACY, MONTGOMERY, ALABAMA

In this building President Jefferson Davis was inaugurated February 18th, 1861. The Alabama Convention assembled here January 7th, 1861, and declared her Independence.

CHORUS:

Three cheers for our army so true,
    Three cheers for Price, Johnston, and Lee ;
Beauregard and our Davis forever,
    The pride of the brave and the free !

When Liberty sounds her war-rattle,
    Demanding her right and her due,
The first land that rallies to battle
    Is Dixie, the shrine of the true ;
Thick as leaves of the forest in summer,
    Her brave sons will rise on each plain,
And then strike, until each Vandal comer
    Lies dead on the soil he would stain.

        Chorus.—Three cheers, etc.

May the names of the dead that we cherish,
    Fill memory's cup to the brim ;
May the laurels they've won never perish,
    " Nor star of their glory grow dim ; "
May the States of the South never sever,
But the champions of freedom e'er be ;
May they flourish Confederate forever,
    The boast of the brave and the free.

        Chorus.—Three cheers, etc.

A CHRISTMAS OF LONG AGO.

By MORTON BRYAN WHARTON, D.D.

I AM thinking to-night in sadness
    Of a Christmas of long ago,
When the air was filled with gladness,
    And the earth was wrapped in snow ;

When the stars like diamonds glistened
    And the night was crisp and cold,
As I eagerly watched and listened
    For the Santa Claus of old.

    The forest was robbed of its treasures,
        The house was a mass of green,
    And I reveled in Christmas pleasures,
        At the dawn of Aurora's sheen ;
    Some talked of the Savior's mission,
        But I of my pretty toys ;
    Some knelt in devout petition—
        I romped and played with the boys.

We went to the pond for skating,
    To the stable to take a ride,
And we found new joys awaiting,
    To whatever spot we hied ;
But the climax of my story
    Was that evening's fireworks show !
Went out in a blaze of glory—
    That Christmas of long ago !

    But in sadness I think of that Christmas,
        For many then happy and gay
    Have gone to the realm of silence
        And sleep in their beds of clay ;
    The hands that filled kindly my stockings,
        I shall grasp in this world no more,
    But when at Heaven's portals I'm knocking
        They'll open the beautiful door.

They will lead me in tenderness clinging,
    And place me before the throne,
Where the choirs angelic are singing
    And the heavenly gifts are strown,

And there in the realm of glory,
    With my loved ones at my side,
I'll repeat the old Bethlehem story
    And join in that Christmas tide.

THE DEATH OF JEFFERSON DAVIS.

By Morton Bryan Wharton, D. D.

My brother, the Rev. Morton Bryan Wharton, D. D., is a writer of poetry, and he writes good poetry. In fact, he has a book of poems. Some of his selections are given in these pages, and to show the appreciation of them, we publish elsewhere a letter of thanks from Mr. Davis upon the receipt of one of these poems.

Our mighty Chieftain breathes no more,
    His noble form, now cold and still,
Has fallen at last, life's conflict o'er,
    Obedient to his Maker's will.
As die the brave and true, he dies,—
    He rests upon a stainless shield,
The great Commander of the skies
    Alone could call him from the field.

    His noble spirit dwells on high,
        Where slanders never vex the soul;
    And fitting 'tis his dust should lie
        Far, far removed from prowling ghoul.
    Among his friends should be his tomb,
        There on old Ocean's utmost verge,
    Where snow-white flowers perennial bloom
        And wild waves chant his funeral dirge.

And he will stand on History's page,
    While cycling years shall onward move,
The victim once of senseless rage,
    Now, idol of his people's love.

When hate is buried in the dust,
    When party strife shall break its spear,
When truth is free and men are just,
    Then will his epitaph appear.

    The Parian quarry asks for time
        In which the marble to mature,
    Destined to speak his fame sublime,
        Worthy to shrine a heart so pure ;
    Till then unmarked we bid him lay,
        With carping critics plead a truce,
    But dear the spot which holds his clay
        As that which holds the heart of Bruce.

PRO MEMORIA.

AIR—There is rest for the weary.

BY INA M. PORTER, of Indiana.

Lo ! the Southland Queen, emerging
    From her sad and wintry gloom,
Robes her torn and bleeding bosom
    In her richest orient bloom.

CHORUS—(Repeat first line three times.)
For her weary sons are resting
By the Edenshore;
They have won the crown immortal,
And the cross of death is o'er !
Where the Oriflamme is burning
On the starlit Edenshore !

    Brightly still, in gorgeous glory,
        God's great jewel lights our sky ;
    Look ! upon the heart's white dial
        There's a SHADOW flitting by !
Chorus—But the weary feet are resting, etc.

Homes are dark and hearts are weary,
    Souls are numb with hopeless pain,
Nor the footfall on the threshold
    Never more to sound again!

    CHORUS—They have gone from us forever,
        Aye, for evermore!
        We must win the crown immortal,
        Follow where they led before,
        Where the Oriflamme is burning
        On the starlit Edenshore.

Proudly, as our Southern forests
    Meet the winter's shafts so keen;
Time-defying memories cluster
    Round our hearts in living green.
    Chorus—They have gone from us forever, etc.

        May our faltering voices mingle
            In the angel-chanted psalm;
        May our earthly chaplets linger
            By the bright celestial palm.
    Chorus—They have gone from us forever, etc.

When the May eternal dawneth
    At the living God's behest,
We will quaff divine Nepenthe,
    We will share the Soldier's rest
    Chorus—Where the weary feet are resting, etc.

        Where the shadows are uplifted
            'Neath the never-waning sun,
        Shout we, Gloria in Excelsis!
            We have lost, but ye have won!
    CHORUS—Our hearts are yours forever,
        Aye, for evermore!
        Ye have won the crown immortal,

And the cross of death is o'er,
Where the Oriflamme is burning
On the starlit Edenshore !

THE SOUTHERN HOMES IN RUIN.

By R. B. Vance, of N. C.

Many a gray-haired sire has died,
    As falls the oak, to rise no more,
Because his son, his prop, his pride,
    Breathed out his last all red with gore.
No more on earth, at morn, at eve,
    Shall age and youth, entwined as one—
Nor father, son, for either grieve—
    Life's work, alas, for both is done !

Many a mother's heart has bled
        While gazing on her darling child,
    As in its tiny eyes she read
        The father's image, kind and mild ;
    For ne'er again his voice will cheer
        The widowed heart, which mourns him dead ;
    Nor kisses dry the scalding tear,
        Fast falling on the orphan's head !

Many a little form will stray
    Adown the glen and o'er the hill,
And watch, with wistful looks, the way
    For him whose step is missing still ;
And when the twilight steals apace
    O'er mead, and brook, and lonely home,
And shadows cloud the dear, sweet face—
    The cry will be, " Oh, papa, come !"

And many a home's in ashes now,
    Where joy was once a constant guest,
And mournful groups there are, I trow,
    With neither house nor place of rest;
And blood is on the broken sill,
    Where happy feet went to and fro,
And everywhere, by field and hill,
    Are sickening sights and sounds of woe!

There is a God who rules on high,
    The widow's and the orphan's friend,
Who sees each tear and hears each sigh,
    That these lone hearts to Him may send!
And when in wrath He tears away
    The reasons vain which men indite,
The record book will plainest say
    Who's in the wrong, and who is right.

THE RAPPAHANNOCK ARMY SONG.

By John C. M'Lemore.

The Rappahannock River, in Virginia, was at one time the dividing line between the two armies. One beautiful moonlight night, as the armies lay behind their breastworks, like two mighty monsters, the band on the Federal side commenced to play "The Star-Spangled Banner." After the band had ceased playing, "Dixie" burst forth from the band on the Southern side; then for a while all was quiet, when some soldier, on one side or the other, it matters not, commenced to sing, "Home, Sweet Home." It was caught up by others; then by the soldiers on the opposite side, until both armies were singing that sweet old song, "Home, Sweet Home." And who can tell the silent tears that were shed behind the breastworks that moonlight night?

THE toil of the march is over—
    The pack will be borne no more—
For we've come for the help of Richmond,
    From the Rappahannock's shore.

The foe is closing round us—
    We can hear his ravening cry;
So, ho! for fair old Richmond!
    Like soldiers we'll do or die.

    We have left the land that bore us,
        Full many a league away,
    And our mothers and sisters miss us,
        As with tearful eyes they pray;
    But this will repress their weeping,
        And still the rising sigh—
    For all, for fair old Richmond,
        Have come to do or die.

We have come to join our brothers
    From the proud Dominion's vales,
And to meet the dark-cheeked soldier,
    Tanned by the Tropic gales;
To greet them all full gladly,
    With hand and beaming eye,
And to swear for fair old Richmond,
    We all will do or die.

    The fair Carolina sisters
        Stand ready, lance in hand,
    To fight as they did in an older war,
        For the sake of their fatherland.
    The glories of Sumter and Bethel
        Have raised their fame full high,
    But they'll fade, if for fair old Richmond
        They swear not to do or die,

Zollicoffer looks down on his people,
    And trusts to their hearts and **arms**,
To avenge the blood he has shed,
    In the midst of the battle's alarms.

JEFFERSON DAVIS AND HIS CABINET

Beginning at the left are Secretaries Mallory, Benjamin, Walker, President Davis, General Lee, Secretaries Regan, Meminger, Vice-President Stephens and Secretary Toombs. This is a reproduction of a rare engraving owned by Mrs. James T. Halsey, President of the "Daughters of the Confederacy" of Philadelphia, and published in this book by special courtesy to the author.

Alabamians, remember the past,
    Be the " South at Manassas," their cry ;
As onward for fair old Richmond,
    They marched to do or die.

        Brave Bartow, from home on high,
            Calls the Empire State to the front,
        To bear once more as she has borne
            With glory the battle's brunt.
        Mississippians who know no surrender,
            Bear the flag of the Chief on high ;
        For he, too, for fair old Richmond,
            Has sworn to do or die.

Fair land of my birth—sweet Florida—
    Your arm is weak, but your soul
Must tell of a purer, holier strength,
    When the drums for the battle roll.
Look within, for your hope in the combat,
    Nor think of your few with a sigh—
If you win not for fair old Richmond,
    At least you can bravely die.

        Onward all ! Oh ! band of brothers !
            The beat of the long roll's heard !
        And the hearts of the columns advancing
            By the sound of its music stirred.
        Onward all ! and never return,
            Till our foes from the borders fly—
        To be crowned by the fair of old Richmond,
            As those who could do or die.

THE SOLDIER IN THE RAIN.

By Julia L. Keyes.

There was never any thought, of course, in the soldiers' life as to what kind of weather we had ; but one of our hardships was, either in camp life or on the march, when it rained. The water would run underneath us and wet our blankets, and pour upon us and saturate our clothing, so there was no escape. The author of this little poem knew something of the soldiers' experience.

Ah me ! the rain has a sadder sound
    Than it ever had before ;
And the wind more plaintively whistles through
    The crevices of the door.

    We know we are safe beneath our roof
        From every drop that falls ;
    And we feel secure and blest, within
        The shelter of our walls.

Then why do we dread to hear the noise
    Of the rapid, rushing rain—
And the plash of the wintry drops, that beat
    Through the blinds, on the window-pane ?

    We think of the tents on the lowly ground,
        Where our patriot soldiers lie ;
    And the sentry's bleak and lonely march,
        'Neath the dark and starless sky.

And we pray, with a tearful heart, for those
    Who brave for us yet more—
And we wish this war, with its thousand ills
    And griefs, was only o'er.

    We pray when the skies are bright and clear,
        When the winds are soft and warm—
    But, oh ! we pray with an aching heart
        'Mid the winter's rain and storm.

We fain would lift these mantling clouds
  That shadow our sunny clime ;
We can but wait—for we know there'll be
  A day, in the coming time,

        When peace, like a rosy dawn, will flood
          Our land with softest light ;
        Then—we will scarcely hearken the rain
          In the dreary winter's night.

TO LILY.

By Morton Bryan Wharton, D. D.

A College Episode.

Here is a love poem of the war times, and my gentle reader must not think it was wholly imaginary. I knew the characters represented in this poem, and my brother was one of them. It would be quite an easy thing to give the name of the fair woman who broke his heart ; but I might add, like men's hearts always, it did not stay broken, but was mended by the very next damsel who came along,

I THOUGHT you an angel and wooed you alone,
    As the dearest of idols earth ever has known ;
Yes, you were my altar, and at the loved shrine
I've paid the pure homage of worship divine.
My soul has delighted your image to keep,
Your form has been near me awake and asleep,
Your eyes, Heaven bless them, so bright and so blue,
Along my dark pathway have thrown their soft hue.
Emotions of rapture would rise in my breast
When your smile, so angelic, has cheered me and blest.
With motives the purest my soul could command
I sought, I entreated, your coveted hand,
For of all the dear treasures that mortals could know
You alone upon me could the richest bestow.
You told me you loved me, I thought you sincere,

My fears were then banished, my sky was then clear.
I did not, I would not, I could not believe
That my own darling Lily could ever deceive.
Yes, you told me in words which I ne'er can forget
(Remembered, alas! with the deepest regret)
That through life you with me would most willingly share
Each pleasure, each sorrow, each blessing, and care.
Oh! you said that whatever my lot might betide
You were mine,—soon to be my companion and bride.
But now in the day of apparent success,
While all was propitious our union to bless,
While my pathway lay scattered with flowers so rare,
And the Lily the richest of all that were there,
While my prayers were ascending to Father and Son
To bless and preserve us forever as one,
You tell me in language how coldly expressed!
That you were "not in earnest but wholly in jest."
Oh, take those words back, though true they may be,
And have not the heart to confess them to me,
" I am just like my sex," have the candor to say,
"I am false, I am fickle, I'm treacherous as they,"
But though, my loved girl, you have broken my heart,
And do not e'en ask of the ruin a part,
Yet know that you've shattered a spirit as true
As e'er was deceived by a lady like you ;
For never, no, never, beneath the blue sky,
Will you meet with a lover so faithful as I.
Oh, had I but honored my Saviour and Lord,
In fervent affection, in deed, or in word,
With half the devotion to you I have paid,
My hopes were not blighted, my love not betrayed.
Yet, yet, I forgive you, and leave you as free
As the bird that, uncaged, flies over the sea,
And in my sad bosom shall linger the prayer
That Heaven may grant you a pardon as fair.

LINCOLN'S TROOPS.

By A. G. Goodlett.

In June, 1865, a battalion of Texas Rangers arrived at Nashville and pitched its camp at the Old Fair Grounds. A. G. Goodlett and Dr. William Minchin walked out to see this noted troop, and while seated on the amphitheatre viewing the men arranging their camp, Goodlett wrote the following lines and handed them to Dr. Minchin, who at once began to sing them to the tune of Dixie. For a time they were quite popular among the Tennessee boys, some of whom may recognize them to-day. None, perhaps, save Dr. Minchin, ever knew their author.

L INCOLN's troops, infatuated fools,
  Taught in Abolition schools,
Are coming South to pull their triggers,
Kill our boys and free our niggers.

  But how cowardly they will feel
  When first approaching Southern steel
  With one hurrah ! we'll sally forth
  And kill those rascals of the North.

Lincoln, in a fit of frenzy,
Will be seized with influenza.
His care's so great he can't be civil,
He'll follow John Brown to the devil.

THE EMPTY SLEEVE.

By Dr. J. R. Bagby, of Virginia.

T OM, old fellow, I grieve to see
  The sleeve hanging loose at your side ;
The arm you lost was worth to me
  Every Yankee that ever died,
But you don't mind it at all,
  You swear you've a beautiful stump,
And laugh at that damnable ball—
  Tom, I knew you were always a trump.

10

A good right arm, a nervy hand,
    A wrist as strong as a sapling oak,
Buried deep in the Malvern sand—
    To laugh at that is a sorry joke.
Never again your iron grip
    Shall I feel in my shrinking palm—
Tom, Tom, I see your trembling lip;
    All within is not calm.

        Well! the arm is gone, it is true;
            But the one that is nearest the heart
        Is left—and that's as good as two;
            Tom, old fellow, what makes you start?
        Why, man, *she* thinks that empty sleeve
            A badge of honor; so do I,
        And all of us—I do believe
            The fellow is going to cry!

" She deserves a perfect man," you say;
    " You were not worth her in your prime;"
Tom! the arm that has turned to clay,
    Your whole body has made sublime;
For you have placed in the Malvern earth
    The proof and pledge of a noble life—
And the rest, henceforward of higher worth
    Will be dearer than all to your wife,

        I see the people in the street
            Look at your sleeve with kindling eyes;
        And you know, Tom, there's naught so sweet
            As homage shown in mute surmise.
        Bravely your arm in battle strove,
            Freely for Freedom's sake you gave it;
        It has perished—but a nation's love
            In proud remembrance will save it.

Go to your sweetheart, then, forthwith—
    You're a fool for staying so long—
Woman's love you'll find no myth,
    But a truth—living, tender, strong.
And when around her slender belt
    Your left is clasped in fond embrace,
Your right will thrill, as if it felt,
    In its grave, the usurper's place.

    As I look through the coming years,
        I see a one-armed married man;
    A little woman, with smiles and tears,
        Is helping as hard as she can
    To put on his coat, to pin his sleeve,
        Tie his cravat, and cut his food;
    And I say, as these fancies I weave,
        " That is Tom, and the woman he wooed."

The years roll on, and then I see
    A wedding picture, bright and fair;
I look closer, and it's plain to me
    That is Tom with the silver hair.
He gives away the lovely bride,
    And the guests linger, loth to leave
The house of him in whom they pride—
    " Brave old Tom with the empty sleeve."

CHICKAMAUGA—"THE STREAM OF DEATH."

CHICKAMAUGA! Chickamauga!
    O'er thy dark and turbid wave
Rolls the death-cry of the daring,
    Rings the war-shout of the brave;
Round thy shore the red fires flashing,
    Startling shot and screaming shell—
Chickamauga, stream of battle,
    Who thy fearful tale shall tell?

Olden memories of horror,
     Sown by scourge of deadly plague,
Long have clothed thy circling forests
     With a terror vast and vague,
Now to gather further vigor
     From the phantoms grim with gore,
Hurried, by war's wilder carnage,
     To their graves on thy lone shore.

          Long, with hearts subdued and saddened,
               As th' oppressor's hosts moved on,
          Fell the arms of freedom backward,
               Till our hopes had almost flown ;
          Till outspoke stern valor's fiat—
               " *Here* th' invading wave shall stay ;
          Here shall cease the foe's proud progress ;
               Here be crushed his grand array ! "

Then their eager hearts all throbbing,
     Backward flashed each battle-flag
Of the veteran corps of Longstreet,
     And the sturdy troops of Bragg ;
Fierce upon the foemen turning,
     All their pent-up wrath breaks out
In the furious battle-clangor,
     And the frenzied battle-shout.

          Roll thy dark waves, Chickamauga,
               Trembles all thy ghastly shore,
          With the rude shock of the onset,
               And the tumult's horrid roar ;
          As the Southern battle-giants
               Hurl their bolts of death along,
          Breckenridge, the iron-hearted,
               Cheatham, chivalric and strong :

ASHBY ON HIS MILK-WHITE STEED

Brigadier-General Turner Ashby of Virginia was killed near Harrisonburg, Virginia, June 6, 1862. This picture is a copy of an old photograph and obtained for this book by Miss Edyth Carter Beveridge.

GENERAL LEE ON "TRAVELER"

Polk and Preston—gallant Buckner,
    Hill and Hindman, strong in might,
Cleburne, flower of manly valor,
    Hood, the Ajax of the fight;
Benning, bold and hardy warrior,
    Fearless, resolute Kershaw;
Mingle battle-yell and death-bolt,
    Volley fierce and wild hurrah!

    At the volleys bleed their bodies,
        At the fierce shout rise their souls,
    While the fiery wave of vengeance
        On their quailing column rolls;
    And the parched throats of the stricken
        Breathe for air the roaring flame,
    Horrors of that hell foretasted
        Who shall ever dare to name!

Borne by those who, stiff and mangled,
    Paid, upon that bloody field,
Direful, cringing, awe-struck homage
    To the sword our heroes wield;
And who felt, by fiery trial,
    That the men who *will* be free,
Though in conflict baffled often,
    Ever will *unconquered* be!

    Learned, though long unchecked they spoil us,
        Dealing desolation round,
    Marking, with the track of ruin,
        Many a rood of Southern ground;
    Yet, whatever course they follow,
        Somewhere in their pathway flows,
    Dark and deep, a Chickamauga,
        Stream of death to vandal foes!

They have found it darkly flowing
 By Manassas' famous plain,
And by rushing Shenandoah
 Met the tide of woe again;
Chickahominy, immortal,
 By the long, ensanguined fight,
Rappahannock, glorious river,
  Twice renowned for matchless fight.

  Heed the story, dastard spoilers,
   Mark the tale these waters tell,
  Ponder well your fearful lesson,
   And the doom that there befell;
  Learn to shun the Southern vengeance,
   Sworn upon the votive sword,
  " *Every* stream a Chickamauga
   To the vile invading horde!"

SAVANNAH.

By Alethea S. Burroughs.

Thou hast not drooped thy stately head,
 Thy woes a wondrous beauty shed!
Not like a lamb to slaughter led,
But with the lion's monarch tread,
Thou comest to thy battle bed,
  Savannah! oh, Savannah!

  Thine arm of flesh is girded strong;
  The blue veins swell beneath thy wrong!
  To thee, the triple cords belong,
  Of woe, and death, and shameless wrong,
  And spirit vaunted long, *too* long!
   Savannah! oh, Savannah!

No blood-stains spot thy forehead fair;
Only the martyrs' blood is there;
It gleams upon thy bosom bare,
It moves thy deep, deep soul to prayer,
And tunes a dirge for thy sad ear,
                Savannah! oh, Savannah!

              Thy clean white hand is opened wide
              For weal or woe, thou Freedom bride,
              The sword-sheath sparkles at thy side,
              Thy plighted troth, whate'er betide,
              Thou hast but Freedom for thy guide,
                          Savannah! oh, Savannah!

What though the heavy storm-cloud lowers—
Still at thy feet the old oak towers;
Still fragrant are thy jessamine bowers,
And things of beauty, love, or flowers,
Are smiling o'er this land of ours,
                My sunny home, Savannah!

              There is no film before thy sight—
              Thou seest woe, and death, and night—
              And blood upon thy banner bright;
              But in thy full wrath's kindled might,
              What carest *thou* for woe, or night?
                          My rebel home, Savannah

Come—for the crown is on thy head;
Thy woes a wondrous beauty shed,
Not like a lamb to slaughter led,
But with the lion's monarch tread,
Oh! come unto thy battle bed,
                Savannah! oh, Savannah!

DIRGE FOR ASHBY.

By Mrs. M. J. Preston.

Heard ye that thrilling word—
  Accent of dread—
Fall, like a thunderbolt,
  Bowing each head?
Over the battle dun,
Over each booming gun—
Ashby, our bravest one!
  Ashby is dead!

    Saw ye the veterans—
      Hearts that had known
    Never a quail of fear,
      Never a groan—
    Sob, though the fight they win,
    Tears their stern eyes within—
    Ashby, our Paladin,
      Ashby is dead!

Dash, dash the tear away—
  Crush down the pain!
Dulce et decus, be
  Fittest refrain!
Why should the dreary pall,
Round *him* be flung at all?
Did not our hero fall
  Gallantly slain?

    Catch the last words of cheer,
      Dropt from his tongue:
    Over the battle's din,
      Let them be rung!
    " Follow *me!* follow *me!*
    Soldier, oh! could there be
    Pæan or dirge for thee,
      Loftier sung?

Bold as the lion's heart—
    Dauntlessly brave—
Knightly as knightliest;
    Bayard might crave;
Sweet, with all Sydney's grace,
Tender as Hampden's face,
Who now shall fill the space,
    Void by his grave?

        'Tis not one broken heart,
            Wild with dismay—
        Crazed in her agony,
            Weeps o'er his clay!
        Ah! From a thousand eyes,
        Flow the pure tears that rise—
        Widowed Virginia lies
            Stricken to-day!

Yet charge as gallantly,
    Ye, whom he led!
Jackson, the victor, still
    Leads at your head!
Heroes! be battle done
Bravelier, every one
Nerved by the thought alone—
    Ashby is dead!

ONLY A SOLDIER'S GRAVE.

By S. A. Jones, of Aberdeen, Mississippi.

Only a soldier's grave! Pass by,
    For soldiers, like other mortals, die.
Parents he had—they are far away;
No sister weeps o'er the soldier's clay;
No brother comes, with a tearful eye:
It's only a soldier's grave—pass by.

True, he was loving, and young, and brave,
Though no glowing epitaph honors his grave ;
No proud recital of virtues known,
Of griefs endured, or of triumphs won ;
No tablet of marble, or obelisk high ;—
Only a soldier's grave—pass by.

Yet bravely he wielded his sword in fight,
And he gave his life in the cause of right !
When his hope was high, and his youthful dream
As warm as the sunlight on yonder stream ;
His heart unvexed by sorrow or sigh ;—
Yet, 'tis only a soldier's grave :—pass by.

Yet, should we mark it—the soldier's grave,
Some one may seek him in hope to save !
Some of the dear ones, far away,
Would bear him home to his native clay ;
'Twere sad, indeed, should they wander nigh,
Find not the hillock, and pass him by.

PROMISE OF SPRING.

THE sun-beguiling breeze,
    From the soft Cuban seas,
With life-bestowing kiss wakes the pride of garden bowers
    And lo ! our city elms,
    Have plumed with buds their helms,
And with tiny spears salute the coming on of flowers.

    The promise of the Spring,
    Is in every glancing wing
That tells its flight in song which shall long survive the
        flight ;

And, mocking Winter's glooms,
Skies, air and earth grow blooms,
With charge as bless'd as ever came with passage of a night!

Ah! could our hearts but share
The promise rich and rare,
That welcomes life to rapture in each happy fond caress,
That makes each innocent thing
Put on its bloom and wing,
Singing for Spring to come to the realm she still would bless!

But, alas for us, no more
Shall the coming hour restore
The glory, sweet and wanted, of the seasons to our souls;
Even as the spring appears,
Her smiling makes our tears
While with each bitter memory the torrent o'er us rolls.

Even as our zephyrs sing
That they bring us in the Spring,
Even as our bird grows musical in ecstasy of flight—
We see the serpent crawl,
With his slimy coat o'er all,
And blended with the song is the hissing of his blight.

We shudder at the blooms,
Which but serve to cover tombs—
At the very sweet of odors which blend venom with the
breath,
Sad shapes look out from trees,
And in sky and earth and breeze,
We behold but the aspect of a Horror worse than Death!

South Carolinian.

SPRING.

By Henry Timrod.

Spring, with that nameless pathos in the air
    Which dwells with all things fair,
Spring, with her golden suns and silver rain,
Is with us once again.

Out in the lonely woods the jasmine burns
Its fragrant lamps, and turns
Into a royal court with green festoons
The banks of dark lagoons.

In the deep heart of every forest tree
The blood is all aglee,
And there's a look about the leafless bowers
As if they dreamed of flowers.

Yet still on every side appears the hand
Of Winter in the land,
Save where the maple reddens on the lawn,
Flushed by the season's dawn ;

Or where, like those strange semblances we find
That age to childhood bind,
The elm puts on, as if in Nature's scorn,
The brown of Autumn corn.

As yet the turf is dark, although you know
That, not a span below,
A thousand germs are groping through the gloom,
And soon will burst their tomb.

Already, here and there, on frailest stems
Appear some azure gems,
Small as might deck, upon a gala day,
The forehead of a fay.

BRIGADIER-GENERAL J. E. B. STUART   LIEUTENANT-GENERAL JUBAL A. EARLY

In gardens you may see, amid the dearth,
The crocus breaking earth;
And near the snowdrop, tender, white and green,
The violet in its screen.

But many gleams and shadows need must pass
Along the budding grass,
And weeks go by, before the enamored South
Shall kiss the rose's mouth.

Still there's a sense of blossoms yet unborn
In the sweet airs of morn;
One almost looks to see the very street
Grow purple at his feet.

At times a fragrant breeze comes floating by
And brings, you know not why,
A feeling as when eager crowds await
Before a palace gate

Some wondrous pageant; and you scarce would start,
If from a beech's heart
A blue-eyed Dryad, stepping forth, should say
" Behold me ! I am May ! "

Ah ! who would couple thoughts of war and crime
With such a blessed time !
Who in the westwind's aromatic breath
Could hear the call of Death !

Yet not more surely shall the Spring awake
The voice of wood and brake,
Than she shall rouse, for all her tranquil charms
A million men to arms.

There shall be deeper hues upon her plains
Than all her sunlight rains,
And every gladdening influence around
Can summon from the ground.

Oh ! standing on this desecrated mould,
Methinks that I behold,
Lifting her bloody daisies up to God,
Spring, kneeling on the sod,

And calling with the voice of all her rills,
Upon the ancient hills,
To fall and crush the tyrants and the slaves
Who turn her meads to graves.

CAROLINA.

By Henry Timrod.

THE despot treads thy sacred sands,
  Thy pines give shelter to his bands,
Thy sons stand by with idle hands,
          Carolina !

    He breathes at ease thy airs of balm,
    He scorns the lances of thy palm ;
    Oh ! who shall break thy craven calm,
            Carolina !

Thy ancient fame is growing dim,
A spot is on thy garment's rim ;
Give to the winds thy battle-hymn,
          Carolina !

    Call on thy children of the hill,
    Wake swamp and river, coast and rill,
    Rouse all thy strength and all thy skill,
            Carolina !

Cite wealth and science, trade and art,
Touch with thy fire the cautious mart,
And pour thee through the people's heart,
          Carolina !

Till even the coward spurns his fears,
And all thy fields, and fens, and meres,
Shall bristle like thy palm, with spears,
                Carolina !

      Hold up the glories of thy dead ;
      Say how thy elder children bled,
      And point to Eutaw's battle-bed,
                      Carolina !

Tell how the patriot's soul was tried,
And what his dauntless breast defied ;
How Rutledge ruled, and Laurens died,
                Carolina !

      Cry ! till thy summons, heard at last,
      Shall fall, like Marion's bugle-blast,
      Re-echoed from the haunted past,
                      Carolina !

I hear a murmur, as of waves
That grope their way through sunless caves.
Like bodies struggling in their graves,
                Carolina !

      And now it deepens ; slow and grand
      It swells, as rolling to the land
      An ocean broke upon the strand,
                      Carolina !

Shout ! let it reach the startled Huns !
And roar with all thy festal guns !
It is the answer of thy sons,
                Carolina !

      They will not wait to hear thee call ;
      From Sachem's head to Sumter's wall
      Resounds the voice of hut and hall,
                      Carolina !

No ! thou hast not a stain, they say,
Or none save what the battle-day
Shall wash in seas of blood away,
                    Carolina !

    Thy skirts, indeed, the foe may part,
    Thy robe be pierced with sword and dart,
    They shall not touch thy noble heart,
                        Carolina !

Ere thou shalt own the tyrant's thrall,
Ten times ten thousand men must fall ;
Thy corpse may hearken to his call,
                    Carolina !

    When by thy bier, in mournful throngs,
    The women chant thy mortal wrongs,
    'Twill be their own funereal songs,
                        Carolina !

From thy dead breast, by ruffians trod,
No helpless child shall look to God ;
All shall be safe beneath thy sod,
                    Carolina !

    Girt with such wills to do and bear,
    Assured in right, and mailed in prayer,
    Thou wilt not bow thee to despair,
                        Carolina !

Throw thy bold banner to the breeze !
Front with thy ranks the threatening seas,
Like thine own proud armorial trees,
                    Carolina !

    Fling down thy gauntlet to the Huns,
    And roar the challenge from thy guns ;
    Then leave the future to thy sons,
                        Carolina !

THE VOICE OF THE SOUTH.

'TWAS a goodly boon that our fathers gave,
  And fits but ill to be held by the slave ;
And sad were the thought, if one of our band
Should give up the hope of so fair a land.

> But the hour has come, and the times that tried
> The souls of men in our days of pride,
> Return once more, and now for the brave,
> To merit the boon which our fathers gave.

And if there be one base spirit who stands
Now, in our peril, with folded hands,
Let his grave at once in the soil be wrought,
With the sword with which his old father fought.

> An oath sublime should the freeman take,
> Still braving the fight and the felon stake ;—
> The oath that his sires brought over the sea,
> When they pledged their swords to Liberty !

'Twas a goodly oath, and in Heaven's own sight,
They battled and bled in behalf of the right ;
'Twas hallowed by God with the holiest sign,
And seal'd with the blood of your sires and mine.

> We cannot forget and we dare not forego,
> The holy duty to them that we owe,
> The duty that pledges the soul of the son
> To keep the freedom his sire hath won.

To suffer no proud transgressor to spoil
One right of our homes, or one foot of our soil,
One privilege pluck from our keeping, or dare
Usurp one blessing 'tis fit that we share !

11

Art ready for this, dear brother, who still
Keep'st Washington's bones upon Vernon's hill?
Art ready for this, dear brother, whose ear.
Should ever the voices of Mecklenburg hear?

Thou art ready, I know, brother nearest my heart,
Son of Eutaw and Ashley, to do thy part;
The sword and the rifle are bright in thy hands,
And wait but the word for the flashing of brands!

And thou, by Savannah's broad valleys,—and thou
Where the Black Warrior murmurs in echoes the vow;
And thou, youngest son of our sires, who roves
Where Apalachicola glides through her groves.

Nor shall Tennessee pause, when like voice from the steep,
The great South shall summon her sons from their sleep;
Nor Kentucky be slow, when our trumpet shall call,
To tear down the rifle that hangs on her wall!

Oh, sound, to awaken the dead from their graves,
The will that would thrust us from place for our slaves,
That, by fraud which lacks courage, and plea that lacks truth,
Would rob us of right without reason or ruth.

Dost thou hearken, brave Creole, as fearless as strong,
Nor rouse thee to combat the infamous wrong?
Ye hear it, I know, in the depth of your souls,
Valiant race, through whose valley the great river rolls.

At last ye are wakened, all rising at length,
In the passion of pride, in the fulness of strength;
And now let the struggle begin which shall see,
If the son, like the sire, is fit to be free.

We are sworn to the State, from our fathers that came,
To welcome the ruin, but never the shame;
To yield not a foot of our soil, nor a right,
While the soul and the sword are still fit for the fight.

Then, brothers, your hands and your hearts, while we draw
The bright sword of right, on the charter of law ;—
Here the record was writ by our fathers, and here,
To keep, with the sword, that old record, we sweare.

Let those who defile and deface it, be sure,
No longer their wrong or their fraud we endure ;
We will scatter in scorn every link of the chain,
With which they would fetter our free souls in vain.

How goodly and bright were its links at the first !
How loathly and foul, in their usage accurst !
We had worn it in pride while it honor'd the brave,
But we rend it, when only grown fit for the slave.

BATTLE HYMN.

LORD of Hosts, that beholds us in battle, defending
  The homes of our sires 'gainst the hosts of the foe.
Send us help on the wings of thy angels descending,
  And shield from his terrors, and baffle his blow.
Warm the faith of our sons, till they flame as the iron,
  Red-glowing from the fire-forge, kindled by zeal ;
Make them forward to grapple the hordes that environ,
  In the storm-rush of battle, through forests of steel !

Teach them, Lord, that the cause of their country makes
   glorious
  The martyr who falls in the front of the fight ;—
That the faith which is steadfast makes ever victorious
  The arm which strikes boldly defending the right ;—
That the zeal, which is roused by the wrongs of a nation,
  Is a war-horse that sweeps o'er the field as his own ;
And the Faith, which is winged by the soul's approbation,
  Is a warrior, in proof, that can ne'er be o'erthrown.

KENTUCKY, SHE IS SOLD.

By J. R. Barbick, of Kentucky.

A tear for " the dark and bloody ground,"
    For the land of hills and caves;
Her Kentons, Boones, and her Shelbys sleep
    Where the vandals tread their graves;
A sigh for the loss of her honored fame,
    Dear won in the days of old;
Her ship is manned by a foreign crew,
    For Kentucky, she is sold.

        The bones of her sons lie bleaching on
            The plains of Tippecanoe,
        On the field of Raisin her blood was shed,
            As free as the summer's dew;
        In Mexico her McRee and Clay
            Were first of the brave and bold—
        A change has been in her bosom wrought,
            For Kentucky, she is sold.

Pride of the free, was that noble State,
    And her banner still were so.
Had the iron heel of the despot not
    Her prowess sunk so low;
Her valleys once were the freeman's home,
    Her valor unbought with gold,
But now the pride of her life is fled,
    For Kentucky, she is sold.

        Her brave would once have scorned to wear
            The yoke that crushes her now,
        And the tyrant grasp, and the vandal tread,
            Would sullen have made her brow;
        Her spirit yet will be wakened up,
            And her saddened fate be told,
        Her gallant sons to the world yet prove
            That Kentucky is not sold.

DISTINGUISHED MEN OF THE CONFEDERACY

Beginning at top and going to right are Judah P. Benjamin, John Slidell, William
L. Yancey, Major-General John C. Breckenridge, Governor Henry A Wise,
James M. Mason, Alexander H. Stephens.

THE SALKEHATCHIE.

By Emily J. Moore.

Written when a garrison, at or near Salkehatchie Bridge, were threatening a raid up in the Fork of Big and Little Salkehatchie.

THE crystal streams, the pearly streams,
　The streams in sunbeams flashing,
The murm'ring streams, the gentle streams,
　The streams down mountains dashing,
　　　　Have been the theme
　　　　Of poets' dream,
　　　And, in wild witching story,
Have been renowned for love's fond scenes,
　　Or some great deed of glory.

　　　　The Rhine, the Tiber, Ayr, and Tweed,
　　　　　The Arno, silver-flowing,
　　　　The Hudson, Charles, Potomac, Don,
　　　　　With poesy are glowing;
　　　　　　　But I would praise
　　　　　　　In artless lays,
　　　　　A stream which well may match ye,
　　　　Though dark its waters glide along—
　　　　　The swampy Salkehatchie.

'Tis not the beauty of its stream,
　Which makes it so deserving
Or honor at the Muses' hands,
　But 'tis the use it's serving,
　　　And 'gainst a raid,
　　　We hope its aid
　Will ever prove efficient,
Its fords remain still overflowed,
　In water ne'er deficient.

If Vandal bands are held in check,
  Their crossing thus prevented,
And we are spared the ravage wild
    Their malice has invented,
    Then we may well
    In numbers tell
  No other stream can match ye,
And grateful we shall ever be
  To swampy Salkehatchie.

THE KNELL SHALL SOUND ONCE MORE.

I KNOW that the knell shall sound once more,
  And the dirge be sung o'er a bloody grave;
And there shall be storm on the beaten shore,
  And there shall be strife on the stormy wave;
And we shall wail, with a mighty wail,
  And feel the keen sorrow through many years,
But shall not our banner at last prevail,
  And our eyes be dried of tears?

There's a bitter pledge for each fruitful tree,
  And the nation whose course is long to run,
Must make, though in anguish still it be,
  The tribute of many a noble son;
The roots of each mighty shaft must grow
  In the blood-red fountain of many hearts;
And to conquer the right from a bloody foe,
  Brings a pang as when soul and body parts!

But the blood and the pang are the need, alas!
  To strengthen the sovereign will that sways
The generations that rise, and pass
  To the full fruition that crowns their days!

'Tis still in the strife, they must grow to life :
 And sorrow shall strengthen the soul for care ;
And the freedom sought must ever be bought
 By the best blood-offerings, held most dear.

Heroes, the noblest, shall still be first
 To mount the red altar of sacrifice ;
Homes the most sacred shall fare the worst,
 Ere we conquer and win the precious prize !—
The struggle may last for a thousand years,
 And only with blood shall the field be bought ;
But the sons shall inherit, through blood and tears,
 The birth-right for which their old fathers fough

" LIBERA NOS, O DOMINE ! "

By James Barron Hope.

WHAT ! ye hold yourselves as freemen ?
 Tyrants love just such as ye !
Go ! abate your lofty manner !
Write upon the State's old banner,
 " *A furore Normanorum,*
 Libera nos, O Domine ! "

  Sink before the federal altar,
   Each one low, on bended knee,
  Pray, with lips that sob and falter,
  This prayer from the coward's psalter,—
   " *A furore Normanorum,*
   Libera nos, O Domine ! "

But ye hold that quick repentance
 In the Northern mind will be ;
This repentance comes no sooner

Than the robbers did, at Luna !
   " *A furore Normanorum,*
   Libera nos, O Domine ! "

      He repented *him :*—the Bishop
        Gave him absolution free ;
      Poured upon him sacred chrism
      In the pomp of his baptism.
       " *A furore Normanorum,*
       Libera nos, O Domine ! "

He repented;—then he sickened !
   Was he pining for the sea ?
In extremis was he shriven,
The viaticum was given,
   " *A furore Normanorum,*
   Libera nos, O Domine ! "

      Then the old cathedral's choir
        Took the plaintive minor key ;
      With the Host upraised before him,
      Down the marble aisles they bore him ;
       " *A furore Normanorum,*
       Libera nos, O Domine ! "

While the bishop and the abbot—
   All the monks of high degree,
Chanting praise to the Madonna,
Came to do him Christian honor !
   " *A furore Normanorum,*
   Libera nos, O Domine ! "

      Now the *miserere's* cadence,
        Takes the voices of the sea ;
      As the music-billows quiver,
      See the dead freebooter shiver !
       " *A furore Normanorum,*
       Libera nos, O Domine ! "

Is it that these intonations
    Thrill him thus from head to knee ?
Lo, his cerements burst asunder !
'Tis a sight of fear and wonder !
    " *A furore Normanorum,*
    Libera nos, O Domine ! "

      Fierce, he stands before the bishop,
        Dark as shape of Destinie.
      Hark ! a shriek ascends, appalling,—
      Down the prelate goes—dead—falling !
        " *A furore Normanorum,*
        Libera nos, O Domine ! "

Hastings lives ! He was but feigning !
    What ! Repentant ? Never he !
Down he smites the priests and friars,
And the city lights with fires !
    " *A furore Normanorum,*
    Libera nos, O Domine ! "

      Ah ! the children and the maidens,
        'Tis in vain they strive to flee !
      Where the white-haired priests lie bleeding,
      Is no place for woman's pleading.
        " *A furore Normanorum,*
        Libera nos, O Domine ! "

Louder swells the frightful tumult—
    Pallid Death holds revelrie !
Dies the organ's mighty clamor,
By the horseman's iron hammer !
    " *A furore Normanorum,*
    Libera nos, O Domine ! "

      So they thought that he'd repented !
        Had they nailed him to the tree,

He had not deserved their pity,
      And they had not—lost their city.
" *A furore Normanorum,*
Libera nos, O Domine! "

      For the moral in this story,
            Which is plain as truth can be:
If we trust the North's relenting,
We shall shriek—too late repenting—
      " *A furore Normanorum,*
      Libera nos, O Domine! "

MY COUNTRY.

By W. D. Porter, of South Carolina.

Go, read the stories of the great and free,
      The nations on the long, bright roll of fame,
Whose noble rage has baffled the decree
      Of tyrants to despoil their life and name;

Whose swords have flashed like lightning in the eyes
      Of robber despots, glorying in their might,
And taught the world, by deeds of high emprise,
      The power of truth and sacredness of right:

Whose people, strong to suffer and endure,
      In faith have wrestled till the blessing came,
And won through woes a victory doubly sure,
      As martyr wins his crown through blood and flame,

The purest virtue has been sorest tried,
      Nor is there glory without patient toil;
And he who woes fair Freedom for his bride,
      Through suffering must be purged of stain and soil.

My country ! in this hour of trial sore,
　　When in the balance trembling hangs thy fate,
Brace thy great heart with courage to the core,
　　Not let one jot of faith or hope abate !

The world's bright eye is fixed upon thee still ;
　　Life, honor, fame—these all are in the scale ;
Endure ! endure ! endure ! with iron will,
　　And by the truth of heaven, thou shalt not fail.

AFTER THE BATTLE.

By Miss Agnes Leonard.

All day long the sun had wandered,
　　Through the slowly creeping hours,
And at last the stars were shining
　　Like some golden-petaled flowers
Scattered o'er the azure bosom
　　Of the glory-haunted night,
Flooding all the sky with grandeur,
　　Filling all the earth with light.

　　　　And the fair moon, with the sweet stars,
　　　　　　Gleamed amid the radiant spheres
　　　　Like " a pearl of great price " shining
　　　　　　Just as it had shone for years,
　　　　On the young land that had risen,
　　　　　　In her beauty and her might,
　　　　Like some gorgeous superstructure
　　　　　　Woven in the dreams of night ;

With her " cities hung like jewels "
　　On her green and peaceful breast,
With her harvest fields of plenty,
　　And her quiet homes of rest.

But a change had fallen sadly
 O'er the young and beauteous land,
Brothers on the field fought madly
 That once wandered hand in hand.

  And " the hearts of distant mountains
   Shuddered," with a fearful wonder,
  As the echoes burst upon them
   Of the canon's awful thunder.
  Through the long hours waged the battle
   Till the setting of the sun,
  Dropped a seal upon the record,
   That the day's mad work was done.

Thickly on the trampled grasses
 Lay the battle's awful traces,
'Mid the blood-stained clover blossoms
 Lay the stark and ghastly faces,
With no mourners bending downward
 O'er a costly funeral pall ;
And the dying daylight softly,
 With the starlight watched o'er all.

  And, where eager, joyous footsteps
   Once perchance were wont to pass,
  Ran a little streamlet making
   One " Blue fold in the dark grass ; "
  And where, from its hidden fountain,
   Clear and bright the brooklet burst
  Two had crawled, and each was bending
   O'er to slake his burning thirst.

Then beneath the solemn starlight
 Of the radiant jewelled skies,
Both had turned, and were intently
 Gazing in each other's eyes.

STATUE TO HENRY CLAY

This beautiful marble statue to Henry Clay was erected in the Capitol Square, Richmond, Virginia, by the Ladies' Clay Association, and dedicated on Clay's Eighty-third Anniversary, April 12, 1860.

Both were solemnly forgiving—
    Hushed the pulse of passion's breath—
Calmed the maddening thirst for battle,
    By the chilling hand of death,

        Then spoke one in bitter anguish :
            " God have pity on my wife,
        And my children, in New Hampshire ;
            Orphans by this cruel strife."
        And the other, leaning closer,
            Underneath the solemn sky,
        Bowed his head to hide the moisture
            Gathering in his downcast eye :

" I've a wife and little daughter,
    'Mid the fragrant Georgia bloom,"—
Then his cry rang sharper, wilder,
    " Oh, God ! pity all their gloom."
And the wounded, in their death-hour,
    Talking of the loved ones' woes,
Nearer drew unto each other,
    Till they were no longer foes.

        And the Georgian listened sadly
            As the other tried to speak,
        While the tears were dropping softly
            O'er the pallor of his cheek :
        " How she used to stand and listen,
            Looking o'er the fields for me,
        Waiting till she saw me coming,
            'Neath the shadowy old plum-tree.
        Never more I'll hear her laughter,
            As she sees me at the gate,
        And beneath the plum-tree's shadows
            All in vain for me she'll wait."

Then the Georgian, speaking softly,
 Said : " A brown-eyed little one
Used to wait among the roses,
 For me, when the day was done ;
And amid the early fragrance
 Of those blossoms, fresh and sweet,
Up and down the old verandah
 I would chase my darling's feet.
But on earth no more the beauty
 Of her face my eye shall greet,
Nevermore I'll hear the music
 Of those merry, pattering feet—
Ah, the solemn starlight, falling
 On the far-off Georgia bloom,
Tells no tale unto my darling
 Of her absent father's doom."

  Through the tears that rose between them
   Both were trying grief to smother,
  An they clasped each other's fingers
   Whispering : " Let's forgive each other."

 * * * * * * *

When the morning sun was walking
 " Up the gray stairs of the dawn,"
And the crimson east was flushing
 All the forehead of the morn,
Pitying skies were looking sadly
 On the " once proud, happy land,"
On the Southron and the Northman,
 Holding fast each other's hand.
Fatherless the golden tresses,
 Watching 'neath the old plum-tree ·
Fatherless the little Georgian,
 Sporting in unconscious glee.

SONG OF THE TEXAS RANGERS.

Air—"The Yellow Rose of Texas."

The name of Wharton occurring in this poem recalls an interesting incident of a few years ago. I was engaged in conducting an evangelistic
service in a little town in Texas. The founder of that town, Captain Kyle,
came out to the meetings and was converted. His confession of faith was
unique. He said, pointing to me: "I followed this man's cousin in many
a hard-fought battle, and now I propose to follow his commander, the
Lord Jesus Christ, for the balance of my days."

THE morning star is paling
    The camp-fires flicker low,
Our steeds are madly neighing,
    For the bugle bids us go,
So put the foot in stirrup,
    And shake the bridle free,
For to-day the Texas Rangers
    Must cross the Tennessee.

    With Wharton for our leader,
        We'll chase the dastard foe,
    Till our horses bathe their fetlocks
        In the deep blue Ohio.

Our men are from the prairies,
    That roll broad and proud and free,
From the high and craggy mountains
    To the murmuring Mexic' sea ;
And their hearts are open as their plains,
    Their thoughts as proudly brave
As the bold cliffs of the San Bernard,
    Or the Gulf's resistless wave.

    Then quick ! into the saddle,
        And shake the bridle free,
    To-day with gallant Wharton,
        We cross the Tennessee.

'Tis joy to be a Ranger!
    To fight for dear Southland ;
'Tis joy to follow Wharton,
    With his gallant, trusty band !
'Tis joy to see our Harrison,
    Plunge like a meteor bright
Into the thickest of the fray,
    And deal his deathly might.

        Oh ! who'd not be a Ranger,
            And follow Wharton's cry !
        To battle for his country—
            And, if needs be—die !

                By the Colorado's waters,
                    On the Gulf's deep murmuring shore,
                On our soft green peaceful prairies
                    Are the homes we may see no more ;
                But in those homes our gently wives,
                    And mothers with silv'ry hairs
                Are loving us with tender hearts,
                    And shielding us with prayers.

                    So, trusting in our country's God,
                        We draw our stout, good brand,
                    For those we love at home,
                        Our altars and our land.

Up, up with the crimson battle-flag—
    Let the blue pennon fly ;
Our steeds are stamping proudly—
    They hear the battle-cry !
The thundering bomb, the bugle's call,
    Proclaim the foe is near ;
We strike for God and native land,
    And all we hold most dear.

        Then spring into the saddle,
            And shake the bridle free—
        For Wharton leads, through fire and blood,
            For Home and Victory !

THE GUERRILLA MARTYRS.

A Y, to the doom—the scaffold and the chain,—
⠀⠀⠀To all your cruel tortures, bear them on,
Ye foul and coward hangmen;—but in vain!—
⠀⠀⠀Ye cannot touch the glory they have won—
And win—thus yielding up the martyr's breath
⠀⠀⠀For freedom!—Theirs is a triumphant death!—
A sacred pledge from Nature, that her womb
⠀⠀⠀Still keeps some sacred fires; that yet shall burst,
Even from the reeking ravage of their doom,
⠀⠀⠀As glorious—ay, more glorious—than the first!
Exult, shout, triumph! Wretches, do your worst!
⠀⠀⠀'Tis for a season only! There shall come
An hour when ye shall feel yourtelves accurst;
⠀⠀⠀When the dread vengeance of a century
Shall reap its harvest in a single day;
⠀⠀⠀And ye shall howl in horror;—and, to die,
Shall be escape and refuge! Ye may slay;—
⠀⠀⠀But to be cruel and brutal, does not make
Ye conquerors; and the vulture yet shall prey
⠀⠀⠀On living hearts; and vengeance fiercely slake
The unappeasable appetite ye wake,
⠀⠀⠀In the hot blood of victims, that have been,
Most eager, binding freemen to the stake,—
⠀⠀⠀Most greedy in the orgies of this sin!

Ye slaughter,—do ye triumph? Ask your chains,
⠀⠀⠀Ye Sodom-hearted butchers!—turn your eyes,
Where reeks yon bloody scaffold; and the pains,
⠀⠀⠀Ungroaned, of a true martyr, ere he dies,
Attest the damned folly of your crime,
⠀⠀⠀Now at its carnival! His spirit flies,
Unscathed by all your fires, through every clime,
⠀⠀⠀Into the world's wide bosom. Thousands rise,

12

Prompt at its call, and principled to strike
    The tyrants and the tyrannies alike!—
Voices, that doom ye, speak in all your deeds,
    And cry to heaven, arm earth, and kindle hell!
A host of freemen, where one martyr bleeds,
    Spring from his place of doom, and make his knell
The tocsin, to arouse a myriad race,
T' avenge Humanity's wrong, and wipe off man's disgrace!

We mourn not for our martyrs!—for they perish,
    As the good perish, for a deathless faith:
Their glorious memories men will fondly cherish,
    In terms and signs that shall ennoble death!
Their blood becomes a principle, to guide,
    Onward, forever onward, in proud flow,
Restless, resistless, as the ocean tide,
    The Spirit heaven yields freedom here below!
How should we mourn the martyrs, who arise,
    Even from the stake and scaffold, to the skies;-
And take their thrones, as stars; and o'er the night,
    Shed a new glory; and to other souls,
Shine out with blessed guidance, and true light,
    Which leads successive races to their goal!

IN MEMORIAM

Of our Right-Reverend Father in God, Leonidas Polk, Lieutenant-General
Confederate States Army.

PEACE, troubled soul!   The strife is done,
    This life's fierce conflicts and its woes are ended:
There is no more—eternity begun,
    Faith merged in sight—hope with fruition blended.
    Peace, troubled soul!

The warrior rests upon his bier,
    Within his coffin calmly sleeping.
        His requiem the cannon peals,
        And heroes of a hundred fields
Their last sad watch are round him keeping.

Joy, sainted soul ! Within the vale
    Of Heaven's great temple, is thy blissful dwelling ;
Bathed in a light, to which the sun is pale,
    Archangels' hymns in endless transports swelling.
        Joy, sainted soul !
Back to her altar which he served,
    The Holy Church her child is bringing.
        The organ's wail then dies away,
        And kneeling priests around him pray,
    As *De Profundis* they are singing.

Bring all the trophies that are owed,
    To him at once so great, so good.
His Bible and his well-used sword—
    His snowy lawn not " stained with blood ! "
No ! pure as when before his God,
    He laid its spotless folds aside,
War's path of awful duty trod,
    And on his country's altar died !

Oh ! Warrior-bishop, Church and State
    Sustain in thee an equal loss ;
But who would call thee from thy weight
    Of glory, back to bear life's cross !
The Faith was kept—thy course was run,
    Thy good fight finished ; hence the word,
" Well done, oh ! faithful child, well done,
    Taste thou the mercies of thy Lord ! "

No dull decay nor lingering pain,
　　By slow degrees, consumed thy health,
A glowing messenger of flame
　　Translated thee by fiery death !
And we who in one common grief
　　Are bending now beneath the rod,
In this sweet thought may find relief,
　　" Our holy father walked with God,
And is not—God has taken him ! "

" LET US CROSS OVER THE RIVER."

Jackson's Last Words.

" A few moments before his death, Stonewall Jackson called out in his delirium : ' Order A. P. Hill to prepare for action. Pass the infantry rapidly to the front. Tell Major Hawks . . . . .' Here the sentence was left unfinished. But, soon after, a sweet smile overspread his face, and he murmured quietly, with an air of relief: ' Let us cross over the river and rest under the shade of the trees.' These were his last words ; and, without any expression of pain, or sign of struggle, his spirit passed away."

COME, let us cross the river, and rest beneath the trees,
　　And list the merry leaflets at sport with every breeze ;
Our rest is won by fighting, and Peace awaits us there.
Strange that a cause so blighting produces fruit so fair !

Come, let us cross the river, those that have gone before,
Crushed in the strife for freedom, await on yonder shore ;
So bright the sunshine sparkles, so merry hums the breeze,
Come, let us cross the river, and rest beneath the trees.

Come, let us cross the river, the stream that runs so dark ;
'Tis none but cowards quiver, so let us all embark.
Come, men with hearts undaunted, we'll stem the tide with
　　　　　　　　　　　　　　　　　　[ease,
We'll cross the flowing river, and rest beneath the trees.

SOLDIERS' MONUMENT AT NEW ORLEANS, LOUISIANA

Come, let us cross the river, the dying hero cried,
And God, of life the giver, then bore him o'er the tide.
Life's wars for him are over, the warrior takes his ease,
There, by the flowing river, at rest beneath the trees.

CHARGE OF HAGOOD'S BRIGADE.

Weldon Railroad, August 31, 1864.

The following lines were written in the summer of 1864, immediately after the charge referred to in them, which was always considered by the brigade as their most desperate encounter.

SCARCE seven hundred men they stand
  In tattered, rude array,
A remnant of that gallant band,
Who erstwhile held the sea-girt strand
Of Morris' Isle, with iron hand
  'Gainst Yankees' hated sway.

  Secessionville their banner claims,
  And Sumter held 'mid smoke and flames
  And the dark battle on the streams
    Of Pocotaligo ;
  And Walthall's Junction's hard-earned fight,
  And Drewry's bluff's embattled height,
  Whence, at the gray dawn of the light,
    They rushed upon the foe.

Tattered and torn those banners now,
But not less proud each lofty brow,
  Untaught as yet to yield ;
With mien unblenched, unfaltering eye,
Forward, where bombshells shrieking fly
Flecking with smoke the azure sky
  On Weldon's fated field.

Sweeps from the woods the bold array,
Not theirs to falter in the fray,
No men more sternly trained than they
      To meet their deadly doom ;
While from a hundred throats agape,
A hundred sulphurous flames escape,
Round shot, and canister, and grape,
      The thundering cannon's boom !

     Swift, on their flank, with fearful crash
     Shrapnel and ball commingling clash,
     And bursting shells, with lurid flash,
       Their dazzled sight confound ;
     Trembles the earth beneath their feet,
     Along their front a rattling sheet
     Of leaden hail concentric meet,
       And numbers strew the ground.

On, o'er the dying and the dead,
O'er mangled limb and gory head,
With martial look, with martial tread,
March Hagood's men to bloody bed,
      Honor their sole reward ;
Himself doth lead the battle line,
      Himself those banners guard.

     They win the height, those gallant few,
     A fiercer struggle to renew,
     Resolved as gallant men to do
       Or sink in glory's shroud ;
     But scarcely gain its stubborn crest,
     Ere, from the ensign's murdered breast,
     An impious foe has dared to wrest
       That banner proud,

Upon him, Hagood, in thy might!
Flash on thy soul th' immortal light
Of those brave deeds that blazon bright
   Our Southern Cross.
He dies.   Unfurl its folds again,
Let it wave proudly o'er the plain ;
The dying shall forget their pain,
   Count not their loss.

   Then, rallying to your chieftain's call,
   Ploughed through by cannon-shot and ball,
   Hemmed in, as by a living wall,
      Cleave back your way,
   Those bannered deeds their souls inspire,
   Borne amid sheets of forked fire,
   By the Two Hundred who retire
      Of that array.

Ah, Carolina ! well the tear
May dew thy cheek ; thy clasped hands rear
In passion o'er their tombless bier,
   Thy fallen chivalry !
Malony, mirror of the brave,
And Sellers lie in glorious grave ;
No prouder fate than theirs, who gave
   Their lives for Liberty.

MUMFORD, THE MARTYR OF NEW ORLEANS.

By INA M. PORTER, of Alabama.

WHERE murdered Mumford lies,
  Bewailed in bitter sighs,
Low-bowed beneath the flag he loved,
Martyrs of Liberty,

Defenders of the Free !
Come, humbly nigh,
And learn to die !

Ah, Freedom, on that day,
Turned fearfully away,
While pitying angels lingered near,
To gaze upon the sod,
Red with a martyr's blood ;
And woman's tear
Fell on his bier !

O God ! that he should die
Beneath a Southern sky !
Upon a felon's gallows swung,
Murdered by tyrant hand,—
While round a helpless band,
On Butler's name
Poured scorn and shame.

But hark ! loud pæans fly
From earth to vaulted sky,
He's crowned at Freedom's holy throne !
List ! sweet-voiced Israel
Tolls far the martyr's knell !
Shout, Southrons, high,
Our battle cry !

Come, all of Southern blood,
Come, kneel to Freedom's God !
Here at her crimsoned altar swear !
Accursed for evermore
The flag that Mumford tore,
And o'er his grave
Our colors wave !

THE COTTON-BURNERS' HYMN.

"On yesterday, all the cotton in Memphis, and throughout the country, was burned. Probably not less than 300,000 bales have been burned in the last three days, in West Tennessee and North Mississippi."—*Memphis Appeal.*

Lo! where Mississippi rolls
　　Oceanward its stream,
Upward mounting, folds on folds,
　　Flaming fire-tongues gleam;
'Tis the planters' grand oblation
On the altar of the nation;
'Tis a willing sacrifice—
Let the golden incense rise—
Pile the cotton to the skies!
　　CHORUS—Lo! the sacrificial flame
　　　　　　Gilds the starry dome of night!
　　　　　　Nations! read the mute acclaim—
　　　　　　'Tis for liberty we fight!
　　　　　　Home! Religion! Right!

Never such a golden light
　　Lit the vaulted sky;
Never sacrifice as bright,
　　Rose to God on high;
Thousands oxen, what were they
To the offering we pay?
And the brilliant holocaust—
When the revolution's past—
In the nation's songs will last!
　　Chorus—Lo! the sacrificial flame, etc.

　　Though the night be dark above,
　　　　Broken though the shield—
　　Those who love us, those we love,
　　　　Bid us never yield;

Never ! though our bravest bleed,
    And the vultures on them feed,
Never ! though the serpents' race—
Hissing hate and vile disgrace—
By the million should menace !
      Chorus—Lo ! the sacrificial flame, etc.

    Pile the cotton to the skies ;
        Lo ! the Northmen gaze ;
    England ! see our sacrifice—
        See the cotton blaze !
    God of nations ! now to Thee,
    Southrons bend th' imploring knee ;
    'Tis our country's hour of need—
    Hear the mothers intercede—
    Hear the little children plead !
      Chorus—Lo ! the sacrificial flame, etc.

ASHES OF GLORY.

By A. J. Requier.

Fold up the gorgeous silken sun,
    By bleeding martyrs blest,
And heap the laurels it has won
    Above its place of rest.

    No trumpet's note need harshly blare—
      No drum funereal roll—
    Nor trailing sables drape the bier
      That frees a dauntless soul !

It lived with Lee, and decked his brow
    From Fate's empyreal Palm ;
It sleeps the sleep of Jackson now—
    As spotless and as calm.

It was outnumbered—not outdone,
    And they shall shuddering tell,
Who struck the blow, its latest gun
    Flashed ruin as it fell.

        Sleep, shrouded Ensign ! not the breeze
            That smote the victor tar,
        With death across the heaving seas
            Of fiery Trafalgar;

Not Arthur's knights, amid the gloom
    Their knightly deeds have starred ;
Nor Gallic Henry's matchless plume,
    Nor peerless-born Bayard ;

        Not all that antique fables feign,
            And Orient dreams disgorge;
        Nor yet the Silver Cross of Spain,
            And Lion of St. George,

Can bid thee pale !   Proud emblem, still
    Thy crimson glory shines
Beyond the lengthened shades that fill
    Their proudest kingly lines.

        Sleep! in thine own historic night,—·
            And by thy blazoned scroll,
        A warrior's Banner takes its flight,
        To greet the warrior's soul!

SOMEBODY'S DARLING.

By Marie La Coste, of Georgia.

Into a ward of the whitewashed halls,
    Where the dead and the dying lay—
Wounded by bayonets, shells and balls,
    Somebody's darling was borne one day—
Somebody's darling, so young and so brave!
    Wearing yet on his sweet, pale face—
Soon to be hid in the dust of the grave—
    The lingering light of his boyhood's grace!

Matted and damp are the curls of gold
    Kissing the snow of that fair young brow,
Pale are the lips of delicate mould—
    Somebody's darling is dying now.
Back from his beautiful blue-veined brow
    Brush his wandering waves of gold;
Cross his hands on his bosom now—
    Somebody's darling is still and cold.

Kiss him once for somebody's sake,
    Murmur a prayer soft and low—
One bright curl from its fair mates take—
    They were somebody's pride you know,
Somebody's hand hath rested there;
    Was it a mother's, soft and white?
Or have the lips of a sister fair
    Been baptized in their waves of light?

God knows best! He has somebody's love;
    Somebody's heart enshrined him there—
Somebody wafted his name above,
    Night and morn, on the wings of prayer.
Somebody wept when he marched away,
    Looking so handsome, brave and grand!
Somebody's kiss on his forehead lay—
    Somebody clung to his parting hand.

LIEUTENANT-GENERAL LEONIDAS POLK

Somebody's watching and waiting for him,
　　Yearning to hold him again to her heart;
And there he lies with his blue eyes dim,
　　And the smiling, child-like lips apart.
Tenderly bury the fair young dead—
　　Pausing to drop on his grave a tear;
Carve on the wooden slab o'er his head—
　　"Somebody's darling slumbers here."

AWAKE—ARISE!

By G. W. Archer, M. D.

Sons of the South—awake—arise!
　　A million foes sweep down amain,
Fierce hatred gleaming in their eyes,
　　And fire and rapine in their train,
　　Like savage Hun and merciless Dane!
　　"We come as brothers!" Trust them not!
　　By all that's dear in heaven and earth,
　　By every tie that hath its birth
　　Within your homes—around your hearth;
Believe me, 'tis a tyrant's plot,
　　Worse for the fair and sleek disguise—
A traitor in a patriot's cloak!
　　　　"Your country's good
　　　　Demands your blood!"
Was it a fiend from hell that spoke?

They point us to the Stripes and Stars;
　　(Our banner erst—the despot's now!)
But let not thoughts of by-gone wars,
　　When beat we back the common foe,
　　And felled them fast and shamed them so,
Divided us at this fearful hour;
　　But think of dungeons and of chains—
　　Think of your violated fanes—
　　Of your loved homestead's gory stains—

Eternal thraldom for your dower!
    No love of country fires their breasts—
The fell fanatics fain would free
            A groveling race,
            And in their place
Would fetter us with fiendish glee!

Sons of the South—awake—awake!
        And strike for rights full dear as those
        For which our struggling sires did shake
        Earth's proudest throne—while freedom rose,
        Baptized in blood of braggart foes.
Awake—that hour hath come again!
        Strike! as ye look to Heaven's high throne—
        Strike! for the Christian patriot's crown—
        Strike! in the name of Washington,
Who taught you once to rend the chain,
        Smiles now from Heaven upon our cause,
So like his own.   His spirit moves
            Through every fight,
            And lends its might
To every heart that freedom loves.

Ye beauteous of the sunny land!
        Unmatched your charms in all the earth,
'Neath freedom's banner take your stand;
        And, though you strike not, prove your worth,
        As wont in days of joy and mirth;
Lavish your praises on the brave—
        Pray when the battle fiercely lowers—
        Smile when the victory is ours—
        Frown on the wretch who basely cowers—
Mourn o'er each fallen hero's grave!
        Lend thus your favors whilst we smile;
Full soon we'll crush this vandal host!—
            With woman's charms
            To nerve their arms,
Oh! when have men their freedom lost!

THE TEXAN MARSEILLAISE.

By James Haines, of Texas.

Sons of the South, arouse to battle!
   Gird on your armor for the fight!
The Northern Thugs with dread " War's rattle,"
   Pour on each vale, and glen, and height;
Meet them as ocean meets in madness
      The frail bark on the rocky shore,
      When crested billows foam and roar,
And the wrecked crew go down in sadness.
         Arm! Arm! ye Southern braves!
         Scatter yon Vandal hordes!
         Despots and bandits, fitting food
         For vultures and your swords.

Shall dastard tyrants march their legions
   To crush the land of Jackson—Lee?
Shall freedom fly to other regions,
   And sons of Yorktown bend the knee?
Or shall their " footprints' base pollution "
      Of Southern soil, in blood be purged,
      And every flying slave be scourged
Back to his snows in wild confusion?
         Arm! Arm! &c.

Vile despots, with their minions knavish,
   Would drag us back to their embrace;
Will freemen brook a chain so slavish?
   Will brave men take so low a place?
O, Heaven! for words—the loathing, scorning
      We feel for such a Union's bands;
      To paint with more than mortal hands,
And sound our loudest notes of warning.
         Arm! Arm! &c.

What! union with a race ignoring
    The charter of our nation's birth!
Union with bastard slaves adoring
    The fiend that chains them to the earth!
No! we reply in tones of thunder—
    No! our staunch hills fling back the sound—
No! our hoarse canon echo round—
    No! evermore remain asunder!
    Arm! Arm! &c.

"MY. MARYLAND."

Written at Pointe Coupre, La., April 26, 1861,

BY LAMAR FONTAINE, Second Virginia Cavalry.

This was one of the most popular songs of the war. It was believed for a long time that Maryland would secede from the Union, so strong was the sympathy for the Southern cause. But though she did not withdraw from the Union, some of the very best troops in the Confederate Army were from that State. This song is a fine specimen of poetry, and breathes as well the spirit of true patriotism.

THE despot's heel is on thy shore,
    Maryland! My Maryland!
His torch is at thy temple door,
        Maryland! My Maryland!
Avenge the patriotic gore
That flecked the streets of Baltimore,
And be the battle-queen of yore,
        Maryland! My Maryland!

    Hark, to an exiled son's appeal,
        Maryland! My Maryland!
    My Mother-State, to thee I kneel,
        Maryland! My Maryland!
    For life and death, for woe and weal,
    Thy peerless chivalry reveal,
    And gird thy beautious limbs with steel!
        Maryland! My Maryland!

Thou wilt not cower in the dust,
   Maryland! My Maryland!
Thy beaming sword shall never rust,
   Maryland! My Maryland!
Remember Carroll's sacred trust,
Remember Howard's warlike thrust,
And all thy slumberers with the just,
   Maryland! My Maryland!

    Come! 'tis the red dawn of the day,
      Maryland! My Maryland!
    Come! with thy panoplied array,
      Maryland! My Maryland!
    With Ringgold's spirit for the fray,
    With Watson's blood at Monterey,
    With fearless Lowe and dashing May,
      Maryland! My Maryland!

Come! for thy shield is bright and strong,
   Maryland! My Maryland!
Come! for thy dalliance does thee wrong,
   Maryland! My Maryland!
Come! to thine own heroic throng,
That stalks with Liberty along,
And ring thy dauntless Slogan-song,
   Maryland! My Maryland!

    Dear Mother! burst the tyrant's chain,
      Maryland! My Maryland!
    Virginia should not call in vain,
      Maryland! My Maryland!
    She meets her sisters on the plain—
    " *Sic semper*," 'tis the proud refrain
    That baffles minions back amain,
      Maryland! My Maryland!
    Arise, in majesty again,
      Maryland! My Maryland!

13

I see the blush upon thy cheek,
   Maryland! My Maryland!
For thou wast ever bravely meek,
   Maryland! My Maryland!
But lo! there surges forth a shriek
From hill to hill, from creek to creek—
Potomac calls to Chesapeake,
   Maryland! My Maryland!

   Thou wilt not yield the Vandal toll,
      Maryland! My Maryland!
   Thou wilt not crook to his control,
      Maryland! My Maryland!
   Better the fire upon thee roll,
   Better the shot, the blade, the bowl,
   Than crucifixion of the soul,
      Maryland! My Maryland!

I hear the distant thunder hum,
   Maryland! My Maryland!
The Old Line bugle, fife, and drum,
   Maryland! My Maryland!
She is not dead, nor deaf, nor dumb—
  Huzza! she spurns the Northern scum!
She breathes—she burns! she'll come! she'll come!
   Maryland! My Maryland!

"OLD BETSY."

By John Killum.

Come, with the rifle so long in your keeping,
    Clean the old gun up and hurry it forth ;
Better to die while " Old Betsy " is speaking,
    Than live with arms folded, the slave of the North.

Hear ye the yelp of the North-wolf resounding,
    Scenting the blood of the warm-hearted South ;
Quick ! or his villainous feet will be bounding
    Where the gore of our maidens may drip from his
        mouth.

Oft in the wildwood " Old Bess " has relieved you,
    When the fierce bear was cut down in his track—
If at that moment she never deceived you,
    Trust her to-day with this ravenous pack.

Then, come, with the rifle so long in your keeping,
    Clean the old girl up and hurry her forth ;
Better to die while " Old Betsy " is speaking,
    Than live with arms folded, the slave of the North.

THE BEAUFORT EXILE'S LAMENT.

Now chant me a dirge for the Isles of the Sea,
    And sing the sad wanderer's psalm—
Ye women and children in exile that flee
    From the land of the orange and palm.

Lament for your homes, for the house of your God,
    Now the haunt of the vile and the low ;
Lament for the graves of your fathers, now trod
    By the foot of the Puritan foe !

No longer for thee, when the sables of night
    Are fading like shadows away,
Does the mocking-bird, drinking the first beams of light,
    Praise God for the birth of a day.

No longer for thee, when the rays are now full,
    Do the oaks form an evergreen glade;
While the drone of the locust o'erhead, seemed to lull
    The cattle that rest in the shade.

No longer for thee does the soft-shining moon
    Silver o'er the green waves of the bay;
Nor at evening, the notes of the wandering loon
    Bid farewell to the sun's dying ray.

Nor when night drops her pall over river and shore,
    And scatters eve's merry-voiced throng,
Does there rise, keeping time to the stroke of the oar,
    The wild chant of the sacred boat-song.

Then the revellers would cease ere the red wine they'd quaff,
    The traveller would pause on his way ;
And maidens would hush their low silvery laugh,
    To list to the negro's rude lay.

" Going home! going home ! " methinks I now hear
    At the close of each solemn refrain ;
'Twill be many a day, aye, and many a year,
    Ere ye'll sing that dear word " Home " again.

Your noble sons slain, on the battle-field lie,
    Your daughters 'mid strangers now roam ;
Your aged and helpless in poverty sigh
    O'er the days when they once had a home.

" Going home! going home ! " for the exile alone
    Can those words sweep the chords of the soul,
And raise from the grave the loved ones who are gone,
    As the tide-waves of time backward roll.

HIS LAST SHOT

An Incident of the deadly charge at Gettysburg.

"Going home ! going home !"   Ah ! how many who pine,
　　Dear Beaufort, to press thy green sod,
Ere then will have passed to shores brighter than thine—
　　Will have gone home at last to their God !

JOHN PEGRAM.

Fell at the Head of his Division, February 6, 1865, Ætat XXXIII,

By W. GORDON McCABE.

WHAT shall we say, now, of our gentle knight,
　　Or how express the measure of our woe,
For him who rode the foremost in the fight,
　　Whose good blade flashed so far amid the foe ?

Of all his knightly deeds what need to tell ?—
　　That good blade now lies fast within its sheath ;
What can we do but point to where he fell,
　　And, like a soldier, met a soldier's death ?

We sorrow not as those who have no hope ;
　　For he was pure in heart as brave in deed—
God pardon us, if blindly we should grope,
　　And love be questioned by the hearts that bleed.

And yet—oh ! foolish and of little faith !
　　We cannot choose but weep our useless tears ;
We loved him so ; we never dreamed that death
　　Would dare to touch him in his brave young years.

Ah dear, browned face, so fearless and so bright !
　　As kind to friend as thou wast stern to foe—
No more we'll see thee radiant in the fight,
　　The eager eyes—the flush on cheek and brow !

No more we'll greet the lithe, familiar form,
    Amid the surging smoke, with deaf'ning cheer;
No more shall soar above the iron storm,
    Thy ringing voice in accents sweet and clear.

Aye ! he has fought the fight and passed away—
    Our grand young leader smitten in the strife !
So swift to seize the chances of the fray,
    And careless only of his noble life.

He is not dead but sleepeth ! well we know
    The form that lies to-day beneath the sod,
Shall rise that time the golden bugles blow,
    And pour their music through the courts of God.

And there amid our great heroic dead—
    The war-worn sons of God, whose work is done—
His face shall shine, as they with stately tread,
    In grand review, sweep past the jasper throne.

Let not our hearts be troubled, few and brief
    His days were here, yet rich in love and faith;
Lord, we believe, help thou our unbelief,
    And grant thy servants such a life and death !

CAPTIVES GOING HOME.

No flaunting banners o'er them wave,
    No arms flash back the sun's bright ray,
No shouting crowds around them throng,
    No music cheers them on their way;
They're going home.   By adverse fate
    Compelled their trusty swords to sheathe;
True soldiers they, even though disarmed—
    Heroes, though robbed of victory's wreath.

Brave Southrons ! 'Tis with sorrowing hearts
    We gaze upon them through our tears,
And sadly feel how vain were all
    Their heroic deeds through weary years ;
Yet, 'mid their enemies they move
    With firm, bold step and dauntless mien ;
Oh, Liberty ! in every age,
    Such have thy chosen heroes been.

    Going home !   Alas, to them the words
        Bring visions fraught with gloom and woe :
    Since last they saw those cherished homes
        The legions of the invading foe
    Have swept them, simoon-like, along,
        Spreading destruction with the wind !
    " They found a garden, but they left
        A howling wilderness behind."

Ah ! in those desolated homes
    To which the " fate of war has come,"
Sad is the welcome—poor the feast—
    Yet loving ones will round him throng,
With smiles more tender, if less gay,
    And joy will brighten pallid cheeks
At sight of the dear boys in gray.

    Aye, give them welcome home, fair South,
        For you they've made a deathless name ;
    Bright through all after-time will glow
        The glorious record of their fame.
    They made a nation.   What, though soon
        Its radiant sun has seemed to set ;
    The past has shown what they can do,
        The future holds bright promise yet.

"OUR LEFT AT MANASSAS."

From dawn to dark they stood,
　　That long midsummer's day !
While fierce and fast
The battle-blast
　　Swept rank on rank away !

　　　　From dawn to dark they fought
　　　　　　With legions swept and cleft,
　　　　While black and wide,
　　　　The battle-tide
　　　　　　Poured ever on our " Left ! "

They closed each ghastly gap !
　　They dressed each shattered rank ;
They knew, how well !
That Freedom fell
　　With that exhausted flank !

　　　　"Oh ! for a thousand men,
　　　　　　Like these that melt away ! "
　　　　And down they came,
　　　　With steel and flame,
　　　　　　Four thousand to the fray !

They left the laggard train ;
　　The panting steam might stay ;
And down they came,
With steel and flame,
　　Head-foremost to the fray !

　　　　Right through the blackest cloud !
　　　　　　Their lightning-path they cleft !
　　　　Freedom and Fame
　　　　With triumph came
　　　　　　To our immortal Left.

Ye ! of your living, sure !
    Ye ! of your dead, bereft !
Honor the brave
Who died to save
    Your all, upon our Left.

ON THE HEIGHTS OF MISSION RIDGE.

By J. Augustine Signaigo.

WHEN the foes, in conflict heated,
    Battled over road and bridge,
While Bragg sullenly retreated
    From the heights of Mission Ridge—
There, amid the pines and wildwood,
    Two opposing colonels fell,
Who had schoolmates been in childhood,
    And had loved each other well.

There, amid the roar and rattle,
    Facing havoc's fiery breath,
Met the wounded two in battle,
    In the agonies of death.
But they saw each other reeling
    On the dead and dying men,
And the old time, full of feeling,
    Came upon them once again.

When that night the moon came creeping,
    With its gold streaks, o'er the slain,
She beheld two soldiers sleeping,
    Free from every earthly pain.
Close beside the mountain heather,
    Where the rocks obscure the sand,
They had died, it seems, together,
    As they clasped each other's hand.

ON TO RICHMOND.

By John R. Thompson, of Virginia.

It need hardly be mentioned here that Richmond, Virginia, was the Capital of the Confederacy, almost the whole of the war, from near its beginning unto the end. When General Lee's forces abandoned Richmond to General Grant and his army, it struck a blow to the Southern cause from which it seemed impossible to recover. From that hour when the last soldier left our Capital city, until the surrender at Appomattox, people saw and accepted the result of the great struggle. It was known on the opposite side, that when Richmond failed, the Confederacy was at an end, and so it proved to be. To-day, that beautiful little city has come forth from the ashes of her ruins the Queen of the South, and stands there the Capital of the Old Commonwealth, the mother of statesmen, and the leader of her sisters of the South.

M AJOR-GENERAL SCOTT
  An order had got
   To push on the columns to Richmond ;
For loudly went forth
From all parts of the North,
The cry that an end of the war must be made
In time for the regular yearly Fall Trade ;
Mr. Greeley spoke freely about the delay,
The Yankees " to hum " were all hot for the fray ;
The chivalrous Grow
Declared they were slow,
And therefore the order
To march from the border
   And make an excursion to Richmond.

Major-General Scott
Most likely was not
Very loth to obey this instruction, I wot ;
In his private opinion
The Ancient Dominion
Deserved to be pillaged, her sons to be shot,
  And the reason is easily noted ;

Though this part of the earth
Had given him birth,
And medals and swords,
Inscribed with fine words,
  It never for Winfield had voted.
Besides, you must know that our First of Commanders
Had sworn quite as hard as the Army in Flanders,
With his finest of armies and proudest of navies,
To wreak his old grudge against Jefferson Davis.
Then " forward the column," he said to McDowell ;
  And the Zouaves, with a shout,
  Most fiercely cried out,
" To Richmond or h—ll " (I omit here the vowel),
And Winfield, he ordered his carriage and four,
A dashing turnout, to be brought to the door,
  For a pleasant excursion to Richmond.

Major-General Scott
Had there on the spot
A splendid array
To plunder and slay ;
In the camp he might boast
Such a numerous host,
As he never had yet
In the battle-field set ;
Every class and condition of Northern society
Were in for the trip, a most varied variety ;
In the camp he might hear every lingo in vogue;
" The sweet German accent, the rich Irish brogue."
The beauthiful boy
  From the banks of the Shannon,
Was there to employ
His excellent cannon
And besides the long files of dragoons and artillery,
  The Zouaves and Hussars,
  All the children of Mars,

There were barbers and cooks
        And writers of books,—
The chef de cuisine with his French bills of fare,
And the artists to dress the young officers' hair.
And the scribblers all ready at once to prepare
        An eloquent story
        Of conquest and glory ;
And servants with numberless baskets of Sillery,
Though Wilson, the Senator, followed the train,
At a distance quite safe, to " conduct the champagne ;"
While the fields were so green and the sky was so blue,
There was certainly nothing more pleasant to do
        On this pleasant excursion to Richmond.

In Congress the talk, as I said, was of action,
To crush out instanter the traitorous faction.
In the press, and the mess,
They would hear of nothing less
Than to make the advance, spite of rhyme or of reason,
And at once put an end to the insolent treason.
There was Greeley,
And Ely,
The bloodthirsty Grow,
And Hickman (the rowdy, not Hickman the beau),
And that terrible Baker
Who would seize on the South, every acre,
And Webb, who would drive us all into the Gulf, or
Some nameless locality smelling of sulphur ;
And with all this bold crew
Nothing would do,
While the fields were so green and the sky was so blue,
        But to march on directly to Richmond.

Then the gallant McDowell
Drove madly the rowel
        Of spur that had never been " won " by him,

THE BATTLE OF MALVERN HILL, JULY 1, 1862

In the flank of his steed,
To accomplish a deed,
  Such as never before had been done by him ;
And the battery called Sherman's
  Was wheeled into line,
While the beer-drinking Germans
  From Neckar and Rhine,
With minie and yager,
Came on with a swagger,
Full of fury and lager,
  (The day and the pageant were equally fine.)
Oh ! the fields were so green and the sky was so blue,
Indeed 'twas a spectacle pleasant to view,
  As the column pushed onward to Richmond.

Ere the march was begun,
In a spirit of fun,
General Scott in a speech
Said this army should teach
The Southrons the lesson the laws to obey,
And just before dusk of the third or fourth day,
  Should joyfully march into Richmond.

He spoke of their drill
And their courage and skill,
And declared that the ladies of Richmond would rave
O'er such matchless perfection, and gracefully wave
In rapture their delicate kerchiefs in air
At their morning parades on the Capitol Square.
But alack ! and alas !
Mark what soon came to pass,
  When this army, in spite of its flatteries,
Amid war's loudest thunder
Must stupidly blunder
  Upon those accursed " masked batteries."

Then Beauregard came,
Like a tempest of flame,
To consume them in wrath
On their perilous path ;
And Johnston bore down in whirlwind to sweep
    Their ranks from the field
    Where their doom had been sealed,
As the storm rushes over the face of the deep !
While swift on the centre our President passed,
    And the foe might descry
    In the glance of his eye
The light that once blazed upon Diomed's crest.
McDowell ! McDowell ! weep, weep for the day
When the Southrons you meet in their battle array ;
To your confident hosts with its bullet and steel
'Twas worse than Culloden to luckless Lochiel.
Oh ! the generals were green and old Scott is now blue,
And a terrible business, McDowell, to you,
    Was that pleasant excursion to Richmond.

TURNER ASHBY.

By John R. Thompson, of Virginia.

To the brave all homage render,
    Weep, ye skies of June !
With a radiance pure and tender,
    Shine, oh saddened moon !
        " Dead upon the field of glory,"
        Hero fit for song and story,
Lies our bold dragoon !

        Well they learned, whose hands have slain him,
            Braver, knightlier foe
        Never fought with Moor nor Paynim—

Rode at Templestowe;
　With a mien how high and joyous,
　'Gainst the hordes that would destroy us,
Went he forth we know.

　　Never more, alas ! shall sabre
　　　Glean around his crest;
　　Fought his fight, fulfilled his labor,
　　　Stilled his manly breast;
　　　　All unheard sweet nature's cadence,
　　　　Trump of fame and voice of maidens—
　　Now he takes his rest.

Earth that all too soon hath bound him,
　Gently wrap his clay;
Linger lovingly around him,
　Light of dying day;
　　Softly fall the summer showers,
　　Birds and bees among the flowers
Make the gloom seem gay.

　　There, throughout the coming ages,
　　　When his sword is rust,
　　And his deeds in classic pages;
　　　Mindful of her trust,
　　　　Shall Virginia, bending lowly,
　　　　Still a ceaseless vigil holy
　　Keep above his dust.

THE MEN.

By Maurice Bell.

In the dusk of the forest shade
  A sallow and dusty group reclined ;
Gallops a horseman up the glade—
  " Where will I your leader find ?
Tidings I bring from the morning's scout—
  I've borne them o'er mound, and moor, and fen."
" Well, sir, stay not hereabout,
  Here are only a few of ' the men.'

        " Here no collar has bar or star,
          No rich lacing adorns a sleeve ;
        Further on our officers are,
          Let them your report receive.
        Higher up, on the hill up there,
          Overlooking this shady glen,
        There are their quarters—don't stop here,
          We are only some of ' the men.'

" Yet stay, courier, if you bear
  Tidings that the fight is near ;
Tell them we're ready, and that where
  They wish us to be we'll soon appear ;
Tell them only to let us know
  Where to form our ranks, and when ;
And we'll teach the vaunting foe
  That they've met a few of ' the men.'

        " We're the men, though our clothes are worn—
          We're the men, though we wear no lace—
        We're the men, who the foe hath torn,
          And scattered their ranks in dire disgrace ;
        We're the men who have triumphed before—
          We're the men who will triumph again ;
        For the dust, and the smoke, and the cannon's roar,
          And the clashing bayonets—' we're the men.' "

" Ye who sneer at the battle-scars,
   Of garments faded, and soiled and bare,
Yet who have for the 'stars and bars'
   Praise and homage and dainty fare ;
Mock the wearers and pass them on,
   Refuse them kindly word—and then
Know, if your freedom is ever won
   By human agents—these are the men ! "

" A REBEL SOLDIER KILLED IN THE TRENCHES BEFORE PETERSBURG, VA., APRIL 15, 1865."

By a Kentucky Girl.

KILLED in the trenches ! How cold and bare
   The inscription graved on the white card there.
'Tis a photograph, taken last Spring, they say,
Ere the smoke of battle had cleared away—
Of a rebel soldier—just as he fell,
When his heart was pierced by a Union shell ;
And his image was stamped by the sunbeam's ray,
As he lay in the trenches that April day.

Oh God ! Oh God ! How my woman's heart
   Thrills with a quick, convulsive pain,
As I view, unrolled by the magic of Art,
   One dreadful scene from the battle-plain :—
White as the foam of the storm-tossed wave,
Lone as the rocks those billows lave—
Gray sky above—cold clay beneath—
A gallant form lies stretched in death !

With his calm face fresh on the trampled clay,
   And the brave hands clasped o'er the manly breast :
Save the sanguine stains on his jacket gray,
   We might deem him taking a soldier's rest.
Ah no ! Too red is that crimson tide—
Too deeply pierced that wounded side ;
Youth, hope, love, glory—manhood's pride—
Have all in vain Death's bolt defied.

14

His faithful carbine lies useless there,
    As it dropped from its master's nerveless ward;
And the sunbeams glance on his waving hair
    Which the fallen cap has ceased to guard—
Oh Heaven! spread o'er it thy merciful shield,
No more to my sight be the battle revealed!
Oh fiercer than tempest—grim Hades as dread—
On woman's eye flashes the field of the dead!

    The scene is changed: In a quiet room,
        Far from the spot where the lone corpse lies,
    A mother kneels in the evening gloom
        To offer her nightly sacrifice,
    The noon is past, and the day is done,
    She knows that the battle is lost or won—
    Who lives? Who died? Hush! be thou still!
    The boy lies dead on the trench-barred hill.

BATTLE OF HAMPTON ROADS.

By Ossian D. Gorman.

Ne'er had a scene of beauty smiled
    On placid waters 'neath the sun,
Like that on Hampton's watery plain,
    The fatal morn the fight begun.
Far toward the silvery Sewell shores,
    Below the guns of Craney Isle,
Were seen our fleet advancing fast,
    Beneath the sun's auspicious smile.

    Oh, fatal night! the hostile hordes
        Of Newport camp spread dire alarms;
    The Cumberland for fight prepares—
        The fierce marines now rush to arms.

The Merrimac, strong cladded o'er,
    In quarters close begins her fire,
Nor fears the rushing hail of shot,
    And deadly missiles swift and dire ,
But, rushing on 'mid smoke and flame,
    And belching thunder long and loud,
Salutes the ship with bow austere,
    And then withdraws in wreaths of cloud.

    The work is done.   The frigate turns
        In agonizing, doubtful poise—
    She sinks! she sinks! along the deck
        I heard a shrieking, wailing noise.
    Engulfed beneath those placid waves
        Disturbed by battle's onward surge,
    The crew is gone ; the vessel sleeps,
        And whistling bombshells sing her dirge.

The battle still is raging fierce ;
    The Congress, " high and dry " aground,
Maintains in vain her boasted power,
    For now the gunboats flock around,
With " stars and bars " at mainmast reared,
    And pour their lightning on the main,
While Merrimac, approaching fast
    Sends forth her shell and hot-shot rain.

    Meantime the Jamestown, gallant boat,
        Engages strong redoubts at land—
    While Patrick Henry glides along,
        To board the Congress, still astrand.
    This done, we turn intently on
        The Minnesota, which replies,
    With whizzing shell to Teaser's gun,
        Whose booming cleaves the distant skies.

The naval combat sounds anew ;
        The hostile fleets are not withdrawn,
Though night is closing earth and sea
        In twilight's pale and mystic dawn.
Strange whistling noises fill the air ;
        The powdered smoke looks dark as night,
And deadly, lurid flames pour forth
        Their radiance on the missiles' flight ;
Grand picture on the noisy waves !
        The breezy zephyrs onward roam,
And echoing volleys float afar,
        Disturbing Neptune's coral home.
The victory's ours, and let the world
        Record Buchanan's name with pride ;
The crew is brave, the banner bright,
        That ruled the day when Hutter died.

KATY WELLS.

You ask what makes this darky sad,
        Why he like others am not gay,
What makes the tear flow down his cheek
        From early morn till close of day ?
My story, darkies, you shall hear
        For in my memory fresh it dwells,
'Twill cause you all to drop a tear
        On the grave of my sweet Katy Wells.

Chorus :

When the birds were singing in the morning,
        And the myrtle and the ivy were in bloom
When the sun o'er the hills was dawning ;
        'Twas then we laid her in the tomb.

TWO INTERESTING PHOTOGRAPHS OF GENERAL ROBERT E. LEE

The first shows General Lee when a student at West Point. This photograph
is published for the first time by the kind permission of Miss Edyth Carter
Beveridge. It is a rare photograph, and of great interest. The other is the
well-known "Three Star Photograph" of the Great General, and is a striking
likeness of him during war time.

Oh, I remember well the day
    When we together roamed the dells,
I kissed her cheek and named the day
    When I should marry Katy Wells,
But death came in my cabin door,
    And stole from me my joy and pride,
And when I found she was no more,
    I laid my banjo down and cried.
The springtime has no charms for me,
    The flowers that bloom around the dells
There's a form I long to see ;
    The form of my sweet Katy Wells. *Chorus—*

    I've sometimes wished that I was dead,
        And laid beside her in the tomb,
    For sorrow now bows down my head
        In silence to the midnight gloom,
    I'm longing for the day to come
        When I shall clasp her to my heart,
    While in the heavenly fields we roam
        And never, never more to part. *Chorus—*

ELLA REE.

A<small>ND</small> Ella Ree so kind and true,
    In the little church yard lies,
Her grave is bright with drops of dew,
    But brighter were her eyes.

C<small>HORUS</small> :

    Then carry me back to Tennessee,
        There let me live and die
    Among the fields of yellow corn,
        In the land where Ella lies.

The summer moon may rise and set
　　And the night birds thrill their lay,
And the possum and coon will softly step
　　Around the grave of Ella Ree.　*Chorus—*

THE BOY-SOLDIER.

H E is acting o'er the battle,
　　With his cap and feather gay,
Singing out his soldier-prattle,
　　In a mockish, manly way—
With the boldest, bravest footstep,
　　Treading firmly up and down,
And his banner waving softly,
O'er his boyish locks of brown.

And I sit beside him sewing,
　　With a busy heart and hand,
For the gallant soldiers going
　　To the far-off battle land—
And I gaze upon my jewel,
　　In his baby spirit bold,
My little blue-eyed soldier,
　　Just a second summer old.

Still a deep, deep well of feeling,
　　In my mother's heart is stirred,
And the tears come softly stealing
　　At each imitative work !
There's a struggle in my bosom
　　For I love my darling boy—
He's the gladness of my spirit,
　　He's the sunlight of my joy !

Yet I think upon my country,
    And my spirit groweth bold—
Oh ! I wish my blue-eyed soldier
    Were but twenty summers old !

    I would speed him to the battle—
        I would arm him for the fight ;
    I would give him to his country,
        For his country's wrong and right !
    I would nerve his hand with blessing
        From the " God of battles " won—
    With His helmet and His armor.
        I would cover o'er my son.

Oh ! I know there'd be a struggle,
    For I love my darling boy ;
He's the gladness of my spirit,
    He's the sunlight of my joy !
Yet in thinking of my country,
    Oh ! my spirit groweth bold,
And I wish my blue-eyed soldier
    Were but twenty summers old !

THE TWO ARMIES.

By Henry Timrod.

Two armies stand enrolled beneath
    The banner with the starry wreath ;
One, facing battle, blight and blast,
Through twice a hundred fields has passed ;
Its deeds against a ruffian foe,
Stream, valley, hill, and mountain know,
Till every wind that sweeps the land
Goes, glory-laden, from the strand.

The other, with a narrower scope,
Yet led by not less grand a hope,
Hath won, perhaps, as proud a place,
And wears its fame with meeker grace.
Wives march beneath its glittering sign,
Fond mothers swell the lovely line ;
And many a sweetheart hides her blush
In the young patriot's generous flush.

No breeze of battle ever fanned
The colors of that tender band ;
Its office is beside the bed,
Where throbs some sick or wounded head.
It does not court the soldier's tomb,
But plies the needle and the loom ;
And, by a thousand peaceful deeds,
Supplies a struggling nation's needs.

Nor is that army's gentle night
Unfelt amid the deadly fight ;
It nerves the son's, the husband's hand,
It points the lover's fearless brand ;
It thrills the languid, warms the cold,
Gives even new courage to the bold.
And sometimes lifts the veriest clod
To its own lofty trust in God.

When Heaven shall blow the trump of peace,
And bid this weary warfare cease,
Their several missions nobly done,
The triumph grasped, and freedom won'
Both armies, from their toils at rest,
Alike may claim the victor's crest,
But each shall see its dearest prize
Gleam softly from the other's eyes.

SONNET.

On Reading a Proclamation for Public Prayer.

BY A SOUTH CAROLINIAN.

OH! terrible, this prayer in the market-place,
    These advertised humilities—decreed
    By proclamation that we may be freed,
And mercy find for once, and saving grace,
Even while we forfeit all that made the race
    Worthy of heavenly favor—and profess
    Our faith and homage only through duress,
And dread of danger which we dare not face.

All working that's done worthily is prayer—
    And honest thought in prayer—the wish, the will
    To mend our ways, maintain our virtues still,
And, losing life, still keep our bosoms fair
In sight of God—with whom humility
And patient working can alone make free.

BATTLE OF BELMONT.

BY J. AUGUSTINE SIGNAIGO.

NOW glory to our Southern cause, and praises be to God,
    That He hath met the Southron's foe, and scourged him
        with His rod ;
On the tented plains of Belmont, in their might the Vandals
    came,
And they gave unto destruction all they found, with sword
    and flame;
But they met a stout resistance from a little band that day,
Who swore nobly they would conquer, or return to mother
    clay.

But the Vandals with presumption—for they came in all their
    might—
Gave free vent unto their feelings, for they thought to win the
    fight ;
And they forced our little cohorts to the very river's brink,
With a breath between destruction and of life's remaining
    link :
When the cannon of McCown, belching fire from out its
    mouth,
Brought destruction to the Vandals and protection to the
    South.

There was Pillow, Polk and Cheatham, who had sworn that
    day on high
That field should see them conquer, or that field should see
    them die ;
And amid the groan of dying, and amid the battle's din,
Came the echo back from Heaven, that they should that
    battle win ;
And amid the boom of cannon, and amid the clash of swords,
Came destruction to the foeman—and the vengeance was the
    Lord's.

When the fight was raging hottest, came the wild and
    cheering cry,
That brought terror to the foeman, and that raised our spirits
    high !
It was " Cheatham ! " " Cheatham ! " " Cheatham ! " that the
    Vandals' ears did sting,
And our boys caught up the echo till it made the welkin
    ring ;
And the moment that the Hessians thought the fight was
    surely won,
From the crackling of our rifles—bravely then they had
    to run !

Then they ran unto their transports in deep terror and dismay,
And their great grandchildren's children will be shamed to
      name that day ;
For the woe they came to bring to the people of the South
Was returned tenfold to them at the cannon's booming mouth;
And the proud old Mississippi ran that day a horrid flood,
For its banks were deeply crimsoned with the hireling
      Northman's blood.

Let us think of those who fell there, fighting foremost with
      the foe,
And who nobly struck for Freedom, dealing Tyranny a blow:
Like the ocean beating wildly 'gainst a prow of adamant,
Or the storm that keeps on bursting, but cannot destroy the
      plant ;
Brave Lieutenant Walker, wounded, still fought on the bloody
      field,
Cheering on his noble comrades, ne'er unto the foe to yield !

None e'er knew him but to love him, the brave martyr to his
      clime—
Now his name belongs to Freedom, to the very end of Time :
And the last words that he uttered will forgotten be by few :
" I have bravely fought them, mother—I have bravely fought
      for you ! "
Let his memory be green in the hearts who love the South,
And his noble deeds the theme that shall dwell in every
      mouth.

In the hottest of the battle stood a Vandal bunting rag,
Proudly to the breeze 'twas floating in defiance to our flag ;
And our Southern boys knew well that, to bring that bunting
      down,
They would meet the angel death in his sternest, maddest
      frown ;

But it could not gallant Armstrong, dauntless Vollmer, or
   brave Lynch,
Though ten thousand deaths confronted, from the task of
   honor flinch !

And they charged upon that bunting, guarded by grim-
   visaged Death,
Who had withered all around it with the blister of his breath;
But they plucked it from his grasp, and brave Vollmer waved
   it high,
On the gory field of battle, wherè the three were doomed to
   die ;
But before their spirits fled came the death-shout of the three,
Cheering for the sunny South and beloved old Tennessee !

Let the horrors of this day to the foe a warning be,
That the Lord is with the South, that His arm is with the
   free ;
That her soil is pure and spotless, as her clear and sunny sky,
And that he who dare pollute it on her soil shall surely die ;
For His fiat hath gone forth, e'en among the Hessian horde,
That the South has got His blessing, for the South is of the
   Lord.

Then glory to our Southern cause, and praises give to God,
That He hath met the Southron's foe and scourged him with
   His rod ;
That He hath been upon our side, with all His strength and
   might,
And battled for the Southern cause in every bloody fight ;
Let us in meek humility, to all the world proclaim,
We bless and glorify the Lord, and battle in His name

ALEXANDER H. STEPHENS
Taken from a steel engraving after a painting made immediately at the close of the war.

THE LEGION OF HONOR

By H. L. Flash.

WHY are we forever speaking
  Of the warriors of old?
Men are fighting all around us,
  Full as noble, full as bold.

    Ever working, ever striving,
      Mind and muscle, heart and soul,
    With the reins of judgment keeping
      Passions under full control.

Noble hearts are beating boldly
  As they ever did on earth;
Swordless heroes are around us,
  Striving ever from their birth.

    Tearing down the old abuses,
      Building up the purer laws,
    Scattering the dust of ages,
      Searching out the hidden flaws.

Acknowledging no " right divine "
  In kings and princes from the rest;
In their creed he is the noblest
  Who has worked and striven best.

    Decorations do not tempt them—
      Diamond stars they laugh to scorn—
    Each will wear a " Cross of Honor "
      On the Resurrection morn.

Warriors they in fields of wisdom—
  Like the noble Hebrew youth,
Striking down Goliath's error,
  With the God-blessed stone of truth.

Marshalled 'neath the Right's broad banner,
    Forward rush these volunteers,
Beating olden wrong away
    From the fast advancing years.

        Contemporaries do not see them
            But the coming times will say
        (Speaking of the slandered present),
            " There were heroes in that day."

Why are we then idly lying
    On the roses of our life,
While the noble-hearted struggle
    In the world-redeeming strife.

        Let us rise and join the legion,
            Ever foremost in the fray—
        Battling in the name of Progress
            For the nobler, purer day.

CLOUDS IN THE WEST.

By A. J. Requier, of Alabama,

HARK ! on the wind that whistles from the West
    A manly shout for instant succor comes,
From men who fight, outnumbered, breast to breast,
    With rage-indented drums !

Who dare for child, wife, country—stream and strand,
    Though but a fraction to the swarming foe,
There—at the flooded gateways of the land,
    To stem a torrent's flow.

To arms ! brave sons of each embattled State,
    Whose queenly standard is a Southern star ;
Who would be free must ride the lists of Fate
    On Freedom's victor-car !

Forsake the field, the shop, the mart, the hum
    Of craven traffic for the mustering clan ;
The dead themselves are pledged that you shall come
    And prove yourself—a man.

That sacred turf where first a thrilling grief
    Was felt which taught you Heaven alone disposes—
God ! can you live to see a foreign thief
    Contaminate its roses?

Blow, summoning trumpets, a compulsive stave,
    Through all the bounds, from Beersheba to Dan ;
Come out ! come out ! who scorns to be a slave,
    Or claims to be a man !

Hark ! on the breezes whistling from the West
    A manly shout for instant succor comes,
From men who fight, outnumbered, breast to breast,
    With rage-indented drums!

Who charge and cheer amid the murderous din,
    Where still your battle-flags unbended wave,
Dying for what your fathers died to win
    And you must fight to save.

Ho ! shrilly fifes that stir the vales from sleep,
    Ho ! brazen thunders from the mountains hoar ;
The very waves are marshaling on the deep,
    While tempests tread the shore.

Arise and swear, your palm-engirdled land
    Shall burial only yield a bandit foe ;
Then spring upon the caitiffs, steel in hand,
    And strike the fated blow.

THE OATH OF FREEDOM.

By James Barron Hope.

Born free, thus we resolve to live ;
    By Heaven we will be free !
By all the stars which burn on high—
By the green earth—the mighty sea—
By God's unshaken majesty,
    We will be free or die !
        Then let the drums all roll !
            Let all the trumpets blow !
                Mind, heart, and soul,
                We spurn control
            Attempted by a foe !

Born free, thus we resolve to live ;
    By Heaven we will be free !
And vainly now the Northmen try
To beat us down—in arms we stand
To strike for this our native land !
    We will be free or die !
        Then let the drums all roll ! etc., etc.

Born free, thus we resolve to live :
    By Heaven we will be free!
Our wives and children look on high,
Pray God to smile upon the right !
And bid us in the deadly fight
    As freemen live or die !
        Then let the drums all roll ! etc., etc.

Born free, thus we resolve to live :
    By Heaven we will be free !
And ere we cease this battle-cry,
Be all our blood, our kindred's spilt,
On bayonet or sabre hilt !
    We will be free or die !
        Then let the drums all roll ! etc., etc.

Born free, thus we resolve to live :
　　By Heaven we will be free !
Defiant let the banners fly,
Shake out their glories to the air,
And, kneeling, brothers, let us swear
　　We will be free or die !
　　　　Then let the drums all roll, etc., etc.

　　Born free, thus we resolve to live :
　　　　By Heaven we will be free !
　　And to this oath the dead reply—
　　Our valiant fathers' sacred ghosts—
　　These with us, and the God of hosts,
　　　　We will be free or die !
　　　　　　Then let the drums all roll ! etc., etc.

ENLISTED TO-DAY.

I KNOW the sun shines, and the lilacs are blowing,
　　And summer sends kisses by beautiful May—
Oh ! to see all the treasures the spring is bestowing,
　　And think—my boy Willie enlisted to-day,

It seems but a day since at twilight, low humming,
　　I rocked him to sleep with his cheek upon mine,
While Robby, the four-year old, watched for the coming
　　Of father, adown the street's indistinct line.

It is many a year since my Harry departed,
　　To come back no more in the twilight or dawn :
And Robby grew weary of watching, and started
　　Alone on the journey his father had gone.

15

It is many a year—and this afternoon sitting
    At Robby's old window, I heard the band play,
And suddenly ceased dreaming over my knitting,
    To recollect Willie is twenty to-day.

And that, standing beside him this soft May-day morning,
    And the sun making gold of his wreathed cigar smoke,
I saw in his sweet eyes and lips a faint warning,
    And choked down the tears when he eagerly spoke:

" Dear mother, you know how these Northmen are crowing,
    They would trample the rights of the South in the dust,
The boys are all fire; and they wish I were going—"
    He stopped, but his eyes said, " Oh, say if I must ! "

I smiled on the boy, though my heart it seemed breaking,
    My eyes filled with tears, so I turned them away,
And answered him, " Willie, 'tis well you are waking—
    Go, act as your father would bid you, to-day ! "

I sit in the window, and see the flags flying,
    And drearily list to the roll of the drum,
And smother the pain in my heart that is lying,
    And bid all the fears in my bosom be dumb.

I shall sit in the window when summer is lying
    Out over the fields, and the honey-bee's hum
Lulls the rose at the porch from her tremulous sighing,
    And watch for the face of my darling to come.

And if he should fall—his young life he has given
    For freedom's sweet sake; and for me, I will pray
Once more with my Harry and Robby in Heaven
    To meet the dear boy that enlisted to-day.

"WOULDST THOU HAVE ME LOVE THEE?"

By Alex. B. Meek.

Wouldst thou have me love thee, dearest!
　　With a woman's proudest heart,
Which shall ever hold thee nearest,
　　Shrined in its inmost part?
Listen, then! My country's calling
　　On her sons to meet the foe!
Leave these groves of rose and myrtle;
　　Drop thy dreamy harp of love!
Like young Korner—scorn the turtle,
　　When the eagle screams above!

　　　　Dost thou pause?—Let dastards dally—
　　　　　　Do thou for thy country fight!
　　　　'Neath her noble emblem rally—
　　　　　　" God, our country, and our right!"
　　　　Listen! now her trumpet's calling
　　　　　　On her sons to meet the foe!
　　　　Woman's heart is soft and tender,
　　　　　　But 'tis proud and faithful, too;
　　　　Shall she be her land's defender?
　　　　　　Lover! Soldier! up and do!

Seize thy father's ancient falchion,
　　Which once flashed as freedom's star!
Till sweet peace—the bow and halcyon,
　　Stilled the stormy strife of war.
Listen! now thy country's calling
　　On her sons to meet her foe!
Sweet is love in moonlight bowers!
　　Sweet the altar and the flame!
Sweet the spring-time with her flowers!
　　Sweeter far the patriot's name!

Should the God who smiles above thee,
 Doom thee to a soldier's grave,
Hearts will break, but fame will love thee,
 Canonized among the brave !
Listen, then ! thy country's calling
 On her sons to meet the foe !
Rather would I view thee lying
 On the last red field of strife,
'Mid thy country's heroes dying,
 Than become a dastard's wife !

THE WAR-CHRISTIAN'S THANKSGIVING.

By George H. Miles, of Baltimore.

OH, God of battles ! once again,
 With banner, trump, and drum,
And garments in the wine-press dyed,
 To give Thee thanks we come.

  No goats or bullocks garlanded,
   Unto Thine altars go ;
  With brothers' blood, by brothers shed,
   Our glad libations flow,

From pest-house and from dungeon foul,
 Where, maimed and torn, they die,
From gory trench and charnel-house,
 Where, heap on heap, they lie.

  In every groan that yields a soul,
   Each shriek a heart that rends,
  With every breath of tainted air,
   Our homage, Lord, ascends.

GENERAL JOHN B. HOOD

GENERAL N. B. FORREST

We thank Thee for the sabre's gash,
    The cannon's havoc wild;
We bless Thee for the widow's tears,
    The want that starves her child!

      We give Thee praise that Thou hast lit
        The torch, and fanned the flame;
      That lust and rapine hunt their prey,
        Kind Father, in Thy name!

That, for the songs of idle joy
    False angels sang of yore,
Thou sendest War on earth—ill-will
    To men for evermore!

      We know that wisdom, truth and right
        To us and ours are given;
      That Thou hast clothed us with the wrath,
        To do the work of Heaven.

We know that plains and cities waste
    Are pleasant in Thine eyes—
Thou lov'st a hearthstone desolate,
    Thou lov'st a mourner's cries.

      Let not our weakness fall below
        The measure of Thy will,
      And while the press hath wine to bleed,
        Oh, tread it with us still!

Teach us to hate—as Jesus taught
    Fond fools, of yore, to love;
Give us Thy vengeance as our own—
    Thy pity, hide above!

      Teach us to turn, with reeking hands,
        The pages of Thy Word,
      And learn the blessed curses there,
        On them that sheathe the sword.

Where'er we tread may deserts spring,
　　'Till none are left to slay;
And when the last red drop is shed,
　　We'll kneel again—and pray!

THE GOOD OLD CAUSE.

By John D. Phelan.

Huzza! huzza! for the Good Old Cause,
　　'Tis a stirring sound to hear,
For it tells of rights and liberties,
　　Our fathers bought so dear;
It brings up the Jersey prison-ship,
　　The spot where Warren fell,
And the scaffold which echoes the dying words
　　Of murdered Hayne's farewell.

　　The Good Old Cause! It is still the same
　　　　Though age upon age may roll;
　　'Tis the cause of the right against the wrong,
　　　　Burning bright in each generous soul;
　　'Tis the cause of all who claim to live
　　　　As freemen on Freedom's sod;
　　Of the widow, who wails her husband and sons,
　　　　By Tyranny's heel down-trod.

And whoever burns with a holy zeal,
　　To behold his country free,
And would sooner see her baptized in blood,
　　Than to bend the suppliant knee;
Must agree to follow her White-Cross flag,
　　Where the storms of battle roll,
A soldier—a soldier!—with arms in his hands,
　　And the love of the South in his soul!

Come one, come all, at your country's call,
    Let none remain behind,
But those too young, and those too old,
    The feeble, the halt, the blind;
Let every man, whether rich or poor,
    Who can carry a knapsack and gun,
Repair to the ranks of our Southern host,
    'Till the cause of the South is won.

      But the son of the South, if such there be,
        Who will shrink from the contest now,
      From a love of ease, or the lust of gain,
        Or through fear of the Yankee foe;
      May his neighbors shrink from his proffered hand,
        As though it was soiled for aye,
      And may every woman turn her cheek
        From his craven lips away;
      May his country's curse be on his head,
        And may no man ever see,
      A gentle bride by the traitor's side,
        Or children about his knee.

Huzza! huzza! for the Good Old Cause,
    'Tis a stirring sound to hear;
For it tells of rights and liberties,
    Our fathers bought so dear;
It summons our braves from their bloody graves,
    To receive our fond applause,
And bids us tread in the steps of those
    Who died for the Good Old Cause.

YOU CAN NEVER WIN THEM BACK.

By Catherine M. Warfield.

You can never win them back,
    never ! never !
Though they perish on the track
    of your endeavor ;
Though their corpses strew the earth
That smiled upon their birth,
And blood pollutes each hearth-
    stone forever !

They have risen to a man,
    stern and fearless ;
Of your curses and your ban
    they are careless.
Every hand is on its knife ;
Every gun is primed for strife ;
Every palm contains a life,
    high and peerless.

You have no such blood as theirs
    for the shedding,
In the veins of Cavaliers
    was its heading.
You have no such stately men
In your abolition den,
To march through foe and fen,
    nothiag dreading.

They may fall before the fire
    of your legions,
Paid in gold for murd'rous hire—
    bought allegiance !

But for every drop you shed
You shall leave a mound of dead ;
And the vultures shall be fed
           in our regions.

    But the battle to the strong
              is not given,
    While the Judge of right and wrong
              sits in Heaven !
    And the God of David still
    Guides each pebble by His will ;
    There are giants yet to kill—
              wrongs unshriven.

CHARLESTON.

By Henry Timrod.

CALM as that second summer which precedes
    The first fall of the snow,
In the broad sunlight of heroic deeds
    The city hides the foe.

    As yet, behind their ramparts, stern and proud,
        Her bolted thunders sleep—
    Dark Sumter, like a battlemented cloud,
        Looms o'er the solemn deep,

No Calpe frowns from lofty cliff or scaur
    To guard the holy strand ;
But Moultrie holds in leash her dogs of war,
    Above the level sand.

    And down the dunes a thousand guns lie crouched,
        Unseen, beside the flood—
    Like tigers in some Orient jungle crouched,
        That wait and watch for blood.

Meanwhile, through streets still echoing with trade,
　　Walk grave and thoughtful men,
Whose hands may one day wield the patriot's blade
　　As lightly as the pen.

　　And maidens, with such eyes as would grow dim
　　　　Over a bleeding hound,
　　Seem, each one, to have caught the strength of him,
　　　　Whose sword she sadly bound.

Thus girt without and garrisoned at home,
　　Day patient following day,
Old Charleston looks from roof, and spire, and dome.
　　Across her tranquil bay.

　　Ships, through a hundred foes, from Saxon lands
　　　　And spicy Indian ports,
　　Bring Saxon steel and iron to her hands,
　　　　And summer to her courts.

But still along yon dim Atlantic line,
　　The only hostile smoke
Creeps like a harmless mist above the brine,
　　From some frail, floating oak.

　　Shall the spring dawn, and she still clad in smiles,
　　　　And with an unscathed brow,
　　Rest in the strong arms of her palm-crowned isles,
　　　　As fair and free as now ?

We know not; in the temple of the Fates
　　God has inscribed her doom ;
And, all untroubled in her faith, she waits
　　The triumph or the tomb.

THE COTTON BOLL.

By Henry Timrod.

WHILE I recline
    At ease beneath
This immemorial pine
Small sphere !—
By dusky fingers brought this morning here,
And shown with boastful smiles,—
I turn thy cloven sheath,
Through which the soft white fibres peer,
That, with their gossamer bands,
Unite, like love, the sea-divided lands,
And slowly, thread by thread,
Draw forth the folded strands,
Than which the trembling line,
By whose frail help yon startled spider fled
Down the tall spear-grass from his swinging bed,
Is scarce more fine ;
And as the tangled skein
Unravels in my hands,
Betwixt me and the noonday light,
A veil seems lifted, and for miles and miles
The landscape broadens on my sight,
As, in the little boll, there lurked a spell
Like that which, in the ocean shell,
With mystic sound,
Breaks down the narrow walls that hem us round,
And turns some city lane
Into the restless main,
With all his capes and isles !

Yonder bird,—
Which floats, as if at rest,
In those blue tracts above the thunder, where

No vapors cloud the stainless air,
And never sound is heard,
Unless at such rare time
When, from the City of the Blest
Rings down some golden chime,—
Sees not from his high place
So vast a cirque of summer space
As widens round me in one mighty field,
Which, rimmed by seas and sands,
Doth hail its earliest daylight in the beams
Of gray Atlantic dawns;
And, broad as realms made up of many lands,
Is lost afar
Behind the crimson hills and purple lawns
Of sunset, among plains which roll their streams
Against the Evening Star!
And lo!
To the remotest point of sight,
Although I gaze upon no waste of snow,
The endless field is white;
And the whole landscape glows,
For many a shining league away,
With such accumulated light
As Polar lands would flash beneath a tropic day!
Nor lack there (for the vision grows,
And the small charm within my hands—
More potent even than the fabled one,
Which oped whatever golden mystery
Lay hid in fairy wood or magic vale,
The curious ointment of the Arabian tale—
Beyond all mortal sense
Doth stretch my sight's horizon, and I see
Beneath its simple influence,
As if, with Uriel's crown,
I stood in some great temple of the Sun,

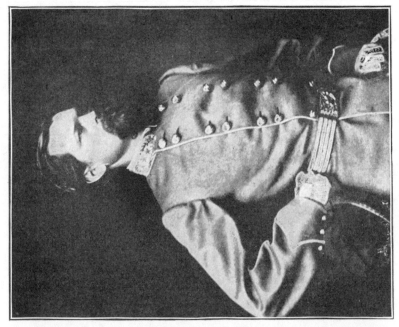

GENERAL JOHN B. GORDON

From Photograph taken during the War.

GENERAL STERLING PRICE

And looked, as Uriel, down)—
Nor lack there pastures rich and fields all green
With all the common gifts of God,
With temperate airs and torrid sheen
Weave Edens of the sod;
Through lands which look one sea of billowy gold
Broad rivers wind their devious ways;
A hundred isles in their embraces fold
A hundred luminous bays;
And through yon purple haze
Vast mountains lift their plumed peaks cloud-crowned;
And, save where up their sides the ploughman creeps,
An unknown forest girds them grandly round,
In whose dark shades a future navy sleeps!
Ye stars, which though unseen, yet with me gaze
Upon this loveliest fragment of the earth!
Thou Sun, that kindlest all thy gentlest rays
Above it, as to light a favorite hearth!
Ye coulds, that in your temples in the West
See nothing brighter than its humblest flowers!
And, you, ye Winds, that on the ocean's breast
Are kissed to coolness ere ye reach its bowers!
Bear witness with me in my song of praise,
And tell the world that, since the world began,
No fairer land hath fired a poet's lays,
Or given a home to man!

But these are charms already widely blown!
His be the meed whose pencil's trace
Hath touched our very swamps with grace,
And round whose tuneful way
All Southern laurels bloom;
The Poet of " The Woodlands," unto whom
Alike are known
The flute's low breathing and the trumpet's tone,

And the soft west-wind's sighs :
But who shall utter all the debt,
O Land ! wherein all powers are met
That bind a people's heart,
The world doth owe thee at this day,
And which it never can repay,
Yet scarcely deigns to own !
Where sleeps the poet who shall fitly sing
The source wherefrom doth spring
That mighty commerce which, confined
To the mean channels of no selfish mart,
Goes out to every shore
Of this broad earth, and throngs the sea with ships
That bear no thunders ; hushes hungry lips
In alien lands ;
Joins with a delicate web remotest strands ;
And gladdening rich and poor,
Doth gild Parisian domes,
Or feed the cottage-smoke of English homes,
And only bounds its blessings by mankind !
In offices like these, thy mission lies,
My Country ! and it shall not end
As long as rain shall fall and Heaven bend
In blue above thee ; though thy foes be hard
And cruel as their weapons, it shall guard
Thy hearthstones as a bulwark ; make thee great
In white and bloodless state ;
And, haply, as the years increase—
Still working through its humbler reach
With that large wisdom which the ages teach—
Revive the half-dead dream of universal peace !

As men who labor in that mine
Of Cornwall, hollowed out beneath the bed
Of ocean, when a storm rolls overhead,

Hear the dull booming of the world of brine
Above them, and a mighty muffled roar
Of winds and waters, and yet toil calmly on,
And split the rock, and pile the massive ore,
Or carve a niche, or shape the arched roof;
So I, as calmly, weave my woof
Of song, chanting the days to come,
Unsilenced, though the quiet summer air
Stirs with the bruit of battles, and each dawn
Wakes from its starry silence to the hum
Of many gathering armies. Still,
In that we sometimes hear,
Upon the Northern winds the voice of woe
Not wholly drowned in triumph, though I know
The end must crown us, and a few brief years
Dry all our tears,
I may sing too gladly. To Thy will
Resigned, O Lord! we cannot all forget
That there is much even Victory must regret.
And, therefore, not too long
From the great burden of our country's wrong
Delay our just release!
And, if it may be, save
These sacred fields of peace
From stain of patriot or of hostile blood!
Oh, help us, Lord! to roll the crimson flood
Back on its course, and, while our banners wing
Northward, strike with us! till the Goth shall cling
To his own blasted altar stones, and crave
Mercy; and we shall grant it, and dictate
The lenient future of his fate
There, where some rotting ships and trembling quays
Shall one day mark the Port which ruled the Western seas.

THE BATTLE OF CHARLESTON HARBOR.

April 7th, 1863.

By Paul H. Hayne.

Two hours, or more, beyond the prime of a blithe April day,
    The Northman's mailed " Invincibles" steamed up fair
        Charleston Bay ;
They came in sullen file, and slow, low-breasted on the wave,
Black as a midnight front of storm, and silent as the grave.

A thousand warrior-hearts beat high as those dread monsters
        drew
More closely to the game of death across the breezeless blue,
And twice ten thousand hearts of those who watched the
        scene afar,
Thrill in the awful hush that bides the battle's broadening Star!

Each gunner, moveless by his gun, with rigid aspect stands,
The ready linstocks firmly grasped in bold, untrembling hands,
So moveless in their marbled calm, their stern heroic guise,
They looked like forms of statued stone with burning human
        eyes!

Our banners on the outmost walls, with stately rustling fold,
Flash back from arch and parapet the sunlight's ruddy gold—
They mount to the deep roll of drums, and widely-echoing
        cheers,
And then—once more, dark, breathless, hushed, wait the grim
        cannoneers.

Onward—in sullen file, and slow, low glooming on the wave,
Near, nearer still, the haughty fleet glides silent as the grave,
When sudden, shivering up the calm, o'er startled flood and
        shore,
Burst from the sacred Island Fort the thunder-wrath of yore !

Ha! brutal Corsairs! tho' ye come thrice-cased in iron mail,
Beware the storm that's opening now, God's vengeance guides
    the hail!
Ye strive the ruffian types of might 'gainst law, and truth,
    and right,
Now quail beneath a sturdier power, and own a mightier
    might!

No empty boast! for while we speak, more furious, wilder,
    higher,
Dart from the circling batteries a hundred tongues of fire.
The waves gleam red, the lurid vault of heaven seems rent
    above.
Fight on! oh! knightly gentlemen! for faith, and home, and
    love!

There's not in all that line of flame, one soul that would not
    rise,
To seize the Victor's wreath of blood, tho' Death must give
    the prize—
There's not in all this anxious crowd that throngs the ancient
    town,
A maid who does not yearn for power to strike *one* despot
    'own.

The strife grows fiercer! ship by ship the proud Armada
    sweeps,
Where hot from Sumter's raging breast the volleyed lightning
    leaps;
And ship by ship, raked, overborne, 'ere burned the sunset
    bloom,
Crawls seaward, like a hangman's hearse bound to his felon
    tomb!

16

Oh! glorious Empress of the Main! from out thy storied
    spires,
Thou well may'st peal thy bells of joy, and light thy festal
    fires—
Since Heaven this day hath striven for thee, hath nerved thy
    dauntless sons,
And thou, in clear-eyed faith hast seen God's angels near the
    guns!

SUMTER IN RUINS.

By W. Gilmore Simms.

Ye batter down the lion's den,
    But yet the lordly beast goes free;
And ye shall hear his roar again,
From mountain height, from lowland glen,
From sandy shore and reedy fen—
Where'er a band of freeborn men
    Bears sacred shrines to liberty.

    The serpent scales the eagle's nest,
        And yet the royal bird in air,
    Triumphant wins the mountain's crest,
    And sworn for strife, yet takes his rest,
    And plumes, to calm, his ruffled breast,
    Till, like a storm-bolt from the West,
        He strikes the invader in his lair.

What's loss of den, or nest, or home,
    If, like the lion, free to go;—
If, like the eagle, wing'd to roam,
We span the rock and breast the foam,
Still watchful for the hour of doom,
When, with the knell of thunder-boom,
    We bound upon the serpent foe!

Oh! noble sons of lion heart!
  Oh! gallant hearts of eagle wing!
What though your batter'd bulwarks part,
Your nest be spoiled by reptile art—
Your souls, on wings of hate, shall start
For vengeance, and with lightning-dart,
  Rend the foul serpent ere he sting!

    Your battered den, your shattered nest,
      Was but the lion's crouching place ;—
    It heard his roar, and bore his crest,
    His, or the eagle's place of rest ;—
    But not the soul in either breast!
    This arms the twain, by freedom bless'd,
      To save and to avenge their race!

FORT WAGNER.

By W. Gilmore Simms.

Glory unto the gallant boys who stood
  At Wagner, and, unflinching, sought the van;
Dealing fierce blows, and shedding precious blood,
  For homes as precious, and dear rights of man!
They've won the meed, and they shall have the glory ;
  Song, with melodious memories, shall repeat
The legend, which shall grow to themes for story,
  Told through long ages, and forever sweet!

High honor to our youth—our sons and brothers,
  Georgians and Carolinians, where they stand!
They will not shame their birthrights, or their mothers,
  But keep, through storm, the bulwarks of the land!
They feel that they must conquer! Not to do it,
  Were worse than death—perdition! Should they fail,
The innocent races yet unborn shall rue it,
  The whole world feel the wound, and nations wail!

No !   They must conquer in the breach or perish !
   Assured in the last consciousness of breath,
That love shall deck their graves, and memory cherish
   Their deeds, with honors that shall sweeten death !
They shall have trophies in long future hours,
   And loving recollections, which shall be
Green as the summer leaves, and fresh as flowers,
   That, through all seasons, bloom eternally !

Their memories shall be monuments, to rise
   Next those of mightiest martyrs of the past ;
Beacons, when angry tempests sweep the skies,
   And feeble souls bend crouching to the blast !
A shrine for thee, young Cheves, well devoted,
   Most worthy of a great, illustrious sire ;—
A niche for thee, young Haskell, nobly noted,
   When skies and seas around thee shook with fire !

And others as well chronicled shall be !
   What though they fell with unrecorded name—
They live among the archives of the free,
   With proudest title to undying fame !
The unchisell'd marble under which they sleep,
   Shall tell of heroes, fearless still of fate ;
Not asking if their memories shall keep,
   But if they nobly served, and saved the State !

For thee, young Fortress Wagner—thou shalt wear
   Green laurels, worthy of the names that now,
Thy sister forts of Moultrie, Sumter, bear !
   See that thou lift'st, for aye, as proud a brow !
And thou shalt be, to future generations,
   A trophied monument, whither men shall come
In homage, and report to distant nations,
   A *shrine*, which foes shall never make a *tomb* !

GENERAL G. T. BEAUREGARD

GENERAL JOSEPH E. JOHNSTON

MORRIS ISLAND.

By W. Gilmore Simms.

Oh ! from the deeds well done, the blood well shed
    In a good cause springs up to crown the land
With ever-during verdure, memory fed,
    Wherever freedom rears one fearless band,
The genius which makes sacred time and place,
Shaping the grand memorials of a race !

The barren rock becomes a monument,
    The sea-shore sands a shrine ;
And each brave life, in desperate conflict spent.
    Grows to a memory which prolongs a line !

Oh ! barren isle—oh ! fruitless shore,
    Oh ! realm devoid of beauty—how the light
From glory's sun streams down for evermore,
    Hallowing your ancient barrenness with bright !

Brief dates, your lowly forts ; but full of glory,
    Worthy a life-long story ;
Remembered to be chronicled and read,
    When all your gallant garrisons are dead ;
        And to be sung
    While liberty and letters find a tongue !

Taught by the grandsires at the ingle-blaze,
    Through the long winter night ;
Pored over, memoried well, in winter days,
    While youthful admiration, with delight,
Hangs, breathless, o'er the tale, with silent praise ;
Seasoning delight with wonder, as he reads
Of stubborn conflict and audacious deeds ;
    Watching the endurance of the free and brave,
    Through the protracted struggle and close fight,

Contending for the lands they may not save,
　　Against the felon and innumerous foe;
Still struggling, though each rampart proves a grave,
　　For home, and all that's dear to man below !

Earth reels and ocean rocks at every blow;
　　But still undaunted, with a martyr's might,
　　　　They make for man a new Thermopylæ ;
　　And perishing for freedom, still go free !
　　Let but each humble islet of our coast
Thus join the terrible issue to the last;
　　And never shall the invader make his boast
Of triumph, though with mightiest panoply
　　He seeks to rend and rive, to blight and blast !

SACRIFICE.

ANOTHER victim for the sacrifice !
　　Oh! my own mother South,
　　How terrible this wail above thy youth,
　　Dying at the cannon's mouth,—
And for no crime—no vice—
No scheme of selfish greed—no avarice,
Or insolent ambition, seeking power;—
But that, with resolute soul and will sublime,
　　They made their proud election to be free,—
To leave a grand inheritance to time,
　　And to their sons and race, of liberty !

Oh ! widow'd woman, sitting in thy weeds,
　　With thy young brood around thee, sad and lone—
Thy fancy sees thy hero where he bleeds,
　　And still thou hear'st his moan !
Dying, he calls on thee—again—again !
　　With blessing and fond memories.　Be of cheer ;

He has not died—he did not bless—in vain ;
For, in the eternal rounds of God, He squares
The account with sorrowing hearts ; and soothes the fears,
And leads the orphans home, and dries the widow's tears.

CAROLINA.

By Anna Peyre Dinnies.

In the hour of thy glory,
    When thy name was far renowned,
When Sumter's glowing story
    Thy bright escutcheon crowned ;
Oh, noble Carolina ! how proud a claim was mine,
That through homage and through duty, and birthright, I
    was thine.

Exulting as I heard thee,
    Of every lip the theme,
Prophetic visions stirred me,
    In a hope-illumined dream ;
A dream of dauntless valor, of battles fought and won,
Where each field was but a triumph—a hero every son.

And now, when clouds arise,
    And shadows round thee fall ;
I lift to Heaven my eyes,
    Those visions to recall ;
For I cannot dream that darkness will rest upon thee long,
Oh, lordly Carolina ! with thine arms and hearts so strong.

Thy serried ranks of pine,
    Thy live oaks spreading wide,
Beneath the sunbeams shine,
    In fadeless robes of pride ;
Thus marshalled on their native soil their gallant sons stand
    forth,
As changeless as thy forests green, defiant of the North.

The deeds of other days,
    Enacted by their sires,
Themes long of love and praise,
    Have wakened high desires
In every heart that beats within thy proud domain,
To cherish their remembrance, and live those scenes again.

Each heart the home of daring,
    Each hand the foe of wrong,
They'll meet with haughty bearing,
    The warship's thunder song;
And though the base invader pollute thy sacred shore,
They'll greet him in their prowess as their fathers did of yore.

His feet may press their soil,
    Or his numbers bear them down,
In his vandal raid for spoil,
    His sordid soul to crown;
But his triumph will be fleeting, for the hour is drawing near,
When the war-cry of thy cavaliers shall strike his startled ear.

A fearful time shall come,
    When thy gathering bands unite,
And the larum-sounding drum
    Calls to struggle for the Right;
" *Pro aris et pro focis,*" from rank to rank shall fly,
As they meet the cruel foeman, to conquer or to die.

Oh, then a tale of glory
    Shall yet again be thine,
And the record of thy story
    The Laurel shall entwine;
Oh, noble Carolina, of proud and lordly State!
Heroic deeds shall crown thee, and the Nations own thee great.

"THE ANGEL OF THE CHURCH."

By W. Gilmore Simms.

The following poem, with its introduction, is given as it came to me. It reminds one of the old story of "God's Providence House" in Chester, England. At the time of a great plague in that ancient city, a prayer was made in a particular house, and the promise was pleaded, "Neither shall any plague come nigh thy dwelling." The family in the house was saved from the plague, and to this day the old habitation stands as a testimony of answered prayer. Such a conviction must have been upon the mind of the author of this poem, who wrote the Preface and the Introduction. He says:

"The enemy, from his camp on Morris Island, has, in frequent letters in the Northern papers, avowed the object at which they aim their shells in Charleston, to be the spire of St. Michael's church. Their *practice* shows that these avowals are true. Thus far, they have not succeeded in their aim. Angels of the Churches, is a phrase applied by St. John, in reference to the Seven Churches of Asia. The Hebrews recognized an Angel of the Church, in their language, 'Sheliack-Zibbor,' whose office may be described as that of a watcher or guardian of the church. Daniel says, iv, 13: 'Behold, a watcher and a Holy one came down from Heaven.' The practice of naming churches after tutelary saints, originated, no doubt, in the conviction that, where the church was pure, and the faith true, and the congregation pious, these guardian angels, so chosen, would accept the office assigned them. They were generally chosen from the Seraphim and Cherubim—those who, according to St. Paul (I Colossians, xvi), represented thrones, dominions, principalities and powers. According to the Hebrew traditions, St. Michael was the head of the first order; Gabriel, of the second; Urial, of the third; and Raphael, of the fourth. St. Michael is the warrior-angel who led the hosts of the sky against the powers of the princes of the air; who overthrew the dragon, and trampled him under foot. The destruction of the Anaconda, in his hands, would be a smaller undertaking. Assuming for our people a hope not less rational than that of the people of Nineveh, we may reasonably build upon the guardianship and protection of God, through his angels, 'a great city of sixty thousand souls, which has been for so long a season the subject of His care. These notes will supply the adequate illustrations for the ode which follows."

Aye, strike with sacrilegious aim
　　The temple of the living God;
Hurl iron bolt and seething flame
　　Through aisles which holiest feet have trod;

Tear up the altar, spoil the tomb,
    And, raging with demoniac ire,
Send down, in sudden crash of doom,
    That grand, old, sky-sustaining spire.

        That spire, for full a hundred years,
            Hath been a people's point of sight;
        That shrine hath warmed their souls to tears,
            With strains well worthy Salem's height;
        The sweet, clear music of its bells,
            Made liquid soft in Southern air,
        Still through the heart of memory swells,
            And wakes the hopeful soul to prayer.

Along the shores for many a mile,
    Long ere they owned a beacon-mark,
It caught and kept the Day-God's smile,
    The guide for every wandering bark;
Averting from our homes the scaith
    Of fiery bolt, in storm-cloud driven,
The Pharos to the wandering faith,
    It pointed every prayer to Heaven!

        Well may ye, felons of the time,
            Still loathing all that's pure and free,
        Add this to many a thousand crime
            'Gainst peace and sweet humanity:
        Ye, who have wrapped our towns in flame,
            Defiled our shrines, befouled our homes,
        But fitly turn your murderous aim
            Against Jehovah's ancient domes.

Yet, though the grand old temple falls,
    And downward sinks the lofty spire,
Our faith is stronger than our walls,
    And soars above the storm and fire,

Ye shake no faith in souls made free
    To tread the paths their fathers trod ;
To fight and die for liberty,
    Believing in the avenging God !

    Think not, though long his anger stays,
        His justice sleeps—His wrath is spent ;
    The arm of vengeance but delays,
        To make more dread the punishment !
    Each impious hand that lights the torch
        Shall wither ere the bolt shall fall ;
    And the bright Angel of the Church,
        With seraph shield avert the ball !

For still we deem, as taught of old,
    That where the faith the alter builds,
God sends an angel from His fold,
    Whose sleepless watch the temple shields,
And to His flock, with sweet accord,
    Yields their fond choice, from *thrones* and *powers;*
Thus Michael, with his fiery sword
    And golden shield, still champions ours!

    And he who smote the dragon down,
        And chained him thousand years of time,
    Need never **fear** the boa's frown,
        Though loathsome in his spite and slime,
    He, from the topmost height, surveys
        And guards the shrines our fathers gave ;
    And we who sleep beneath his gaze,
        May well believe his power to save !

Yet, if it be that for our sin
    Our angel's term of watch is o'er,
With proper prayer, true faith must win
    The guardian watcher back once more !

Faith, brethren of the Church, and prayer—
  In blood and sackcloth, if it need ;
And still our spire shall rise in air,
  Our temple, though our people bleed !

THE CAMEO BRACELET.

By James S. Randall, of Maryland.

Eva sits on the ottoman there,
  Sits by a Psyche carved in stone,
With just such a face, and just such an air,
  As Esther upon her throne.

She's sifting lint for the brave who bleed,
  And I watch her fingers float and flow
Over the linen, as, thread by thread,
  It flakes to her lap like snow.

A bracelet clinks on her delicate wrist,
  Wrought, as Cellini's were at Rome,
Out of the tears of the amethyst,
  And the wan Vesuvian foam.

And full on the bauble-crest alway—
  A cameo image keen and fine—
Glares thy impetuous knife, Corday,
  And the lava-locks are thine !

I thought of the war-wolves on our trail,
  Their gaunt fangs sluiced with gouts of blood :
Till the Past, in a dead, mesmeric veil,
  Drooped with a wizard flood,

Till the surly blaze through the iron bars
  Shot to the hearth with a pang and cry—
And a lank howl plunged from the Champ de Mars
  To the Column of July—

ATTACK ON CHARLESTON, AUGUST 23 TO SEPTEMBER 29, 1863.

Till Corday sprang from the gem, I swear,
 And the dove-eyed damsel I knew had flown—
For Eva was not on the ottoman there,
 By the Psyche carved in stone.

She grew like a Pythoness flushed with fate,
 With the incantation in her gaze,
A lip of scorn—an arm of hate—
 And a dirge of the " Marseillaise !"

Eva, the vision was not wild,
 When wreaked on the tyrants of the land—
For you were transfigured to Nemesis, child,
 With the dagger in your hand !

ZOLLICOFFER.

BY H. L. FLASH, of Alabama.

FIRST in the fight, and first in the arms
 Of the white-winged angels of glory,
With the heart of the South at the feet of God,
 And his wounds to tell the story :

And the blood that flowed from his hero heart,
 On the spot where he nobly perished,
Was drunk by the earth as a sacrament
 In the holy cause he cherished.

In Heaven a home with the brave and blessed,
 And, for his soul's sustaining,
The apocalyptic eyes of Christ—
 And nothing on earth remaining.

But a handful of dust in the land of his choice,
 A name in song and story,
And Fame to shout with her brazen voice,
 " Died on the Field of Glory !"

BEAUREGARD.

By Miss WARFIELD, of Mississippi.

L ET the trumpet shout once more,
                    Beauregard!
Let the battle-thunders roar,
                    Beauregard!
And again by yonder sea,
Let the swords of all the free
Leap forth to fight with thee,
                    Beauregard!

Old Sumter loves thy name,
                    Beauregard!
Grim Moultrie guards thy fame,
                    Beauregard!
Oh! first in Freedom's fight!
Oh! steadfast in the right!
Oh! brave and Christian Knight!
                    Beauregard!

St. Michael, with his host,
                    Beauregard!
Encamps by yonder coast,
                    Beauregard!
And the Demon's might shall quail
And the Dragon's terrors fail,
Were he trebly clad in mail,
                    Beauregard!

Not a leaf shall fall away,
                    Beauregard!
From the laurel won to-day,
                    Beauregard!
While the ocean breezes blow,
While the billows lapse and flow
O'er the Northman's bones below,
                    Beauregard!

Let the trumpet shout once more,
> Beauregard!
Let the battle-thunders roar,
> Beauregard!
From the centre to the shore,
From the sea to the land's core
Thrills the echo, evermore,
> Beauregard!

THE FIEND UNBOUND.

No more, with glad and happy cheer,
  And smiling face, doth Christmas come,
But usher'd in with sword and spear,
  And beat of the barbarian drum!
No more, with ivy-circled brow,
  And mossy beard all snowy white,
He comes to glad the children now,
  With sweet and innocent delight.

  The merry dance, the lavish feast,
    The cheery welcome, all are o'er;
  The music of the viol ceased,
    The gleesome ring around the floor.
  No glad communion greets the hour,
    That welcomes in a Saviour's birth,
  And Christmas, to a hostile power,
    Yields all the sway that made its mirth.

The Church, like some deserted bride,
  In trembling, at the Altar waits,
While raging fierce on every side,
  The foe is thundering at her gates.
No ivy green, nor glittering leaves,
  Nor crimson berries deck her walls;
But blood, red dripping from her eaves,
  Along the sacred pavement falls.

Her silver bells no longer chime,
    In summons to her sacred home ;
Nor holy song at matin prime,
    Proclaims the God within the dome.
Nor do the fireside's happy bands
    Assemble fond, with greetings dear,
While Patriarch Christmas spreads his hands
    To glad with gifts and crown with cheer.

    In place of that beloved form,
        Benignant, bland and blessing all,
    Comes one begirt with fire and storm,
        The raging shell, the hissing ball!
    Type of the Prince of Peace, no more,
        Evoked by those who bear His name,
    The Fiend, in place of Saint of yore,
        Now hurls around Satanic flame.

In hate,—evoked by kindred lands,
    But late beslavering with caress,
Lo, Moloch, dripping crimson, stands,
    And curses where he cannot bless.
He wings the bolt and hurls the spear,
    A demon loosed, that rends in rage,
Sends havoc through the homes most dear,
    And butchers youth and tramples age !

    With face of Fox—with glee that grins,
        And apish arms, with fingers claw'd,
    To snatch at all his brother wins,
        And straight secrete, with stealth and fraud;—
    Lo ! Mammon, kindred Demon, comes,
        And lurks, as dreading ill, in rear ;
    He blows the trumpet, beats the drums,
        Inflames the torch, and sharps the spear !

And furious, following in their train,
    What hosts of lesser Demons rise;
Lust, Malice, Hunger, Greed and Gain,
    Each raging for its special prize,
Too base for freedom, mean for toil,
    And reckless all of just and right,
They rage in peaceful homes for spoil,
    And where they cannot butcher, blight.

    A Serpent lie from every mouth,
        Coils outward ever,—sworn to bless;
    Yet, through the gardens of the South,
        While spreading evils numberless,
    By locust swarms the fields are swept,
        By frenzied hands the dwelling flames,
    And virgin beds, where Beauty slept,
        Polluted blush, from worst of shames.

The Dragon, chain'd for thousand years,
    Hath burst his bonds and rages free ;—
Yet, patience, brethren, stay your fears ;—
    Loosed for "a little season," he
Will soon, beneath th' Ithuriel sword,
    Of heavenly judgment, crush'd and driven,
Yield to the vengeance of the Lord,
    And crouch beneath the wrath of Heaven !

    " A little season," and the Peace,
        That now is foremost in your prayers,
    Shall crown your harvest with increase,
        And bless with smiles the home of tears;
    Your wounds be healed ; your noble sons,
        Unhurt, unmutilated—free—
    Shall limber up their conquering guns,
        In triumph grand of Liberty !

A few more hours of mortal strife,—
    Of faith and patience, working still,
In struggle for the immortal life,
    With all their soul, and strength, and will;
And, in the favor of the Lord,
    And powerful grown by heavenly aid,
Your roof trees all shall be restored,
    And ye shall triumph in their shade.

"DEAR MOTHER I'VE COME HOME TO DIE."

By E. Bowers.

The following beautiful lines are based upon facts, and will call forth the sympathy of every mother's heart. Many a boy wounded, or sick, and changed in health, came home to die, and many, alas, were not permitted to look into the faces of their loved ones again. I attended the funeral of a young fellow, whose last words were: "Give my love to mother, and tell her I will meet her in Heaven." As the years wear on the reunions are occurring in a better land, and many a boy has been restored to the circle which was broken by the rude red hand of war.

Dear mother, I remember well
    The parting kiss you gave me,
When merry rang the village bell—
    My heart was full of joy and glee;
I did not dream that one short year
    Would crush the hopes that soared so high !
Oh, mother dear, draw near to me ;
    Dear mother, I've come home to die.

Chorus:

Call sister, brother, to my side,
    And take your soldier's last good-by,
Oh, mother dear, draw near to me !
    Dear mother, I've come home to die.

Hark ! mother, 'tis the village bell ;
    I can no longer with thee stay ;
My country calls, to arms ! to arms !
    The foe advances in fierce array !
The vision's past—I feel that now
    For country I can only sigh.
Oh, mother dear, draw near to me !
    Dear mother ! I've come home to die.

    Dear mother, sister, brother, all,
        One parting kiss—to all good-by :
    Weep not, but clasp your hand in mine,
        And let me like a soldier die !
    I've met the foe upon the field,
        Where hosts contending scorned to fly ;
    I fought for right—God bless you all !—
        Dear mother, I've come home to die.

NO LAND LIKE OURS.

By J. R. BARRICK, of Kentucky.

THOUGH other lands may boast of skies
    Far deeper in their blue,
Where flowers in Eden's pristine dyes,
    Bloom with a richer hue ;
And other nations pride in kings,
    And worship lordly powers ;
Yet every voice of nature sings,
    There is no land like ours.

    Though other scenes than such as grace
        Our forests, fields, and plains,
    May lend the earth a sweeter face
        Where peace incessant reigns ;

But dearest still to me the land
    Where sunshine cheers the hours,
For God hath shown, with His own hand,
    There is ho land like ours!

        Though other streams may softer flow
            In vales of classic bloom,
        And rivers clear as crystal glow,
            That wear no tinge of gloom;
        Though other mountains lofty look,
            And grand seem olden towers,
        We see, as in an open book,
            There is no land like ours!

Though other nations boast of deeds
    That live in old renown,
And other peoples cling to creeds
    That coldly on us frown;
On pure religion, love, and law
    Are based our ruling powers—
The world but feels, with wondering awe,
    There is no land like ours!

        Though other lands may boast their brave,
            Whose deeds are writ in fame,
        Their heroes ne'er such glory gave
            As gilds our country's name;
        Though others rush to daring deeds,
            Where the darkening war-cloud lowers,
        Here, each alike for freedom bleeds—
            There is no land like ours!

Though other lands Napoleon
    And Wellington adorn,
America, her Washington,
    And later heroes born;
        Yet Johnston, Jackson, Price, and Lee,
            Bragg, Buckner, Morgan towers,
        With Beauregard, and Hood, and Bee—
            There is no land like ours!

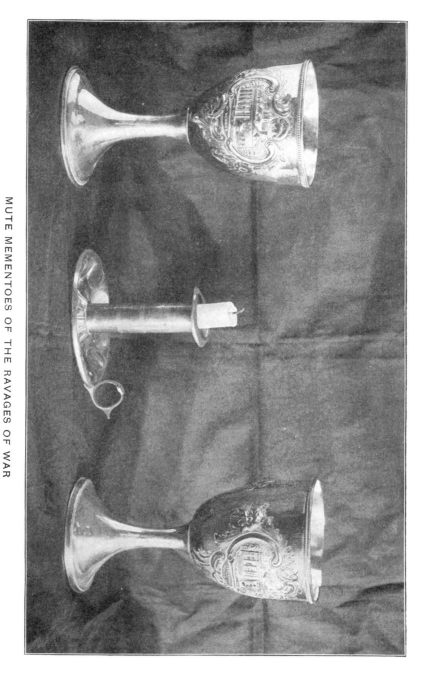

MUTE MEMENTOES OF THE RAVAGES OF WAR

Two Silver Goblets rescued from their hiding-place after the war: The one at the left has engraved upon it the home of Washington at Mount Vernon; the one at the right Thomas Jefferson's home at Monticello. The Candlestick was found on the field of Fredericksburg.

READING THE LIST.

ANONYMOUS.

"Is there any news of the war?" she said.
  "Only a list of the wounded and dead,"
    Was the man's reply
    Without lifting his eye
    To the face of the woman standing by.
"'Tis the very thing I want," she said;
"Read me a list of the wounded and dead."
He read the list; 'twas a sad array
Of the wounded and killed in the fatal fray.

    In the very midst was a pause to tell
    Of a gallant youth who fought so well
    That his comrades asked: "Who is he, pray?"
    "The only son of the Widow Gray,"
      Was the proud reply
      Of his captain nigh . . . .

What ails the woman standing near?
Her face has the ashen hue of fear;
"Well, well, read on; is he wounded? Quick!
O God! but my heart is sorrow-sick!
    Is he wounded?" "No; he fell, they say,
    Killed outright on that fatal day!"
    But see, the woman has swooned away!
Sadly she opened her eyes to the light;
Slowly recalled the events of the fight;
Faintly, she murmured: "Killed outright!
    It has cost me the life of my only son;
    But the battle is fought, and the victory won,
    The will of the Lord, let it be done!"
God pity the cheerless Widow Gray,
And send from the halls of eternal day
The light of His peace to illumine her way.

O, TEMPORA! O, MORES!

BY JOHN DICKSON BRUNS, M. D.

" GREAT Pan is dead! " so cried an airy tongue
    To one who, drifting down Calabria's shore,
Heard the last knell, in starry midnight rung,
    Of the old Oracles, dumb for evermore.

A low wail ran along the shuddering deep,
    And as, far off, its flaming accents died,
The awe-struck sailors, startled from their sleep,
    Gazed, called aloud: no answering voice replied;

Nor ever will—the angry Gods have fled,
    Closed are the temples, mute are all the shrines,
The fires are quenched, Dodona's growth is dead,
    The Sibyl's leaves are scattered to the winds.

No mystic sentence will they bear again,
    Which, sagely spelled, might ward a nation's doom;
But we have left us still some god-like men,
    And some great voices pleading from the tomb.

If we would heed them, they might save us yet,
    Call up some gleams of manhood in our breasts,
Truth, valor, justice, teach us to forget
    In a grand cause our selfish interests.

But we have fallen on evil times indeed,
    When public faith is but the common shame,
And private morals held an idiot's creed,
    And old-world honesty an empty name.

And lust, and greed, and gain are all our arts!
    The simple lessons which our fathers taught
Are scorned and jeered at; in our sordid marts
    We sell the faith for which they toiled and fought.

Each jostling each in the mad strife for gold,
    The weaker trampled by the reckless throng
Friends, honor, country lost, betrayed, or sold,
    And lying blasphemies on every tongue.

Cant for religion, sounding words for truth,
    Fraud leads to fortune, gelt for guilt atones,
No care for hoary age or tender youth,
    For widows' tears or helpless orphans' groans,

The people rage, and work their own wild will,
    They stone the prophets, drag their highest down,
And as they smite, with savage folly still
    Smile at their work, those dead eyes wear no frown.

The sage of " Drainfield " tills a barren soil,
    And reaps no harvest where he sowed the seed,
He has but exile for long years of toil ;
    Nor voice in council, though his children bleed.

And never more shall " Redcliff's " oaks rejoice,
    Now bowed with grief above their master's bier ;
Faction and party stilled that mighty voice,
    Which yet could teach us wisdom, could we hear.

And " Woodland's " harp is mute; the gray, old man
    Broods by his lonely hearth and weaves no song ;
Or, if he sing, the note is sad and wan,
    Like the pale face of one who's suffered long.

So all earth's teachers have been overborne
    By the coarse crowd, and fainting droop or die;
They bear the cross, their bleeding brows the thorn,
    And ever hear the clamor—" Crucify ! "

Oh, for a man with godlike heart and brain !
    A god in stature, with a god's great will,
And fitted to the time, that not in vain
    Be all the blood we've spilt and yet must spill.

Oh, brothers ! friends ! shake off the Circean spell !
　Rouse to the dangers of impending fate !
Grasp your keen swords, and all may yet be well—
　More gain, more pelf, and it will be, too late !

　　　　　　　-Charleston Mercury, 1864.

OUR MARTYRS.

By Paul E. Hayne.

I am sitting lone and weary
　On the hearth of my darkened room,
And the low wind's *miserere*
　Makes sadder the midnight gloom ;
There's a terror that's nameless nigh me—
　There's a phantom spell in the air,
And methinks that the dead glide by me,
　And the breath of the grave's in my hair !

　　'Tis a vision of ghastly faces,
　　　All pallid and worn with pain,
　　Where the splendor of manhood's graces
　　　Give place to a gory stain ;
　　In a wild and weird procession
　　　They sweep by my startled eyes,
　　And stern with their fate's fruition,
　　　Seem melting in blood-red skies.

Have they come from the shores supernal,
　Have they passed from the spirit's goal,
'Neath the veil of the life eternal,
　To dawn on my shrinking soul ?
Have they turned from the choiring angels,
　Aghast at the woe and dearth
That war, with his dark evangels,
　Have wrought in the loved of earth ?

Vain dream! 'mid the far-off mountains
　　They lie where the dew-mists weep,
And the murmur of mournful fountains
　　Breaks over their painful sleep;
On the breast of the lonely meadows,
　　Safe, safe from the despot's will,
They rest in the star-lit shadows,
　　And their brows are white and still!

　　　　Alas! for the martyred heroes
　　　　　　Cut down at their golden prime,
　　　　In a strife with the brutal Neroes,
　　　　　　Who blacken the path of Time?
　　　　For them is the voice of wailing,
　　　　　　And the sweet blush-rose departs
　　　　From the cheeks of the maidens, paling
　　　　　　O'er the wreck of their broken hearts!

And alas! for the vanished glory
　　Of a thousand household spells!
And alas! for the tearful story
　　Of the spirit's fond farewells!
By the flood, on the field, in the forest,
　　Our bravest have yielded breath,
But the shafts that have smitten sorest,
　　Were launched by a viewless death!

　　　　Oh, Thou that hast charms of healing,
　　　　　　Descend on a widowed land,
　　　　And bind o'er the wounds of feeling
　　　　　　The balms of Thy mystic hand!
　　　　Till the hearts that lament and languish,
　　　　　　Renewed by the touch divine,
　　　　From the depths of a mortal anguish,
　　　　　　May rise to the calm of Time!

OUR DEPARTED COMRADES.

By J. Marion Shirer.

I am sitting alone by a fire
    That glimmers on Sugar Loaf's-height,
But before I to rest shall retire
    And put out the fast-fading light—
While the lanterns of heaven are ling'ring
    In silence all o'er the deep sea,
And loved ones at home are yet mingling
    Their voices in converse of me—
While yet the lone seabird is flying
    So swiftly far o'er the rough wave,
And many fond mothers are sighing
    For the noble, the true, and the brave ;
Let me muse o'er the many departed
    Who slumber on mountain and vale ;
With the sadness which shrouds the lone-hearted,
    Let me tell of my comrades a tale.

    Far away in the green, lonely mountains,
        Where the eagle makes bloody his beak,
    In the mist, and by Gettysburg's fountains,
        Our fallen companions now sleep !
    Near Charleston, where Sumter still rises
        In grandeur above the still wave,
    And always at evening discloses
        The fact that her inmates yet live—
    On islands, and fronting Savannah,
        Where dark oaks o'ershadow the ground,
    Round Macon and smoking Atlanta,
        How many dead heroes are found !
    And out on the dark swelling ocean,
        Where vessels go, riding the waves,
    How many, for love and devotion,
        Now slumber in warriors' graves !

No memorials have yet been erected
    To mark where these warriors lie,
All alone, save by angels protected,
    They sleep 'neath the sea and the sky !
But think not that they are forgotten,
    By those who the carnage survive :
When their headboards will all have grown rotten,
    And the night-winds have levelled their graves,
Then hundreds of sisters and mothers,
    Whose freedom they perished to save,
And fathers, and empty-sleeved brothers,
    Who surmounted the battle's red wave ;
Will crowd from their homes in the Southward,
    In search of the loved and the blest,
And, rejoicing, will soon return homeward
    And lay our dear martyrs to rest.

THE BROKEN MUG.

By John Esten Cooke.

Many are the relics of those days that are gone, and everyone with a history. Elsewhere in this book may be found a picture of two silver goblets, which was given to us by Mrs. James T. Halsey, the daughter of General D. H. Maury, of Virginia. As will be seen in her account of them they are solid silver communion goblets, which were found in a desolate church, the goblets all mashed out of recognition under the ruins of the house which General Sherman's men had destroyed. But the day will come when those who drank the communion wine from that cup, and for whom was poured out the bitter cup of sorrow, will sit down with joy at the marriage supper of the Lamb, at perfect peace with all the world, and they shall greet, as their friends, those who once were enemies, and the days of difference, and of antagonism, and of war, will be remembered no more !

My mug is broken, my heart is sad !
    What woes can fate still hold in store
The friend I cherished a thousand days
    Is smashed to pieces on the floor !
    Is shattered and to Limbo gone,
        I'll see my Mug no more !

Relic it was of joyous hours
    Whose golden memories still allure—
When coffee made of rye we drank,
    And gray was all the dress we wore!
    When we were paid some cents a month,
        But never asked for more!

    In marches long, by day and night,
        In raids, hot charges, shocks of war,
    Strapped on the saddle at my back
        This faithful comrade still I bore—
        This old companion, true and tried,
        I'll never carry more!

From the Rapidan to Gettysburg—
    "Hard bread" behind, "sour krout" before—
This friend went with the cavalry
    And heard the jarring cannon roar
    In front of Cemetery Hill—
        Good heavens! how they did roar!

    Then back again, the foe behind,
        Back to the "Old Virginia shore"—
Some dead and wounded left—some holes
        In flags, the sullen graybacks bore;
        This mug had made the great campaign,
        And we'd have gone once more!

Alas! we never went again!
    The red cross banner, slow but sure.
"Fell back"—we bade to sour krout
    (Like the lover of Lenore)
    A long, sad, lingering farewell—
        To taste its joys no more.

A MEMORIAL OF MARYLAND VALOR

A monument erected in Baltimore, and unveiled May 2, 1903, to Maryland soldiers and sailors who fought for the Confederacy. On its face it bears the following inscription: "Gloria Victis. To the Soldiers and Sailors of Maryland in the Service of the Confederate States of America. 1861-1865."

But still we fought, and ate hard bread,
    Or starved—good friend, our woes deplore
And still this faithful friend remained—
    Riding behind me as before—
    The friend on march, in bivouac,
      When others were no more.

    How oft we drove the horsemen blue
      In Summer bright, or Winter frore !
    How oft before the Southern charge
      Through field and wood the blue-birds tore !
      I'm " harmonized," but long to hear
        The bugles ring once more.

Oh yes ! we're all " fraternal " now,
    Purged of our sins, we're clean and pure,
Congress will " reconstruct " us soon—
    But no gray people on *that* floor !
    I'm harmonized—" so-called "—but long
      To see those times once more !

    Gay days ! the sun was brighter then,
      And we were happy, though so poor !
That past comes back as I behold
      My shattered friend upon the floor,
      My splintered, useless, ruined mug,
        From which I'll drink no more.

How many lips I'll love for aye,
    While heart and memory endure.
Have touched this broken cup and laughed—
      How they did laugh !—in days of yore !
      Those days we'd call " a beauteous dream,"
        If they had been no more !

Dear comrades, dead this many a day,
　　I saw you weltering in your gore,
After those days amid the pines
　　　On the Rappahannock shore!
　　When the joy of life was much to me
　　　　But your warm hearts were more!

Yours was the grand heroic nerve
　　That laughs amid the storm of war—
Souls that " loved much " your native land,
　　Who fought and died therefor!
　　You gave your youth, your brains, your arms,
　　　　Your blood—you had no more!

You lived and died true to your flag!
　　And now your wounds are healed—but sore
Are many hearts that think of you
　　Where you have " gone before."
　　Peace, comrade! God bound up those forms,
　　　　They are " whole " forevermore!

Those lips this broken vessel touched,
　　His, too!—the man's we all adore—
That cavalier of cavaliers,
　　Whose voice will ring no more—
　　Whose plume will float amid the storm
　　　　Of battle never more!

Not on this idle page I write
　　That name of names, shrined in the core
Of every heart!—peace! foolish pen,
　　Hush! words so cold and poor!
　　His sword is rust; the blue eyes dust,
　　　　His bugle sounds no more!

Never was cavalier like ours !
   Not Rupert in the years before !
And when his stern, hard work was done,
     His griefs, joys, battles o'er—
     His mighty spirit rode the storm,
       And led his men once more!

He lies beneath his native sod,
     Where violets spring, or frost is hoar;
He recks not—charging squadrons watch
     His raven plume no more!
     That smile we'll see, that voice we'll hear,
       That hand we'll touch no more !

My foolish mirth is quenched in tears :
     Poor fragments strewed upon the floor,
Ye are the types of nobler things
     That find their use no more—
     Things glorious once, now trodden down—
       That makes us smile no more !

Of courage, pride, high hopes, stout hearts—
     Hard, stubborn nerve, devotion pure,
Beating his wings against the bars,
     The prisoned eagle tried to soar ;
     Outmatched, o'erwhelmed, we struggled still—
       Bread failed—we fought no more !

Lies in the dust the shattered staff
     That bore aloft on sea and shore,
That blazing flag, amid the storm !
     And none are now so poor,
     So poor to do it reverence,
       Now when it flames no more !

But it is glorious in the dust,
    Sacred till Time shall be no more;
Spare it, fierce editors! your scorn—
    The dread " Rebellion's " o'er!
    Furl the great flag—hide cross and star,
    Thrust into darkness star and bar,
    But look! across the ages far
      It flames for evermore!

MELT THE BELLS.

By F. V. Rockett.

The following lines were written on General Beauregard's appeal to the people to contribute their bells, that they may be melted into cannon:

Melt the bells, melt the bells,
    Still the tinkling on the plains,
And transmute the evening chimes
Into war's resounding rhymes,
    That the invaders may be slain
      By the bells.

Melt the bells, melt the bells,
    That for years have called to prayer,
And, instead, the cannon's roar
Shall resound the valleys o'er,
    That the foe may catch despair
      From the bells.

Melt the bells, melt the bells,
    Though it cost a tear to part
With the music they have made,
Where the friends we love are laid,
    With pale cheek and silent heart,
      'Neath the bells.

Melt the bells, melt the bells,
 Into cannon, vast and grim,
And the foe shall feel the ire
From each heaving lungs of fire,
 And we'll put our trust in Him
  And the bells.

   Melt the bells, melt the bells,
    And when foes no more attack,
   And the lightning cloud of war
   Shall roll thunderless and far,
    We will melt the cannon back
    Into bells.

Melt the bells, melt the bells,
 And they'll peal a sweeter chime,
And remind of all the brave
Who have sunk to glory's grave,
 And will sleep thro' coming time
  'Neath the bells.—*Memphis Appeal.*

      ———

SEA-WEEDS.

By Annie Chambers Ketchum.

Friend of the thoughtful mind and gentle heart !
 Beneath the citron-tree—
Deep calling to my soul's profounder deep—
 I hear the Mexique Sea.

While through the night rides in the spectral surf
 Along the spectral sands,
And all the air vibrates, as if from harps
 Touched by phantasmal hands.

Bright in the moon the red pomegranate flowers
 Lean to the Yucca's bells,
While with her chrism of dew, sad Midnight fills
 The milk-white asphodels.

18

Watching all night—as I have done before—
    I count the stars that set,
Each writing on my soul some memory deep
    Of Pleasure or Regret;

Till, wild with heart-break, toward the East I turn,
    Waiting for dawn of day;—
And chanting sea, and asphodel and star
    Are faded, all, away.

Only within my trembling, trembling hands—
    Brought unto me by thee—
I clasp these beautiful and fragile things,
    Bright sea-weeds from the sea,

Fair bloom the flowers beneath these Northern skies,
    Pure shine the stars by night,
And grandly sing the grand Atlantic waves
    In thunder-throated might;

But, as the sea-shell in her chambers keeps
    The murmur of the sea,
So the deep-echoing memories of my home
    Will not depart from me.

Prone on the page they lie, these gentle things!
    As I have seen them cast
Like a drowned woman's hair, along the beach,
    When storms were over-past;

Prone, like mine own affections, cast ashore
    In Battle's storm and blight;
Would they had died, like sea-weeds! Pray forgive me,
    But I must weep to-night.

Tell me again, of Summer fields made fair
    By Spring's precursing plough;
Of joyful reapers, gathering tear-sown harvests—
    Talk to me,—will you—now!

THE MOUNTAIN PARTISAN.

(Anonymous.)

M Y rifle, pouch, and knife !
   My steed ! And then we part !
One loving kiss, dear wife,
   One press of heart to heart !
Cling to me yet awhile,
   But stay the sob, the tear !
Smile—only try to smile—
   And I go without a fear.

Our little cradled boy,
   He sleeps—and in his sleep,
Smiles, with an angel joy,
   Which tells thee not to weep
I'll kneel beside, and kiss—
   He will not wake the while,
Thus dreaming of the bliss,
   That bids thee, too, to smile.

Think not, dear wife, I go,
   With a light thought at my heart :
'Tis a pang akin to woe,
   That fills me as we part ;
But when the wolf was heard
   To howl around our lot,
Thou know'st, dear mother-bird,
   I slew him on the spot !

Aye, panther, wolf, and bear,
   Hath perish'd 'neath my knife ;
Why tremble, then, with fear,
   When now I go, my wife ?
Shall I not keep the peace,
   That made our cottage dear ;
And 'till these wolf-curs cease
   Shall I be housing here ?

One loving kiss, dear wife,
　　　One press of heart to heart;
Then for the deadliest strife,
　　　For freedom I depart!
I were of little worth,
　　　Were these Yankee wolves left free
To ravage 'round the bearth,
　　　And bring one grief to thee!

　　　God's blessing on thee, wife,
　　　　　God's blessing on the young:
　　　Pray for me through the strife,
　　　　　And teach our infant's tongue.
　　　Whatever haps in fight,
　　　　　I shall be true to thee—
　　　To the home of our delight—
　　　　　To my people of the free.

JOHN PELHAM.

By James R. Randall.

Just as the spring came laughing through the strife
　　　With all its gorgeous cheer;
In the bright April of historic life
　　　Fell the great cannoneer.

　　　The wondrous lulling of a hero's breath
　　　　　His bleeding country weeps—
　　　Hushed in the alabaster arms of death,
　　　　　Our young Marcellus sleeps.

Nobler and grander than the Child of Rome,
　　　Curbing his chariot steeds;
The knightly scion of a Southern home
　　　Dazzled the land with deeds.

GENERAL A. P. HILL

GENERAL KIRBY SMITH

Gentlest and bravest in the battle brunt,
 The champion of the truth,
He bore his banner to the very front
 Of our immortal youth.

  A clang of sabres 'mid Virginian snow,
   The fiery pang of shells—
  And there's a wail of immemorial woe
   In Alabama dells.

The pennon drops that led the sacred band
 Along the crimson field !
The meteor blade sinks from the nerveless hand
 Over the spotless shield.

  We gazed and gazed upon that beauteous face,
   While 'round the lips and eyes,
  Couched in the marble slumber, flashed the grace
   Of a divine surprise.

Oh, mother of a blessed soul on high !
 Thy tears may soon be shed—
Think of thy boy with princes of the sky,
 Among the Southern dead.

  How must he smile on this dull world beneath,
   Fevered with swift renown—
  He—with the martyr's amaranthine wreath
   Twining the victor's crown !

"YE BATTERIES OF BEAUREGARD."

By J. R. BARRICK, of Kentucky.

" Ye batteries of Beauregard!"
        Pour your hail from Moultrie's wall;
Bid the shock of your deep thunder
        On their fleet in terror fall;
Rain your storm of leaden fury
        On the black invading host—
Teach them that their step shall never
        Press on Carolina's coast.

        " Ye batteries of Beauregard!"
                Sound the story of our wrong;
        Let your tocsin wake the spirit
                Of a people brave and strong;
        Her proud names of old remember—
                Marion, Sumter, Pinckney, Greene;
        Swell the roll whose deeds of glory
                Side by side with theirs are seen,

" Ye batteries of Beauregard!"
        From Savannah on them frown;
By the majesty of Heaven
        Strike their " grand armada " down;
By the blood of many a freeman,
        By each dear-bought battle-field,
By the hopes we fondly cherish,
        Never ye the victory yield.

        " Ye batteries of Beauregard!"
                All along our Southern coast,
        Let, in after-time, your triumphs,
                Be a nation's pride and boast;

Send each missile with a greeting
 To the vile, ungodly crew ;
Make them feel they ne'er can conquer
 People to themselves so true.

" Ye batteries of Beauregard ! "
 By the glories of the past,
By the memory of Old Sumter,
 Whose renown will ever last,
Speed upon their vaunted legions
 Volleys thick of shot and shell,
Bid them welcome, in your glory,
 To their own appointed hell.

VIRGINIA.

By Catherine M. Warfield.

Glorious Virginia ! Freedom sprang
 Light to her feet at thy trumpet's clang
At the first sound of that clarion blast,
Foes like the chaff from the whirlwind passed—
Passed to their doom; from that hour no more
Triumphs their cause by sea or shore.

Glorious Virginia ! noble the blood
That hath bathed thy fields in a crimson flood ;
On many a wide-spread and sunny plain,
Like leaves of autumn they dead have lain ;
The Southron heart is their funeral urn !
The Southron slogan their requiem stern !

Glorious Virginia ! to thee, to thee
We lean, as the shoots to the parent tree ;
Bending in awe at thy glance of might ;—
First in the council, first in the fight !
While our flag is fanned by the breath of fame,
Glorious Virginia ! we'll bless thy name.

"WHEN PEACE RETURNS."

By Olivia Tully Thomas

WHEN " war has smoothed his wrinkled front,"
        And meek-eyed peace returning,
Has brightened hearts that long were wont
        To sigh in grief and mourning—
How blissful then will be the day
        When, from the wars returning,
The weary soldier wends his way
        To dear ones that are yearning.

                To clasp in true love's fond embrace,
                        To gaze with looks so tender
                Upon the war-worn form and face
                        Of Liberty's defender;
                To count with pride each cruel scar,
                        That mars the manly beauty,
                Of him who proved so brave in war,
                        So beautiful in duty.

When peace returns, throughout our land,
        Glad shouts of welcome render
The gallant few of Freedom's band
        Whose cry was " no surrender "
Who battled bravely to be free
        From tyranny's oppressions,
And won, for Southern chivalry,
        The homage of all nations !

                And when again, in Southern bowers
                        The ray of peace is shining,
                Her maidens gather fairest flowers,
                        And honor's wreaths are twining,

To bind the brows victorious
　On many a field so gory,
Whose names renowned and glorious,
　Shall live in song and story,

　　Then will affection's tear be shed,
　　　And pity, joy restraining,
　　For those, the lost, lamented dead,
　　　Are all beyond our plaining ;
　　They fell in manhood's prime and might ;
　　　And we should not weep the story
　　That tells of Fame, a sacred light,
　　　Above each grave of glory !

GOD SAVE THE SOUTH.

By George H. Miles, of Baltimore.

God save the South !
　God save the South !
Her altars and firesides—
　God save the South !
Now that the war is nigh—
Now that we arm to die—
Chanting our battle-cry,
　Freedom or death !

　　God be our shield !
　　At home or a-field,
　　Stretch Thine arm over us,
　　　Strengthen and save !
　　What though they're five to one,
　　Forward each sire and son,
　　Strike till the war is done,
　　　Strike to the grave.

God make the right
Stronger than might !
Millions would trample us
    Down in their pride.
Lay, Thou, their legions low ;
Roll back the ruthless foe;
Let the proud spoiler know
    God's on our side !

    Hark ! honor's call,
    Summoning all—
    Summoning all of us
        Up to the strife.
    Sons of the South, awake !
    Strike till the brand shall break !
    Strike for dear honor's sake,
        Freedom and Life !

Rebels before
Were our fathers of yore ;
Rebel, the glorious name
    Washington bore.
Why, then, be ours the same
Title be snatched from shame ;
Making it first in fame,
    Odious no more.

    War to the hilt !
    Their's be the guilt,
    Who fetter the freeman
        To ransom the slave.
    Up, then, and undismayed,
    Sheathe not the battle-blade,
    Till the last foe is laid
        Low in the grave.

God save the South!
God save the South!
Dry the dim eyes that now
    Follow our path.
Still let the light feet rove
Safe through the orange grove;
Still keep the land we love
    Safe from all wrath.

    God save the South!
    God save the South!
    Her altars and firesides—
        God save the South!
    For the rude war is nigh,
    And we must win or die;
    Chanting our battle-cry
        Freedom or Death!

THE SOUTHERN CROSS.

By E. K. Blunt.

In the name of God! Amen!
    Stand for our Southern rights;
On our side, Southern men,
    The God of battles fights:
Fling the invaders far—
    Hurl back their work of woe—
Thy voice is the voice of a brother,
    But the hands are the hands of a foe.
They come with a trampling army,
    Invading our native sod—
Stand, Southrons! fight and conquer
    In the name of the mighty God

They are singing our song of triumph,
      Which proclaimed us proud and free—
While breaking away the heartstrings
      Of our nation's harmony.
Sadly it floateth from us,
      Sighing o'er land and wave;
Till, mute on the lips of the poet,
      It sleeps in its Southern grave.
Spirit and song departed!
      Minstrel and minstrelsy!
We mourn ye, heavy hearted,—
      But we will—we will be free!

            They are waving our flag above us,
                  With the despot's tyrant will;
            With our blood they have stained its colors,
                  And they call it holy still.
            With tearful eyes, but steady hand,
                  We'll tear its stripes apart,
            And fling them, like broken fetters,
                  That may not bind the heart.
            But we'll save our stars of glory,
                  In the might of the sacred sign
            Of Him who has fixed forever
                  One "Southern Cross" to shine.

Stand, Southrons! fight and conquer!
      Solemn, and strong, and sure!
The fight shall not be longer
      Than God shall bid endure.
By the life that but yesterday
      Waked with the infant's breath!
By the feet which, ere morning, may
      Tread to the soldier's death!
By the blood which cries to heaven—
      Crimson upon our sod!
Stand, Southrons! fight and conquer,
      In the name of the mighty God!

GENERAL CLEMENT A. EVANS

Successor to General "Stonewall" Jackson in Command of Division Army of Western Virginia, C. S. A., 1864-1865.

GENERAL "STONEWALL" JACKSON

THE NEW STAR.

By B. M. Anderson.

Another star arisen ; another flag unfurled ;
  Another name inscribed among the nations of the world ;
Another mighty struggle 'gainst a tyrant's fell decree,
And again a burdened people have uprisen, and are free.

The spirit of the fathers in the children liveth yet ;
Liveth still the olden blood which dimmed the foreign bayonet ;
And the fathers fought for freedom, and the sons for freedom
        fight ;
Their God was with the fathers—and is still the God of right !

Behold ! the skies are darkened ! A gloomy cloud hath lowered !
Shall it break before the sun of peace, or spread in rage
        impowered ?
Shall we have the smile of friendship, or shall it be the blow ?
Shall it be the right hand to the friend, or the red hand to the
        foe ?

In peacefulness we wish to live, but not in slavish fear ;
In peacefulness we dare not die, dishonored on our bier.
To our allies of the northern land we offer heart and hand,
But if they scorn our friendship—then the banner and the
        brand !

Honor to the new-born nation ! and honor to the brave !
A country freed from thraldom, or a soldier's honored grave.
Every step shall be contested ; every rivulet run red,
And the invader, should he conquer, find the conquered in the
        dead.

But victory shall follow where the sons of freedom go,
And the signal for the onset be the death-knell of the foe ;
And hallowed shall the spot be where he was so bravely met,
And the star which yonder rises, rises never more to set.

GIVE BACK THY SWORD.

Virginia to Winfield Scott.

A voice is heard in Ramah !
  High sounds are on the gale !
Notes to wake buried patriots !
  Notes to strike traitors pale !
Wild notes of outraged feeling
  Cry aloud and spare him not !
'Tis Virginia's strong appealing,
  And she calls to Winfield Scott !

Oh ! chief among ten thousand !
  Thou whom I loved so well,
Star that has set, as never yet
  Since son of morning fell !
I call not in reviling,
  Nor to speak thee what thou art ;
I leave thee to thy death-bed,
  And I leave thee to thy heart !

But by every mortal hope,
  And by every mortal fear ;
By all that man deems sacred,
  And that woman holds most dear ;
Yea ! by thy mother's honor,
  And by thy father's grave,
By hell beneath, and heaven above,
  Give back the sword I gave !

Not since God's sword was planted
  To guard life's heavenly tree,
Has ever blade been granted,
  Like that bestowed on thee !

To pierce me with the steel I gave
To guard mine honor's shrine,
Not since Iscariot lived and died,
Was treason like to thine !

Give back the sword and sever
Our strong and mighty tie !
We part, and part forever,
To conquer or to die !
In sorrow, not in anger,
I speak the word, " We part ! "
For I leave thee to thy death-bed,
And I leave thee to thy heart !

SEVENTY-SIX AND SIXTY-ONE.

By JOHN W. OVERALL, of Louisiana.

YE spirits of the glorious dead !
Ye watchers in the sky !
Who sought the patriot's crimson bed,
With holy trust and high—
Come, lend your inspiration now,
Come, fire each Southern son,
Who nobly fights for freemen's rights,
And shouts for sixty-one.

Come, teach them how, on hill, on glade,
Quick leaping from your side,
The lightning flash of sabres made
A red and flowing tide—
How well ye fought, how bravely fell,
Beneath our burning sun ;
And let the lyre, in strains of fire,
So speak of sixty-one.

There's many a grave in all the land,
    And many a crucifix,
Which tells how that heroic band
    Stood firm in seventy-six—
Ye heroes of the deathless past,
    Your glorious race is run,
But from your dust springs freemen's trust,
    And blows for sixty-one.

        We build our altars where you lie,
            On many a verdant sod,
        With sabres pointing to the sky,
            And sanctified of God ;
        The smoke shall rise from every pile,
            Till freedom's cause is won,
        And every mouth throughout the South,
            Shall shout for sixty-one.

_____

FROM THE RAPIDAN—1863.

A LOW wind in the pines !
    And a dull pain in the breast !
And oh ! for the sigh of her lips and eyes—
One touch of the hand I pressed !

        The slow, sad lowland wind,
            It sighs through the livelong day,
        While the splendid mountain breezes blow,
            And the autumn is burning away.

Here the pines sigh ever above,
    And the broomstraw sighs below ;
And far from the bare, bleak, wintry fields
    Comes the note of the drowsy crow.

There the trees are crimson and gold,
  Like the tints of a magical dawn,
And the slender form, in the dreamy days,
  By the slow stream rambles on.

  Oh, day that weighs on the heart!
    Oh, wind in the dreary pines!
  Does she think on me 'mid the golden hours,
    Past the mountain's long blue lines?

The old house, lonely and still,
  By the sad Shenandoah's waves,
Must be touched to-day by the sunshine's gleam,
  As the spring flowers bloom on graves.

  Oh, sunshine, flitting and sad,
    Oh, wind, that forever sighs!
  The hall may be bright, but my life is dark
    For the sunshine of her eyes!

"IS THERE, THEN, NO HOPE FOR THE NATIONS?"

IS THERE, then, no hope for the nations?
  Must the record of Time be the same?
And shall History, in all her narrations,
  Still close each last chapter in shame?
Shall the valor which grew to be glorious,
  Prove the shame, as the pride of a race:
And a people, for ages victorious,
  Through the arts of the chapman, grow base?

  Greek, Hebrew, Assyrian and Roman,
    Each strides o'er the scene and departs!
  How valiant their deeds 'gainst the foeman,
    How wondrous their virtues and arts!

19

Rude valor, at first, when beginning,
　　The nation through blood took its name;
Then the wisdom, which hourly winning
　　New heights in its march, rose to Fame!

　　How noble the tale for long ages,
　　　　Blending Beauty with courage and might!
　　What Heroes, what Poets, and Sages,
　　　　Made eminent stars for each height!
　　While their people, with reverence ample,
　　　　Brought tribute of praise to the Great,
　　Whose wisdom and virtuous example,
　　　　Made virtue the pride of the State!

Ours, too, was as noble a dawning,
　　With hopes of the Future as high;
Great men, each a star of the morning,
　　Taught us bravely to live and to die!
We fought the long fight with our foeman,
　　And through trial—well-borne—won a name,
Not less glorious than Grecian or Roman,
　　And worthy as lasting a fame!

　　　*　　　*　　　*　　　*　　　*　　　*　　　*

　　Shut the Book!　We must open another!
　　　　O Southron! if taught by the Past,
　　Beware, when thou choosest a brother,
　　　　With what ally thy fortunes are cast!
　　Beware of all foreign alliance,
　　　　Of their pleadings and pleasings beware,
　　Better meet the old snake with defiance,
　　　　Than find in his charming a snare!

HYMN TO THE NATIONAL FLAG.

By Mrs. M. J. Preston.

Float aloft, thou stainless banner!
    Azure cross and field of light;
Be thy brilliant stars the symbol
    Of the pure and true and right.
Shelter freedom's holy cause—
Liberty and sacred laws;
Guard the youngest of the nations—
    Keep her virgin honor bright.

From Virginia's storied border,
    Down to Tampa's furthest shore—
From the blue Atlantic's clashings
    To the Rio Grande's roar—
Over many a crimson plain,
    Where our martyred ones lie slain—
Fling abroad thy blessed shelter,
    Stream and mount and valley o'er.

In thy cross of heavenly azure
    Has our faith its emblem high;
In thy field of white, the hallow'd
    Truth for which we'll dare and die;
In thy red, the patriot blood—
Ah! the consecrated flood.
Lift thyself, resistless banner!
    Ever fill our Southern sky!

Flash with living, lightning motion
    In the sight of all the brave!
Tell the price at which we purchased
    Room and right for thee to wave

Freely in our God's free air,
Pure and proud and stainless fair,
Banner of the youngest nation—
   Banner we would die to save!

      Strike thou for us! King of armies!
         Grant us room in thy broad world!
      Loosen all the despot's fetters,
         Back be all his legions hurled!
      Give us peace and liberty,
      Let the land we love be free—
      Then, oh! bright and stainless banner!
      Never shall thy folds be furled!

AT FORT PILLOW.

You shudder as you think upon
   The carnage of the grim report,
The desolation when we won
   The inner trenches of the fort.

      But there are deeds you may not know,
         That scourge the pulses into strife;
      Dark memories of deathless woe
         Pointing the bayonet and knife.

The house is ashes where I dwelt,
   Beyond the mighty inland sea;
The tombstones shattered where I knelt,
   By that old church at Pointe Coupee.

      The Yankee fiends that came with fire,
         Camped on the consecrated sod,
      And trampled in the dust and mire
         The Holy Eucharist of God!

"STONEWALL" JACKSON MONUMENT IN THE CAPITOL SQUARE,
RICHMOND, VIRGINIA

From photograph made for this work by Edyth Carter Beveridge.

The spot where darling mother sleeps,
　　Beneath the glimpse of yon sad moon,
Is crushed, with splintered marble heaps,
　　To stall the horse of some dragoon.

　　　　God! when I ponder that black day
　　　　　　It makes my frantic spirit wince;
　　　　I marched—with Longstreet—far away,
　　　　　　But have beheld the ravage since.

The tears are hot upon my face,
　　When thinking what bleak fate befell
The only sister of our race—
　　A thing too horrible to tell.

　　　　They say that, ere her senses fled,
　　　　　　She rescue of her brothers cried;
　　　　Then feebly bowed her stricken head,
　　　　　　Too pure to live thus—so she died.

Two of those brothers heard no plea;
　　With their proud hearts forever still—
John shrouded by the Tennessee,
　　And Arthur there at Malvern Hill.

　　　　But I have heard it everywhere,
　　　　　　Vibrating like a passing knell;
　　　　'Tis as perpetual as the air,
　　　　　　And solemn as a funeral bell.

By scorched lagoon and murky swamp
　　My wrath was never in the lurch;
I've killed the picket in his camp,
　　And many a pilot on his perch.

With steady rifle, sharpened brand,
  A week ago, upon my steed,
With Forrest and his warrior band,
  I made the hell-hounds writhe and bleed.

    You should have seen our leader go
      Upon the battle's burning marge,
    Swooping like falcon, on the foe,
      Heading the gray line's iron charge!

All outcasts from our ruined marts,
  We heard th' undying serpent hiss,
And in the desert of our hearts
  The fatal spell of Nemesis.

    The Southern yell rang loud and high
      The moment that we thundered in,
    Smiting the demons hip and thigh,
      Cleaving them to the very chin.

My right arm bared for fiercer play,
  The left one held the rein in slack;
In all the fury of the fray
  I sought the white man, not the black.

    The dabbled clots of brain and gore
      Across the swirling sabres ran;
    To me each brutal visage bore
      The front of one accursed man.

Throbbing along the frenzied vein,
  My blood seemed kindled into song—
The death-dirge of the sacred slain,
  The slogan of immortal wrong.

It glared athwart the dripping glaves,
   It blazed in each avenging eye—
The thought of desecrated graves,
   And some lone sister's desperate cry !

JACKSON, THE ALEXANDRIA MARTYR.

By Wm. H. Holcombe, M. D., of Virginia.

When Colonel Ellsworth with his forces entered the city of Alexandria, Virginia, there was a hotel known as the Marshall House, kept by one Jackson. Over the house a Confederate flag was floating. Colonel Ellsworth ordered it down, but Jackson refused to remove it. Colonel Ellsworth then proceeded to take it down himself, when Jackson shot him dead. Of course, he in turn was immediately shot to death by Ellsworth's soldiers.

'TWAS not the private insult galled him most,
      But public outrage of his country's flag,
To which his patriotic heart had pledged
Its faith as to a bride.   The bold, proud chief,
Th' avenging host, and the swift-coming death
Appalled him not.   Nor life with all its charms,
Nor home, nor wife, nor children could weigh down
The fierce, heroic instincts to destroy
The insolent invader.   Ellsworth fell
And Jackson perished 'mid the pack of wolves,
Befriended only by his own great heart
And God approving.   More than Roman soul !
O type of our impetuous chivalry !
May this young nation ever boast her sons
A vast and inconceivable multitude,
Standing like thee in her extremest van,
Self-poised and ready, in defence of rights
Or in revenge of wrongs, to dare and die !

SONG OF OUR GLORIOUS SOUTHLAND.

By Mrs. Mary Ware.

Oh, sing of our glorious Southland,
    The pride of the golden sun !
'Tis the fairest land of flowers
    The eye e'er looked upon.

        Sing of her orange and myrtle
            That glitter like gems above ;
        Sing of her dark-eyed maidens
            As fair as a dream of love.

Sing of her flowing rivers—
    How musical their sound !
Sing of her dark green forests,
    The Indian hunting-ground.

        Sing of the noble nation
            Fierce struggling to be free;
        Sing of the brave who barter
            Their lives for liberty !

Weep for the maid and matron
    Who mourn their loved ones slain ;
Sigh for the light departed,
    Never to shine again :

        'Tis the voice of Rachel weeping,
            That never will comfort know ;
        'Tis the wail of desolation,
            The breaking of hearts in woe !

Ah ! the blood of Abel crieth
    For vengeance from the sod !
'Tis a brother's hand that's lifted
    In the face of an angry God !

Oh! brother of the Northland,
    We plead from our father's grave;
We strike for our homes and altars,
    He fought to build and save!

    A smouldering fire is burning,
        The Southern heart is steeled—
    Perhaps 'twill break in dying,
        But never will it yield.

HOSPITAL DUTIES.

FOLD away all your bright-tinted dresses,
    Turn the key on your jewels to-day,
And the wealth of your tendril-like tresses
    Braid back in a serious way;
No more delicate gloves, no more laces,
    No more trifling in boudoir or bower,
But come with your souls in your faces
    To meet the stern wants of the hour.

    Look around! By the torchlight unsteady
        The dead and the dying seem one—
    What! trembling and paling already,
        Before your dear mission's begun?
    These wounds are more precious than ghastly—
        Time presses her lips to each scar,
    While she chants of that glory which vastly
        Transcends all the horrors of war.

Pause here by this bedside. How mellow
    The light showers down on that brow!
Such a brave, brawny visage, poor fellow!
    Some homestead is missing him now.

Some wife shades her eyes in the clearing,
    Some mother sits moaning distressed,
While the loved one lies faint but unfearing,
    With the enemy's ball in his breast.

    Here's another—a lad—a mere stripling,
        Picked up in the field almost dead,
    With the blood through his sunny hair rippling
        From the horrible gash in the head.
    They say he was first in the action ;
        Gay-hearted, quick-headed, and witty :
    He fought till he dropped with exhaustion
        At the gates of our fair Southern city.

Fought and fell 'neath the guns of that city,
    With a spirit transcending his years—
Lift him up in your large-hearted pity,
    And wet his pale lips with your tears.
Touch him gently ; most sacred the duty
    Of dressing that poor shattered hand !
God spare him to rise in his beauty,
    And battle once more for his land !

    Pass on ! it is useless to linger
        While others are calling your care ;
    There is need for your delicate finger,
        For your womanly sympathy there.
    There are sick ones athirst for caressing,
        There are dying ones raving at home,
    There are wounds to be bound with a blessing,
        And shrouds to make ready for some.

They have gathered about you the harvest
    Of death in its ghastliest view ;
The nearest as well as the furthest
    Is there with the traitor and true,

And crowned with your beautiful patience,
　Made sunny with love at the heart,
You must balsam the wounds of the nations,
　Nor falter nor shrink from your part.

And the lips of the mother will bless you,
　And angels, sweet-visaged and pale,
And the little ones run to caress you,
　And the wives and the sisters cry hail!
But e'en if you drop down unheeded,
　What matter?　God's ways are the best;
You have poured out your life where 'twas needed,
　And He will take care of the rest.

THEY CRY, " PEACE, PEACE," WHEN THERE IS NO PEACE.

THEY are ringing peace on my heavy ear—
　No peace to my heavy heart!
They are ringing peace, I hear! I hear!
　O God! how my hopes depart!

　　They are ringing peace from the mountain side;
　　　With a hollow voice it comes—
　　They are ringing peace o'er the foaming tide
　　　And its echoes fill our homes.

They are ringing peace, and the spring-time blooms
　Like a garden fresh and fair;
But our martyrs sleep in their silent tombs—
　Do they hear that sound—do they hear?

　　They are ringing peace, and the battle cry
　　　And the bayonet's work are done,
　　And the armor bright they are laying by,
　　　From the brave sire to the son.

And the musket's clang, and the soldier's drill,
　　And the tattoo's nightly sound;
We shall hear no more with a joyous thrill,
　　Peace! Peace! they are ringing round!

　　There are women, still as the stifled air
　　　　On the burning desert's track,
　　Not a cry of joy, not a welcome cheer—
　　　　And the brave ones coming back!

There are fair young heads in their morning pride,
　　Like the lilies pale they bow;
Just a memory left to the soldier's bride—
　　Ah, God! sustain her now!

　　There are martial steps that we may not hear!
　　　　There are forms we may not see!
　　Death's muster roll they have answered clear,
　　　　They are free! thank God, they are free!

Not a fetter fast, nor a prisoner's chain
　　For the noble army gone—
No conqueror comes o'er the heavenly plain—
　　Peace! Peace! to the dead alone!

　　They are ringing peace, but strangers tread
　　　　O'er the land where our fathers trod,
　　And our birthright joys, like a dream have fled,
　　　　And Thou! where art Thou, O God?

They are ringing peace! not here, not here,
　　Where the victor's mark is set,
Roll back to the North its mocking cheer—
　　No peace to the Southland yet!

The Constitution

of the

Confederate States of

America

We, the people of the Confederate States, each State acting for itself, and in its sovereign and independent character, in order to form a permanent Federal Government, establish justice, ensure domestic tranquility, and secure the blessings of liberty to ourselves and our posterity — to which ends we invoke the favor and guidance of Almighty God — do ordain and establish this Constitution for the Confederate States of America —

FIRST PAGE OF THE PERMANENT CONSTITUTION OF THE CONFEDERATE STATES AS REPORTED BY THE COMMITTEE

This is the handwriting of General Thomas R. B. Cobb, who was a member of the Committee. Taken from the original which is in possession of Mr. A. L. Hull, Athens, Georgia, and used by permission.

We may sheathe the sword, and the rifle-gun
    We may hang on the cottage wall,
And the bayonet brave, sharp duty done,
    From the soldier's arm it may fall.

But peace ! No peace ! till the same good sword,
    Drawn out from its scabbard be,
And the wide world list to my country's word,
    And the South ! Oh, the South, be free!

BALLAD—"WHAT HAVE YE THOUGHT?"

WHAT ! have ye thought to pluck
    Victory from chance and luck,
Triumph from clamorous shout, without a will?
    Without the heart to brave
    All peril to the grave,
And battle on its brink, unshrinking still?

    And did ye dream success
    Would still unvarying bless
Your arms, nor meet reverse in some dread field?
    And shall an adverse hour
    Make ye mistrust the power
Of virtue, in your souls, to make your enemy yield?

    Oh ! from this dreary sleep
    Arise, and upward leap,
Nor let your hearts grow palsied with dismay !
    Fling out your banner high,
    Still challenging the sky,
While thousand strong arms bear it on its way.

Forth, as a sacred band,
Sworn saviours of the land,
Chosen by God, the champions of the right!
And never doubt that He
Who made will keep you free,
If thus your souls resolve to triumph in the fight!

The felon foe, no more
Trampling the sacred shore,
Shall leave defiling footprint on the sod;
Where, desperate in the strife,
Reckless of wounds and life,
Ye brave your myriad foes beneath the eye of God!

On brothers, comrades, men,
Rush to the field again;
Home, peace, love, safety—freedom—are the price!
Strike! while the arm can bear
Weapon—and do not spare—
Ye break a felon bond in every foe that dies!

JACKSON.

Not midst the lightning of the stormy fight,
    Nor in the rush upon the vandal foe,
Did kingly death, with his resistless might,
        Lay the great leader low.

His warrior soul its earthly shackles broke,
In the full sunshine of a peaceful town:
When all the storm was hushed, the trusty oak
        That propped our cause went down.

Though his alone the blood that flocks the ground,
Recalling all his grand heroic deeds
Freedom herself is writhing with the wound,
        And all the country bleeds.

He entered not the nation's promised land,
  At the red belching of the cannon's mouth :
But broke the house of bondage with his hand—
    The Moses of the South !

O gracious God ! not gainless in the loss ;
A glorious sunbeam gilds the sternest frown ;
And while his country staggers with the cross,
    He rise with the crown !

MISSING.

In the cool, sweet hush of a wooded nook,
  Where the May buds sprinkle the green old mound,
And the winds and the birds and the limpid brook,
  Murmur their dreams with a drowsy sound ;
Who lies so still in the plushy moss,
  With his pale cheek pressed on a breezy pillow,
Couched where the light and the shadows cross
  Through the flickering fringe of the willow ?
    Who lies, alas !
So still, so chill, in the whispering grass ?

A soldier clad in the Zouave dress,
  A bright-haired man, with his lips apart,
One hand thrown up o'er his frank, dead face,
  And the other clutching his pulseless heart,
Lies here in the shadows, cool and dim,
  His musket swept by a trailing bough,
With a careless grace in each quiet limb,
  And a wound on his manly brow
    A wound, alas !
Whence the warm blood drips on the quiet grass.

The violets peer from their dusky beds,
    With a tearful dew in their great, pure eyes;
The lilies quiver their shining heads,
    Their pale lips full of a sad surprise;
And the lizard darts through the glistening fern—
    And the squirrel rustles the branches hoary;
Strange birds fly out, with a cry, to bathe
    Their wings in the sunset glory;
        While the shadows pass
O'er the quiet face and the dewy grass.

God pity the bride who waits at home,
    With her lily cheeks and her violet eyes,
Dreaming the sweet old dreams of love,
    While her lover is walking in Paradise;
God strengthen her heart as the days go by,
    And the long, drear nights of her vigil follow,
Nor bird, nor moon, nor whispering wind,
    May breathe the tale of the hollow;
        Alas! alas!
The secret is safe with the woodland grass.

SONNET.

Rise from your gory ashes stern and pale,
    Ye martyred thousands! and with dreadful ire,
A voice of doom, a front of gloomy fire,
Rebuke those faithless souls, whose querulous wail
Disturbs your sacred sleep!—"The withering hail
Of battle, hunger, pestilence, despair,
Whatever of mortal anguish man may bear,
We bore unmurmuring! strengthened by the mail
Of a most holy purpose! then we died!—
Vex not our rest by cries of selfish pain,
But to the noblest measure of your powers
Endure the appointed trial! Griefs defied,
But launch their threatening thunderbolts in vain,
And angry storms pass by in gentlest showers!"

ODE—"SOULS OF HEROES."

Souls of heroes, ascended from fields ye have won,
 Still smile on the conflict so greatly begun;
Bring succor to comrade, to brother, to son
  Now breasting the battle in ranks of the brave;
And the dastard that loiters, the conflict to shun,
 Pursue him with scorn to the grave!

Pursue him with furies that goad to despair,
Hunt him out, where he crouches in crevice and lair,
Drive him forth, while the wife of his bosom cries—"There
  Goes the coward that skulks, though his sister and wife
Tremble nightly in sleep, overshadowed by fear
 Of a sacrifice dearer than life."

There are thousands that loiter, of historied claim,
Who boast of the heritage shrined in each name—
Sting their souls to the quick, till they shrink from the shame
  Which dishonors the names and the past of their boast;
Even now they may win the best guerdon of fame,
 And retrieve the bright honors they've lost!

Even now, while their country is torn in the toils,
While the wild boar is raging to raven the spoils,
While the boa is spreading around us the coils
  Which would strangle the freedom our ancestors gave;
But each soul must be quickened until it o'er-boils,
 Every muscle be corded to save!

Still the cause is the same which, in long ages gone,
Roused up your great sires, so gallantly known,
When, braving the tyrant, the sceptre and throne,
  They rushed to the conflict, despising the odds;
Armed with bow, spear, and scythe, and with sling and with
   stone,
 For their homes and their family goods!

20

Shall we be less worthy the sacrifice grand,
The heritage noble we took at their hand,
The peace and the comfort, the fruits of the land ;
    And, sunk in a torpor as hopeless as base,
Recoil from the shock of the Sodomite band,
    That would ruin the realm and the race ?

Souls of heroes, ascended from fields ye have won,
Your toils are not closed in the deeds ye have done ;
Touch the souls of each laggard and profligate son,
    The greed and the sloth, and the cowardice shame ;
Till we rise to complete the great work ye've begun,
    And with freedom make conquest of fame !

THE OLD RIFLEMAN.

By Frank Ticknor, of Georgia.

Now bring me out my buckskin suit !
    My pouch and powder, too !
We'll see if seventy-six can shoot
    As sixteen used to do.

    Old Bess ! we've kept our barrels bright !
        Our trigger quick and true !
    As far, if not as fine a sight,
        As long ago we drew !

And pick me out a trusty flint !
    A real white and blue,
Perhaps 'twill win the other tint
    Before the hunt is through !

Give boys your brass percussion caps !
Old "shut-pan " suits as well !
There's something in the sparks : perhaps
There's something in the smell !

We've seen the red-coat Briton bleed !
The red-skin Indian, too !
We've never thought to draw a bead
On Yankee-doodle-doo !

But, Bessie ! bless your dear old heart !
Those days are mostly done ;
And now we must revive the art
Of shooting on the run !

If Doodle must be meddling, why,
There's only this to do—
Select the black spot in his eye,
And let the daylight through !

And if he doesn't like the way
That Bess presents the view,
He'll maybe change his mind, and stay
Where the good Doodles do !

We'll teach these shot-gun boys the tricks
By which a war is won ;
Especially how Seventy-six
Took Tories on the run.

SONNET—THE SHIP OF STATE.

Here lie the peril and necessity
    That need a race of giants—a great realm,
    With not one noble leader at the helm ;
And the great Ship of State still driving high,
    'Midst breakers, on a lee shore—to the rocks.
    With ever and anon most terrible shocks—
The crew aghast, and fear in every eye.
Yet in the gracious Providence still nigh ;
    And, if our cause be just, our hearts be true,
    We shall save goodly ship and gallant crew,
Nor suffer shipwreck of our liberty !
    It needs that as a people we arise,
    With solemn purpose that even fate defies,
And brave all perils with unblenching eye !

"IN HIS BLANKET ON THE GROUND."

By Caroline H. Gervais, Charleston.

Weary? weary lies the soldier,
    In his blanket on the ground
With no sweet "Good-night" to cheer him,
    And no tender voice's sound,
Making music in the darkness,
    Making light his toilsome hours,
Like a sunbeam in the forest,
    Or a tomb wrestled o'er with flowers.

Thoughtful, hushed, he lies, and tearful,
    As his memories sadly roam
To the "cozy little parlor"
    And the loved ones of his home ;

GENERAL BRAXTON BRAGG

GENERAL WADE HAMPTON

And his waking and his dreaming
    Softly braid themselves in one,
As the twilight is the mingling
    Of the starlight and the sun.

    And when sleep descends upon him,
        Still his thought within his dream
    Is of home, and friends, and loved ones,
        And his busy fancies seem
    To be real, as they wander
        To his mother's cherished form.

As she gently said, in parting,
    "Thine in sunshine and in storm :
Thine in helpless childhood's morning,
    And in boyhood's joyous time,
Thou must leave me now—God watch thee
    In thy manhood's ripened prime."

    Or, mayhap, amid the phantoms
        Teeming thick within his brain,
    His dear father's locks, o'er-silvered,
        Come to greet his view again ;
    And he hears his trembling accents,
        Like a clarion ringing high,
    "Since not mine are youth and strength, boy,
        Thou must victor prove, or die."

Or perchance he hears a whisper
    Of the faintest, faintest sigh,
Something deeper than word-spoken,
    Something breathing of a tie
Near his soul as bounding heart-blood :
    It is hers, that patient wife—
And again that parting seemeth
    Like the taking leave of life :

And her last kiss he remembers,
    And the agonizing thrill,
And the " Must you go ? " and answer,
    " I but know my Country's will."

        Or the little children gather,
            Half in wonder, round his knees;
        And the faithful dog, mute, watchful,
            In the mystic glass he sees ;
        And the voice of song, and pictures,
            And the simplest homestead flowers,
        Unforgotten, crowd before him
            In the solemn midnight hours.

Then his thoughts in Dreamland wander
    To a sister's sweet caress,
And he feels her dear lips quiver
    As his own they fondly press ;
And he hears her proudly saying,
    (Though sad tears are in her eyes),
" Brave men fall, but live in story,
    For the Hero never dies ! "

        Or, perhaps, his brown cheek flushes,
            And his heart beats quicker now,
        As he thinks of one who gave him
            Him, the loved one, love's sweet vow ;
        And, ah, fondly he remembers
            He is still her dearest care,
        Even in his star-watched slumber
            That she pleads for him in prayer.

Oh, the soldier will be dreaming,
    Dreaming often of us all,
(When the damp earth is his pillow,
    And the snow and cold sleet fall),

Of the dear, familiar faces,
 Of the cozy, curtained room,
Of the flitting of the shadows
 In the twilight's pensive gloom.

  Or when summer suns burn o'er him,
   Bringing drought and dread disease,
  And the throes of wasting fever
   Come his weary frame to seize—
  In the restless sleep of sickness,
   Doomed, perchance, to martyr death,
  Hear him whisper " Home " sweet cadence,
   With his quickened, labored breath.

Then God bless him, bless the soldier,
 And God nerve him for the fight;
May He lend his arm new prowess
 To do battle for the right.
Let him feel that while he's dreaming
 In his fitful slumber bound,
That we're praying—God watch o'er him
 In his blanket on the ground.

THE UNKNOWN DEAD.

By Henry Timrod.

THE rain is plashing on my sill,
 But all the winds of heaven are still;
And so, it falls with that dull sound
Which thrills us in the churchyard ground,
When the first spadeful drops like lead
Upon the coffin of the dead.
Beyond my streaming window-pane,
I cannot see the neighboring vane,
Yet from its old familiar tower
The bell comes, muffled, through the shower.
What strange and unsuspected link

Of feeling touched has made me think—
While with a vacant soul and eye
I watch that gray and stony sky—
Of nameless graves on battle plains,
Washed by a single winter's rains,
Where, some beneath Virginian hills,
And some by green Atlantic rills,
Some by the waters of the West,
A myriad unknown heroes rest.
Ah! not the chiefs who, dying, see
Their flags in front of victory,
Or, at their life-blood's noblest cost
Pay for a battle nobly lost,
Claim from their monumental beds
The bitterest tears a nation sheds.
Beneath yon lonely mound—the spot,
By all save some fond few forgot—
Lie the true martyrs of the fight,
Which strikes for freedom and for right.
Of them, their patriot zeal and pride,
The lofty faith that with them died,
No grateful page shall further tell
Than that so many bravely fell;
And we can only dimly guess
What worlds of all this world's distress,
What utter woe, despair, and dearth,
Their fate has brought to many a hearth.
Just such a sky as this should weep
Above them, always, where they sleep;
Yet, haply, at this very hour,
Their graves are like a lover's bower;
And Nature's self, with eyes unwet
Oblivious of the crimson debt
To which she owes her April grace,
Laughs gayly o'er their burial place.

ENGLAND'S NEUTRALITY.

A Parliamentary Debate.

By John R. Thompson, of Richmond, Virginia.

All ye who with credulity the whispers hear of fancy,
 Or yet pursue with eagerness hope's wild extravagancy,
Who dream that England soon will drop her long miscalled
  neutrality,
And give us, with a hearty shake, the hand of nationality.

Read, as we give, with little fault of statement or omission,
The next debate in Parliament on Southern Recognition;
They're all so much alike, indeed, that one can write it off, I see,
As truly as the *Times'* report, without the gift of prophecy.

Not yet, not yet to interfere does England see occasion,
But treats our good commissioner with coolness and evasion;
Such coolness in the premises, that really 'tis refrigerant
To think that two long years ago she called us a belligerent.

But, further, Downing Street is dumb, the Premier deaf to
  reason,
As deaf as is the *Morning Post*, both in and out of season;
The working men of Lancashire are all reduced to beggary,
And yet they will not listen unto Roebuck or to Gregory.

" Or any other man," to-day, who counsels interfering,
While all who speak on t'other side obtain a ready hearing—
As, per exemple, Mr. Bright, that pink of all propriety,
That meek and mild disciple of the blessed Peace Society.

" Why, let 'em fight," says Mr. Bright, " those Southerners, I
  hate 'em,
And hope the Black Republicans will soon exterminate 'em;
If freedom can't rebellion crush, pray tell me what's the use
  of her?"
And so he chuckles o'er the fray as gleefully as Lucifer.

Enough of him—an abler man demands our close attention—.
The Maximus Apollo of strict non-intervention—
With pitiless severity, though decorous and calm his tone,
Thus spake the " old man eloquent," the puissant Earl of
        Palmerston :

" What though the land run red with blood, what though the
        lurid flashes
Of cannon light, at dead of night, a mournful heap of ashes
Where many an ancient mansion stood—what though the
        robber pillages
The sacred home, the house of God, in twice a hundred villages.

" What though a fiendish, nameless wrong, that makes revenge
        a duty,
Is daily done" (O Lord, how long?) " to tenderness and beauty!"
(And who shall tell this deed of hell, how deadlier far a curse it is
Than even pulling temples down and burning universities)?

" Let arts decay, let millions fall, aye, let freedom perish,
With all that in the Western world men fain would love and
        cherish ;
Let universal ruin there become a sad reality ;
We cannot swerve, we must preserve our rigorous neutrality,"

Oh, Pam ! oh, Pam ! hast ever read what's writ in holy pages,
How blessed the peace-makers are, God's children of the ages?
Perhaps you think the promise sweet was nothing but a
        platitude ;
'Tis clear that you have no concern in that divine beatitude.

But " hear ! hear ! hear ! " another Peer, that mighty man of
        muscle,
Is on his legs, what slender pegs ! "Ye noble Earl " of Russell ;
Thus might he speak, did not of speech his shrewd reserve
        the folly see,
And thus unfold the subtle plan of England's secret policy.

"John Bright was right, yes, let 'em fight, these fools across
    the water,
'Tis no affair at all of ours, their carnival of slaughter;
The Christian world, indeed, may say we ought not to allow
    it, sirs,
But still, " 'tis music in our ears, this roar of Yankee howitzers.

"A word or two of sympathy, that costs us not a penny,
We give the gallant Southerners, the few against the many;
We say their noble fortitude of final triumph presages,
And praise in ' Blackwood's Magazine,' Jeff. Davis and his
    messages.

"Of course, we claim the shining fame of glorious Stonewall
    Jackson,
Who typifies the English race, a sterling Anglo-Saxon ;
To bravest song his deeds belong, to Clio and Melpomene "—
(And why not for a British stream demand the Chicka-
    hominy?)

" But for the cause in which we fell we cannot lift a finger,
'Tis idle on the question any longer here to linger;
'Tis true the South has freely bled, her sorrows are
    Homeric, oh !
Her case is like to his of old who journeyed unto Jericho.

" The thieves have stripped and bruised, although as yet they
    have not bound her,
We'd like to see her slay 'em all to right and left around her;
We shouldn't cry in parliament if Lee should cross the
    Raritan,
But England never yet was known to play the Good Samaritan,

" And so we pass the other side, and leave them to their glory,
To give new proofs of manliness, new scenes for song and story;
These honeyed words of compliment may possibly bam-
    boozle 'em,
But ere we intervene, you know, we'll see 'em in—Jerusalem.

" Yes, let 'em fight, till both are brought to hopeless deso-
    lation.
Till wolves troop round the cottage door in one and t'other
    nation,
Till, worn and broken down, the South shall prove no more
    refractory,
And rust eats up the silent looms in every Yankee factory.

" Till bursts no more the cotton boll o'er fields of Carolina,
And fills with snowy flosses the dusky hands of Dinah ;
Till war has dealt its final blow, and Mr. Seward's knavery
Has put an end in all the land to freedom and to slavery.

" The grim Bastile, the rack, the wheel, without remorse of pity,
May flourish with the guillotine in every Yankee city ;
No matter should old Abe revive the brazen bull of Phalaris,
' Tis no concern at all of ours ' (sensation in the galleries.).

" So shall our ' merry England ' thrive on trans-Atlantic
    troubles,
While India, on her distant plains, her crop of cotton doubles;
And just so long as North or South shall show the least
    vitality,
We cannot swerve, we must preserve our rigorous neutrality."

Your speech, my lord, might well become a Saxon legislator,
When the " fine old English gentlemen " lived in a state of
    natur',
When Vikings quaffed from human skulls their fiery draughts
    of honey mead,
Long, long before the barons bold met tyrant John at Runny-
    mede.

But 'tis a speech so plain, my lord, that all may understand it,
And so we quickly turn again to fight the Yankee bandit,
Convinced that we shall fairly win at last our nationality,
Without the help of Britain's arm, in spite of her neutrality.

GENERAL STEPHEN D. LEE

GENERAL FITZHUGH LEE
The Hero of Two Wars.

THE SEA-KINGS OF THE SOUTH.

By Edward C. Bruce, of Winchester, Va.

Full many have sung of the victories our warriors have won,
From Bethel, by the eastern tide, to sunny Galveston,
On fair Potomac's classic shore, by sweeping Tennessee,
Hill, rock, and river shall tell forever the vengeance of the free.

The air still rings with the cannon-shot, with battle's breath
is warm;
Still on the hills their swords have saved our legions wheel
and form;
And Johnston, Beauregard, and Lee, with all their gallant
train,
Wait yet at their head, in silence dread, the hour to charge
again.

But a ruggeder field than the mountain-side—a broader field
than the plain,
Is spread for the fight in the stormy wave and the globe-
embracing main.
'Tis there the keel of the goodly ship must trace the fate of
the land,
For the name ye write in the sea-foam white shall first and
longest stand.

For centuries on centuries, since first the hallowed tree
Was launched by the lone mariner on some primeval sea,
No stouter stuff than the heart of oak, or tough elastic pine.
Had floated beyond the shallow shoal to pass the burning Line.

The Naiad and the Dryad met in billow and in spar;
The forest fought at Salamis, the grove at Trafalgar.
Old Tubalcain had sweated amain to forge the brand and ball;
But failed to frame the mighty hull that held enfortressed all.

Six thousand years had waited for our gallant tars to
      show
That iron was to ride the wave and timber sink below.
The waters bland that welcomed first the white man to our
      shore,
Columbus, of an iron world, the brave Buchanan bore.

Not gun for gun, but thirty to one, the odds he had to
      meet!
One craft, untried of wind or tide, to beard a haughty fleet!
Above her shattered relics now the billow break and pour;
But the glory of that wondrous day shall be hers fore ever-
      more.

See yonder speck on the mist afar, as dim as in a dream!
Anear it speeds, there are masts like reeds and a tossing plume
      of steam!
Fleet, fierce, and gaunt, with bows aslant, she dashes proudly
      on,
Whence and whither, her prey to gather, the foe shall learn
      anon.

Oh, broad and green is her hunting-park, and plentiful the
      game!
From the restless bay of old Biscay to the Carib' sea she
      came.
The catchers of the whale she caught; swift Ariel overhauled;
And made Hatteras know the hardest blow that ever a tar
      appalled.

She bears the name of a noble State, and sooth she bears it
      well.
To us she hath made it a word of pride, to the Northern ear
      a knell.
To the Puritan in the busy mart, the Puritan on his deck,
With "Alabama" visions start of ruin, woe, and wreck.

In vain his lubberly squadrons round her magic pathway
    swoop—
Admiral, captain, commodore, in gunboat, frigate, sloop.
Save to snatch a prize, or a foe chastise, as their feeble art she
    foils,
She will scorn a point from her course to veer, to baffle all their
    toils.

And bravely doth her sister-ship begin her young career.
Already hath her gentle name become a name of fear ;
The name that breathes of the orange-bloom, of soft lagoons
    that roll
Round the home of the Roman of the West -the unconquered
    Seminole.

Like the albatross and the tropic-bird, forever on the wing,
For them nor night nor breaking morn may peace nor shelter
    bring.
All dripping from the weary cruise or shattered from the
    fight,
No dear home-haven opes to them its arms of welcome bright.

Then side by side, in our love and pride, be our men of the
    land and sea ;
The fewer these, the sterner task, the greater their guerdon be !
The fairest wreaths of amaranth the fairest hands shall twine
For the brows of our preux chevaliers, the Bayards of the
    brine !

The " stars and bars " of our sturdy tars as gallantly shall
    wave
As long shall live in the storied page, or the spirit-stirring
    stave,
As hath the red cross of St. George or the raven-flag of
    Thor,
Or flag of the sea, whate'er it be, that ever unfurled to war.

Then flout full high to their parent sky those circled stars of ours,
Where'er the dark-hulled foeman floats, where'er his emblem
      towers!
Speak for the right, for the truth and light, from the gun's
      unmuzzled mouth,
And the fame of the Dane revive again, ye Vikings of the South!

CLOSE THE RANKS.

By JOHN L. O'SULLIVAN.

THE fell invader is before!
    Close the ranks! Close up the ranks!
We'll hunt his legions from our shore.
    Close the ranks! Close up the ranks!
Our wives, our children are behind,
Our mothers, sisters, dear and kind,
Their voices reach us on the wind,
    Close the ranks! Close up the ranks!

    Are we to bend to slavish yoke?
        Close the ranks! Close up the ranks!
    We'll bend when bends our Southern oak.
        Close the ranks! Close up the ranks!
    On with the line of serried steel,
    We all can die, we none can kneel
    To crouch beneath the Northern heel.
        Close the ranks! Close up the ranks!

We kneel to God, and God alone.
    Close the ranks! Close up the ranks!
One heart in all—all hearts as one.
    Close the ranks! Close up the ranks!
For home, for country, truth and right,
We stand or fall in freedom's fight:
In such a cause the right is might.
    Close the ranks! Close up the ranks!

We're here from every Southern home.
    Close the ranks! Close up the ranks!
Fond, weeping voices bade us come.
    Close the ranks! Close up the ranks!
The husband, brother, boy, and sire,
All burning with one holy fire—
Our country's love our only hire.
    Close the ranks! Close up the ranks!

    We cannot fail, we will not yield!
        Close the ranks! Close up the ranks!
    Our bosoms are our country's shield.
        Close the ranks! Close up the ranks!
    By Washington's immortal name,
        By Stonewall Jackson's kindred fame,
    Their souls, their deeds, their cause the same,
        Close the ranks! Close up the ranks!

By all we hope, by all we love,
    Close the ranks! Close up the ranks!
By home on earth, by heaven above,
    Close the ranks! Close up the ranks!
By all the tears, and heart's blood shed,
By all our hosts of martyred dead,
We'll conquer, or we'll share their bed.
    Close the ranks! Close up the ranks!

    The front may fall, the rear succeed,
        Close the ranks! Close up the ranks!
    We smile in triumph as we bleed,
        Close the ranks! Close up the ranks!
    Our Southern Cross above us waves,
    Long shall it bless the sacred graves.
    Of those who died, but were not slaves.
        Close the ranks! Close up the ranks!

21

THE RETURN.

THREE years!   I wonder if she'll know me?
       I limp a little, and I left one arm
At Petersburg; and I am grown as brown
       As the plump chestnuts on my little farm:
And I'm as shaggy as the chestnut burrs—
But ripe and sweet within, and wholly hers.

The darling! how I long to see her!
       My heart outruns this feeble soldier pace,
For I remember, after I had left,
       A little Charlie came to take my place,
Ah! how the laughing, three-year-old, brown eyes—
His mother's eyes—will stare with pleased surprise!

Surely, they will be at the corner watching!
       I sent them word that I should come to-night:
The birds all know it, for they crowd around,
       Twittering their welcome with a wild delight;
And that old robin, with a halting wing—
I saved her life, three years ago last spring.

Three years! perhaps I am but dreaming!
       For, like the pilgrim of the long ago,
I've tugged, a weary burden at my back,
       Through summer's heat and winter's blinding snow;
Till now, I reach my home, my darling's breast,
There I can roll my burden off, and rest.

       *   *   *   *   *

When morning came, the early rising sun
       Laid his light fingers on a soldier sleeping—
Where a soft covering of bright green grass
       Over two mounds was lightly creeping;
But waked him not: his was the rest eternal,
Where the brown eyes reflected love supernal.

OUR CHRISTMAS HYMN.

By JOHN DICKSON, M. D., of Charleston, S. C.

"GOOD-WILL and peace! peace and good-will!"
　　The burden of the Advent song,
What time the love-charmed waves grew still
　　To hearken to the shining throng;
The wondering shepherds heard the strain
　　Who watched by night the slumbering fleece,
The deep skies echoed the refrain,
　　"Peace and good-will, good-will and peace!"

And wise men hailed the promised sign,
　　And brought their birth-gifts from the East,
Dear to that Mother as the wine
　　That hallowed Cana's bridal feast;
But what to these are myrrh or gold,
　　And what Arabia's costliest gem,
Whose eyes the Child divine behold,
　　The blessed Babe of Bethlehem.

"Peace and good-will, good-will and peace!"
　　They sing, the bright ones overhead;
And scarce the jubilant anthems cease
　　Ere Judah wails her first-born dead;
And Rama's wild, despairing cry
　　Fills with great dread the shuddering coast,
And Rachel hath but one reply,
　　"Bring back, bring back my loved and lost."

So, down two thousand years of doom
　　That cry is borne on wailing winds,
But never star breaks through the gloom
　　No cradled peace the watcher finds;

And still the Herodian steel is driven,
   And breaking hearts make ceaseless moan,
And still the mute appeal to Heaven
   Man answers back with groan for groan.

     How shall we keep our Christmas tide?
       With that dread past, its wounds agape,
     Forever walking by our side,
       A fearful shade, an awful shape;
     Can any promise of the spring
       Make green the faded autumn leaf?
     Or who shall say that time will bring
       Fair fruit to him who sows but grief?

Wild bells! that shake the midnight air
   With those dear tones that custom loves,
You wake no sounds of laughter here,
   Nor mirth in all our silent groves;
On one broad waste, by hill or flood,
   Of ravaged lands your music falls,
And where the happy homestead stood
   The stars look down on roofless halls.

     At every board a vacant chair
       Fills with quick tears some tender eye,
     And at our maddest sports appear
       Those well-loved forms that will not die.
     We lift the glass, our hand is stayed—
       We jest, a spectre rises up—
     And weeping, though no word is said,
       We kiss and pass the silent cup.

And pledge the gallant friend who keeps
   His Christmas-eve on Malvern's height,
And him, our fair-haired boy, who sleeps
   Beneath Virginian snows to-night;

WINNIE DAVIS MONUMENT IN "HOLLYWOOD,"
RICHMOND, VIRGINIA

Erected by the "Daughters of the Confederacy."
From photograph made for this work by Edyth Carter Beveridge.

While, by the fire, she, musing, broods
  On all that was and might have been,
If Shiloh's dank and oozing woods
  Had never drunk that crimson stain.

      O happy Yules of buried years!
        Could ye but come in wonted guise,
      Sweet as love's earliest kiss appears,
        When looking back through wistful eyes,
      Would seem those chimes whose voices tell
        His birth-night with melodious burst,
      Who, sitting by Samaria's well,
        Quenched the lorn widow's life-long thirst.

Ah! yet I trust that all who weep,
  Somewhere, at last, will surely find
His rest, if through dark ways they keep
  The child-like faith, the prayerful mind:
And some far Christmas morn shall bring
  From human ills a sweet release
To loving hearts, while angels sing
  " Peace and good-will, good-will and peace!"

CHRISTMAS.

By HENRY TIMROD, of South Carolina.

How grace this hallowed day?
  Shall happy bells, from yonder ancient spire,
Send their glad greetings to each Christmas fire
  Round which the children play?

      Alas! for many a moon,
That tongueless tower hat cleaved the Sabbath air,
Mute as an obelisk of ice aglare
      Beneath an Arctic noon.

Shame to the foes that drown
Our psalms of worship with their impious drum,
The sweetest chimes in all the land lie dumb
    In some far rustic town.

There, let us think, they keep,
Of the dead Yules which here beside the sea
They've ushered in with old-world English glee,
    Some echoes in their sleep.

How shall we grace the day?
With feast and song, and dance, and antique sports,
And shout of happy children in the courts,
    And tales of ghost and fay?

Is there indeed a door
Where the old pastimes, with their lawful noise,
And all the merry wound of Christmas joys,
    Could enter as of yore.

Would not some pallid face
Look in upon the banquet, calling up
Dread shapes of battle in the wassail cup,
    And trouble all the place?

How could we bear the mirth,
While some loved reveller of a year ago
Keeps his mute Christmas now beneath the snow,
    In cold Virginian earth?

How shall we grace the day?
Ah! let the thought that on this holy morn
The Prince of Peace—the Prince of Peace was born,
    Employ us, while we pray!

Pray for the peace which long
Hath left this tortured land, and haply now
Holds its white court on some far mountain's brow,
    There hardly safe from wrong.

Let every sacred fane
Call its sad votaries to the shrine of God,
And, with the cloister and the tented sod,
 Join in one solemn strain!

With pomp of Roman form,
With the grave ritual brought from England's shore,
And with the simple faith which asks no more
 Than that the heart be warm.

He, who till time shall cease,
Shall watch that earth, where once, not all in vain,
He died to give us peace, will not disdain
 A prayer whose theme is—peace.

Perhaps, ere yet the spring
Hath died into the summer, over all
The land, the peace of His vast love shall fall
 Like some protecting wing.

Oh, ponder what it means!
Oh, turn the rapturous thought in every way!
Oh, give the vision and the fancy play,
 And shape the coming scenes!

Peace in the quiet dales,
Made rankly fertile by the blood of men;
Peace in the woodland, and the lonely glen,
 Peace in the peopled vales!

Peace in the crowded town,
Peace in a thousand fields of waving grain,
Peace in the highway and the flowery lane,
 Peace on the wind-swept down!

Peace on the furthest seas,
Peace in our sheltered bays and ample streams,
Peace wheresoe'er our starry garland gleams,
 And peace in every breeze!

Peace on the whirring marts,
Peace where the scholar thinks, the hunter roams,
Peace, God of Peace! peace, peace in all our homes,
And peace in all our hearts!

CHARLESTON.

By Miss E. B. Cheeseborough.

Proudly she stands by the crystal sea,
    With the fires of hate around her,
But a cordon of love as strong as fate,
    With adamant links surround her,
Let them hurl their bolts through the azure sky,
    And death-bearing missiles send her,
She finds in our God a mighty shield,
    And in Heaven a sure defender.

Her past is a page of glory bright,
    Her present a blaze of splendor,
You may turn o'er the leaves of the jewell'd tome,
    You'll not find the word surrender;
For sooner than lay down her trusty arms,
    She'd build her own funeral pyre,
And the flames that give her a martyr's fate
    Will kindle her glory higher.

How the demons glare as they see her stand
    In majestic pride serenely,
And gnash with the impotent rage of hate,
    Creeping up slowly, meanly;
While she cries, " Come forth from your covered dens.
    All your hireling legions send me,
I'll bare my breast to a million swords,
    Whilst God and my sons defend me."

Oh, brave old town, o'er thy sacred form
　　Whilst the fiery rain is sweeping,
May He whose love is an armor strong
　　Embrace thee in tender keeping;
And when the red war-cloud has rolled away,
　　Anoint thee with holy chrism,
And sanctified, chastened, regenerate, true,
　　Thou surviv'st this fierce baptism.

GATHERING SONG.

AIR—" Bonnie Blue Flag."

BY ANNIE CHAMBERS KETCHUM.

COME, brothers! rally for the right!
　　The bravest of the brave
Sends forth her ringing battle-cry
　　Beside the Atlantic wave!
She leads the way in honor's path!
　　Come, brothers, near and far,
Come, rally 'round the Bonnie Blue Flag
　　That bears a single star!

　　　　We've borne the Yankee trickery,
　　　　　　The Yankee gibe and sneer,
　　　　Till Yankee insolence and pride
　　　　　　Know neither shame nor fear;
　　　　But ready now with shot and steel
　　　　　　Their brazen front to mar,
　　　　We hoist aloft the Bonnie Blue Flag
　　　　　　That bears a single star!

Now Georgia marches to the front,
　　And close beside her come
Her sisters by the Mexique Sea,
　　With pealing trump and drum!

Till, answering back from hill and glen
    The rallying cry afar,
A Nation hoists the Bonnie Blue Flag
    That bears a single star !

    By every stone in Charleston Bay,
      By each beleaguered town,
    We swear to rest not, night nor day,
      But hunt the tyrants down !
    Till, bathed in valor's holy blood
      The gazing world afar
    Shall greet with shouts the Bonnie Blue Flag
      That bears the cross and star !

THE BAND IN THE PINES.
(Heard after Pelham Died.)
By John Esten Cooke.

OH, band in the pine-wood, cease!
    Cease with your splendid call ;
The living are brave and noble,
    But the dead were bravest of all !

    They throng to the martial summons,
      To the loud, triumphant strain ;
    And the dear bright eyes of long dead friends
      Come to the heart again !

They come with the ringing bugle,
    And the deep drum's mellow roar ;
Till the soul is faint with longing
    For the hands we clasp no more !

    Oh, band in the pine-wood cease !
      Or the heart will melt in tears,
    For the gallant eyes and the smiling lips,
      And the voices of old years !

CAPTAIN MAFFIT'S BALLAD OF THE SEA.

Though winds are high and skies are dark,
 And the stars scarce show us a meteor spark ;
Yet buoyantly bounds our gallant barque,
 Through billows that flash in a sea of blue ;
We are coursing free, like the Viking shark,
 And our prey, like him, pursue !

At each plunge of our prow we bare the graves,
Where, heedless of roar among winds and waves,
The dead have slept in their ocean caves,
 Never once dreaming—as if no more
They hear, though the Storm-God ramps and raves
 From the deeps to the rock-bound shore.

Brave sailors were they in the ancient times,
Heroes or pirates—men of all climes,
That had never an ear for the Sabbath chimes,
 Never once called on the priest to be shriven ;
They died with the courage that still sublimes,
 And, haply, may fit for Heaven.

Never once asking the when or why,
But ready, all hours, to battle and die,
They went into fight with a terrible cry,
 Counting no odds, and, victors or slain,
Meeting fortune or fate with an equal eye,
 Defiant of death and pain.

Dread are the tales of the wondrous deep,
And well do the billows their secrets keep,
And sound should those savage old sailors sleep,
 If sleep they may after such a life ;
Where every dark passion, alert and aleap,
 Made slumber itself a strife

What voices of horror, through storm and surge,
Sang in the perishing ear its dirge,
As, raging and reading, o'er Hell's black verge,
    Each howling soul sank to its doom ;
And what thunder-tones from the deeps emerge,
    As yawns for its prey the tomb !

We plough the same seas which the rovers trod,
But with better faith in the saving God,
And bear aloft and carry abroad
    The starry cross, our sacred sign,
Which, never yet sullied by crime or fraud,
    Makes light o'er the midnight brine.

And we rove not now on a lawless quest,
With passions foul in the hero's breast,
Moved by no greed at the fiend's behest,
    Gloating in lust o'er a bloody prey ;
But from tyrant robber the spoil to wrest,
    And tear down his despot sway !

'Gainst the spawn of Europe, and all the lands,
British and German—Norway's sands,
Dutchland and Irish—the hireling bands
    Bought for butchery—recking no rede,
But, flocking like vultures, with felon hands,
    To fatten the rage of greed.

With scath they traverse both land and sea,
And with sacred wrath we must make them flee ;
Making the path of the nations free,
    And planting peace in the heart of strife ;
In the star of the cross, our liberty
    Brings light to the world, and life !

Paid Out by
Capt. Wm. E. Duncan

D. M. Z. Brigade
This 1st April 1863.

CONFEDERATE NOTE WITH SOLDIER'S ENDORSEMENT

(See Poem.)

Let Christendom cower 'neath Stripes and Stars
Cloaking her shame under legal bars,
Not too moral for traffic, but shirking wars,
  While the Southern cross, floating topmast high,
Though torn, perchance, by a thousand scars,
  Shall light up the midnight sky !

THE PRIDE OF BATTERY B.

Sᴏᴜᴛʜ Mountain towering on our right,
  Far off the river lay,
And over on the wooded height
  We held their lines at bay.

  At last the muttering guns were still,
    The day died slow and wan ;
  At last the gunners' pipes did fill,
    The sergeant's yarns began.

When, as the wind a moment blew
  Aside the fragrant flood
Our brierwoods raised, within our view
  A little maiden stood.

  A tiny tot of six or seven,
    From fireside fresh she seemed
  (Of such a little one in heaven
    One soldier often dreamed).

And as we stared, her little hand
  Went to her curly head
In grave salute. " And who are you ? "
  At length the sergeant said.

" And where's your home? " He growled again,
    She lisped out, " Who is me?
Why, don't you know? I'm little Jane,
    The pride of Battery B.

    " My home? Why, that was burned away,
        And Pa and Ma are dead,
    And so I ride the guns all day,
        Along with Sergeant Ned.

" And I've a drum that's not a toy,
    A cap with feathers, too,
And I march beside the drummer boy
    On Sundays at review.

    " But now, our 'bacca's all give out,
        The men can't have their smoke.
    And so they're cross. Why, even Ned
        Won't play with me and joke!

" And the big colonel said to-day—
    I hate to hear him swear—·
He'd give a leg for a good pipe
    Like the Yank had over there.

    " And so I thought, when beat the drum,
        And the big guns were still,
    I'd creep beneath the tent and come
        Down here across the hill,

" And beg, good Master Yankee men,
    You give me some Lone Jack,
Please do; when we get some again
    I'll surely bring it back.

    " Indeed! I will, for Ned, says he,
        If I do what I say
    I'll be a general yet, maybe,
        And ride a prancing bay.'

We brimmed her tiny apron o'er;
    You should have heard her laugh
And each man from his scanty store
    Shook out a generous half!

        To kiss the little mouth, stooped down
            A score of grimy men,
        Until the sergeant's husky voice
            Said, "'Tention, squad!" and then

We gave her escort, till good-night
    The pretty waif we bid,
And watched her toddle out ot sight
    Or else 'twas tears that hid

        Her tiny form—nor turned about
            A man, not spoke a word,
        Till after awhile a far, hoarse shout
            Upon the wind we heard.

We sent it back, then cast sad eyes
    Upon the scene around ;
A baby's hand had touched the ties
    That brothers once had bound.

        That's all—save when the dawn awoke
            Again the work of hell,
        And through the sullen clouds of smoke
            The screaming missiles fell.

Our general often rubbed his glass
    And marveled much to see
Not a single shell that whole day fell
    In the camp of Battery B.

THE DEAD MAN THAT LAY AT MY DOOR.

BY A. L. MOORE.

In June, 1863, a Kentucky brigade was encamped at Jackson, Miss. While there the writer of the following lines was confined with fever in what was formerly the Dixon House, then temporarily converted into a hospital under the charge of the Sisters of Mercy. The place being destitute of the necessary equipments, those who died over night were left in the hallway to await the morning for burial.

At last through the casement is streaming
 The soft mellow light of the dawn.
And night, with its visions and dreaming,
 Thank Heaven ! forever is flown.
Ah ! fearful the night was to me
 As, noiseless, I crept o'er the floor,
With my eyes closed fast, lest I see
 The dead man that lay at my door.

The wind o'er the chimney top sighing,
 Wailed fitfully out on the night,
Like the wail of some lost spirit flying
 Amid the dread regions of fright.
It seemed that all nature, in sorrow,
 Did the fate of my comrade deplore,
And with howlings of pity awaited the morrow,
 For the dead man that lay at my door.

The lamp on the mantel was burning,
 And fitfully lighted the room ;
The shadows were dancing and turning
 Like spectres that peopled the gloom.
In vain did I strive to forget me
 In events that had passed long before,
But the demon of dread would not let me—
 The dead man that lay at my door.

The rats, in the wainscot at work,
　　Their stores were moving about,
Whose rattling noise seemed the knock
　　Of some wandering spirit without.
It was in vain I strove to withstand
　　The dread impression it bore—
That it came from the cold, withered hand
　　Of the dead man that lay at my door.

　　　Naught but the deep breathing around
　　　　Betrayed that the living was near,
　　And they in their slumbers profound,
　　　　Like the dead lay quietly there.
　　'Twas fruitless to try to awake them—
　　　　Their names did I call o'er and o'er:
　　As well might I strive to awaken
　　　　The dead man that lay at my door.

I can bear it no longer!　To see
　　This sentinel grim at my door,
A feeling too potent for me
　　To withstand led me out on the floor,
And there, on his lone, little bed,
　　So still, so calm and so hoar,
Lay the stark, frozen form of the dead—
　　This dead man that lay at my door.

　　　A hand on my shoulder was laid,
　　　　A voice in my ear, low and kind,
　　In tones of sweet sympathy said:
　　　　" Come, get thee to bed, my poor friend
　　I pointed my finger, and she,
　　　　The direction her eyes glancing o'er,
　　Started and screamed, there to see
　　　　This dead man that lay at my door.

22

On my couch again am I lain,
  And in whispers they bade me forget
The visions so freighted with pain,
  That my mind in its weakness beset.
But their voices were husky and drear,
  And wild was the look that they wore;
They, too, felt a dread and a fear;
  Of the dead man that lay at my door.

  But the sun in my window shines warm,
    And with night have my tears passed away,
  And broken's the spell and alarm,
    For none fear the dead during day.
  I have heard them ! They've nailed down the lid,
    And slowly and sadly they bore
  Away—off! forever away—
    The dead man that lay at my door.

MOONSTRUCK.

BY MORTON BRYAN WHARTON, D. D.

I LOOKED and the stars like diamonds shone,
  Till the moon's pale mantle was over them thrown,
And she then appeared as the queen of the night,
Though every one knew that she borrowed her light.

  And thus in the lower human sphere,
  I have seen great galaxies disappear,
  The geniuses of the land decline,
  And fools with reflected glory shine.

The Senate was once a shaft of light
And it gilded the land with effulgence bright,
But its Websters, Clays, Calhouns are gone,
And political hucksters mount the throne.

The Church once gleamed a luminous band,
Obedient all, to the Lord's command,
But the good and pure to the rear repair,
And the vile her holy vestments wear.

The Pulpit once o'er the nations flamed,
And God's pure gospel alone proclaimed,
But the clown and jester entered in,
And it lost its power o'er the world of sin.

Society, too, was refined and pure,
And woman her modest garments wore,
But cards, and wine, and dances gay,
Have banished the light of home away.

The nation itself begins to fail,
The stars on its banner are dead and pale,
The dream of the fathers has faded soon,
And all for the light of the glittering moon !

O what is this moon that with baleful light
Obscureth the great and pure from sight,
That draweth the tides of life awry,
And crazeth the souls that are struck thereby ?

The answer from out the sky is rolled
In thunder tones—"it is gold, gold, gold ! "
A deceptive orb, and of sordid worth,
But the stars all fade when it blazes forth !

O moon, withdraw thy arrogant face,
O stars, come forth from your hiding place,
Shine on till the glorious god of day,
Shall banish the mists of the land away !

THE RIGHT ABOVE THE WRONG.

By John W. Overall.

In other days our fathers' love was loyal, full, and free,
  For those they left behind them in the Island of the Sea ;
They fought the battles of King George, and toasted him in
    song,
For then the Right kept proudly down the tyranny of the
    Wrong.

But when the King's weak, willing slaves laid tax upon the tea,
The Western men rose up and braved the Island of the Sea ;
And swore a fearful oath to God, those men of iron might,
That in the end the Wrong should die, and up should go the
    Right.

The King sent over hireling hosts—the Briton, Hessian, Scot—
And swore in turn those Western men, when captured, should
    be shot ;
While Chatham spoke with earnest tongue against the hireling
    throng,
And mournfully saw the Right go down, and place given to
    the Wrong.

But God was on the righteous side, and Gideon's sword was out,
With clash of steel, and rattling drum, and freeman's thunder-
    shout ;
And crimson torrents drenched the land through that long,
    stormy fight,
But in the end, hurrah ! the Wrong was beaten by the Right !

And when again the foeman came from out the Northern Sea,
To desolate our smiling land and subjugate the free,
Our fathers rushed to drive them back, with rifles keen and
    long,
And swore a mighty oath, the Right should subjugate the
    Wrong.

THE WHITE HOUSE OF THE CONFEDERACY, RICHMOND, VIRGINIA

President Jefferson Davis lived in this imposing building during the war. The large grounds attached to the house were beautifully laid out and adorned with statuary, flowers and fountains. (See description elsewhere.)

And while the world was looking on, the strife uncertain grew,
But soon aloft arose our stars amid a field of blue ;
For Jackson fought on red Chalmette, and won the glorious
  fight,
And then the Wrong went down, hurrah ! and triumph
  crowned the Right !

The day has come again, when men who love the beauteous
  South,
To speak, if needs be, for the Right, though by the cannon's
  mouth ;
For foes accursed of God and man, with lying speech and song,
Would bind, imprison, hang the Right, and defy the Wrong.

But canting knave of pen and sword, nor sanctimonious fool,
Shall never win this Southern land, to cripple, bind, and rule ;
We'll muster on each bloody plain, thick as the stars of night,
And, through the help of God, the Wrong shall perish by the
  Right.

CARMEN TRIUMPHALE.

By Henry Timrod.

Go forth and bid the land rejoice,
  Yet not too gladly, oh my song !
  Breathe softly, as if mirth would wrong
The solemn rapture of thy voice.

  Be nothing lightly done or said
    This happy day ! Our joy should flow
    Accordant with the lofty woe
  That wails above the noble dead.

  Let him whose brow and breast were calm
    While yet the battle lay with God,
    Look down upon the crimson sod
  And gravely wear his mournful palm ;

And him, whose heart still weak from fear
    Beats all too gayly for the time,
    Know that intemperate glee is crime
While one dead hero claims a tear.

    Yet go thou forth, my song ! and thrill,
        With sober joy, the troubled days ;
        A nation's hymn of grateful praise
    May not be hushed for private ill.

Our foes are fallen !   Flash, ye wires !
    The mighty tidings far and nigh !
    Ye cities ! write them on the sky
In purple and in emerald fires !

    They came with many a haughty boast ;
        Their threats were heard on every breeze ;
        They darkened half the neighboring seas,
    And swooped like vultures on the coast.

False recreants on all knightly strife,
    Their way was wet with woman's tears ;
    Behind them flamed the toil of years,
And bloodshed stained the sheaves of life.

    They fought as tyrants fought, or slaves ;
        God gave the dastards to our hands ;
        Their bones are bleaching on the sands,
    Or smouldering slow in shallow graves.

What though we hear about our path
    The heavens with howls of vengeance rent ;
    The venom of their hate is spent ;
We need not heed their fangless wrath.

    Meantime the stream we strove to chain
        Now drinks a thousand springs, and sweeps,
        With broadening breast, and mightier deeps,
    And rushes onward to the main ;

While down the swelling current glides
    Our ship of state before the blast,
With streamers poured from every mast,
Her thunders roaring from her sides.

        Lord ! bid the frenzied tempest cease,
            Hang out thy rainbow on the sea !
            Laugh round her, waves ! in silver glee,
        And speed her to the ports of peace !

ODE—"OUR CITY BY THE SEA."

By W. Gilmore Simms.

Charleston, South Carolina, might well be called the Rome of the Early
Confederacy, for from that little city went forth the first influences that
startled our great Government and shocked the world. She has ever been
noted for her splendid harbor, and is the Queen City of the Palmetto State.

Our city by the sea,
    As the rebel city known,
With a soul and spirit free
    As the waves that make her zone,
Stands in wait for the fate
From the angry arm of hate ;
But she nothing fears the terror of his blow ;
She hath garrisoned her walls,
And for every son that falls,
She will spread a thousand palls
    For the foe !

        Lo ! rising at his side,
            As if emulous to share
        His old historic pride,
            The vast form of Sumter there !
        Girt by waves, which
        Do ye quail, as on yon little islet
        They have planted the feet that defile it ?

Make its sands pure of taint, by the stroke of the sword,
And by torrents of blood in red sacrifice pour'd !
Doubts are traitors, if once they persuade you to fear,
That the foe, in his foothold, is safe from your spear !
When the foot of pollution is set on your shores,
What sinew and soul should be stronger than yours?
By the fame—by the same—of your sires.

Set on, though each freeman expires ;
Better fall, grappling fast with the foe, to their graves,
Than groan in your fetters, the slaves of your slaves.

The voice of your loud exultation
Hath rung, like a trump, through the nation,
How loudly, how proudly, of deeds to be done,
The blood of the sire in the veins of the son !
Old Moultrie and Sumter still keep at your gates,
And the foe in his foothold as patiently waits.
He asks, with a taunt, by your patience made bold,
If the hot spur of Percy grows suddenly cold—
Makes merry with boasts of your city his own,
And the Chivalry fled, ere his trumpet is blown ;
Upon them, O sons of the mighty of yore,
And fatten the sands with their Sodomite gore !

Where's the dastard that cowers and falters
In the sight of his hearthstones and altars ?
With the faith of the free in the God of the brave,
Go forth ; ye are mighty to conquer and save !
By the blue Heaven shining above ye,
By the pure-hearted thousands that love ye,
Ye are armed with a might to prevail in the fight,
And an ægis to shield and a weapon to smite !
Then fail not, and quail not ; the foe shall prevail not :
With the faith and the will, ye shall conquer him still.
To the knife—with the knife, Carolinians,
For your homes, and your sacred dominions.

THE COAT OF FADED GRAY.

BY G. W. HARRIS.

A LOW hut rests in Lookout's shade,
  As rots its moss-grown roof away,
While sundown's glories softly fade,
  Closing another weary day.
The battle's din is heard no more,
    No more the hunted stand at bay,
The breezes through the lowly door
    Swing mute a coat of faded gray,
      A tattered relic of the fray,
      A threadbare coat of faded gray.

'Tis hanging on the rough log wall,
    Near to the foot of a widow's bed,
By a white plume and well-worn shawl—
    His gift the happy morn they wed;
By the wee slip their dead child wore—
    The one they gave the name of May:
By her rag doll and pinafore—
    By right 'tis here that coat of gray
      A red-fleck'd relic of the fray,
      An armless coat of faded gray.

Her all of life now drapes that wall;
    But poor and patient, still she waits
On God's good time to gently call
    Her, too, within the jewell'd gates;
And all she craves is here to die—
    To part from these and pass away,
To join her love eternally
    That wore that—the coat of gray,
      The shell-torn relic of the fray
      Her soldier's coat of faded gray.

" 'TWAS JUST LIKE JIM."

By L. W. Canady.

'Twas just like Jim, in his schoolboy days,
    To protect the lad who threw
The paper wad at the big blackboard,
    On the wall, with aim so true ;
'Twas just like Jim to say, " 'Twas I,"
    And the master's wrath defy—
To shift the blame from a weaker lad,
    Jim faltered not at a lie.

'Twas just like Jim, when, in sixty-one,
    There came the appeal to arms,
And the pleading voice of Peace was hushed
    By War and his rude alarms ;
'Twas just like Jim to march away—
    Tap of drum and music gay—
Looking so handsome, so brave and true,
    In his suit of homespun gray.

*   *   *   *   *

'Twas just like Jim, that April day,*
When the broken and sullen lines of gray
Turned anon like a stag at bay,
Rallied and fought, then filed away ;
'Twas just like Jim, I say ;
    To be the last
On guard at the bridge where his comrades passed.
Firm and motionless, gaunt and grim,
" *No surrender for me !* " said Jim.
Alone he stood, close by the bridge,
When Sheridan's troops rode over the ridge.

* The day before the surrender of Lee.

A "Yankee shout" a "Rebel yell"
Three troopers from their saddles fell.
Fewer the living moments grew
For Jim, but his *aim* was never more true;
And when the foe the bridge had gained
Not a ball in his cartridge box remained;
But never a sabre that squadron drew—
They rode him down, those lines of blue!

*   *   *   *   *

At Appomattox they called the roll,
But Jim answered not. His wayward soul
Had gone to God, to be judged by *Him*,
No surrender! Ah! hat was like *Jim*.

THE DYING SOLDIER BOY.

By A. B. Cunningham of Louisiana.

Air—"Maid of M terey."

Upon Manassa's bloody plain a s ldier boy lay dying!
  The gentle winds above his rm, in softest tones were
    sighing;
The god of day had slowly sunk be eath the verge of day,
And the silver moon was gliding al ve the Milky Way.

The stars were shining brightly, a d the sky was calm and
    blue;
Oh! what a beautiful scene was this for human eyes to
    view;
The river rolled in splendor, and the wavelets danc'd around
But the banks were strewed with dead men, and gory was the
    ground.

But the hero boy was dying, and his thoughts were very deep,
For the death-wound in his young side was wafting him to sleep.
He thought of home and kindred away on a distant shore,
All of whom he must relinquish, and never see them more.

And as the breeze passed by, in whispers o'er the dead,
Sweet memories of olden days came rushing to his head ;
But his mind was weak and deaden'd, so he turned over
	where he lay,
As the Death Angel flitted by, and called his soul away !

FIRST CONFEDERATE FLAG.

The first flag raised as an emhlem of confederacy by South Carolina,
the mother State in the afterward named "Confederate States of America,"
during the Civil War, was eight feet long by six feet broad. The body of
it was turkey red, and the immense star and crescent in the upper left-hand
corner were of white. It was sewed together by the ladies of Charleston,
S. C., on the eve of that State's declaration of secession, December, 1860.
and was hoisted the next morning over the Charleston custom house;
Shortly afterward, the "Dixie," a small privateer and blockade runner,
started on its depredations, and as the young confederacy had as yet
adopted no official banner, the Charleston custom house flag was presented
as its colors. In the spring of 1863 the "Dixie" was captured by the United
States steamer "Keystone State."—*The Confederate Veteran.*

LAST MEETING OF GENERALS LEE AND "STONEWALL" JACKSON
AT THE BATTLE OF CHANCELLORSVILLE, VA.

From the original and celebrated painting by Julio in the Arsenal of the Washington
Artillery, New Orleans, La.   Size, 10 x 12 feet.   Value, $5,000.

"THE ENEMY SHALL NEVER REACH YOUR CITY."

Andrew Jackson's Address to the People of New Orleans.

In the engagement of Fort Sumter with the enemy's fleet, April 7, 1861, the spray thrown above the walls by their enormous missiles was formed into a beautiful sunbow, seeing which, General Ripley, with the piety of Constantine, exclaimed : " *In hoc signo vinces !* "

NEVER, while such as ye are in the breach,
    Oh ! brothers, sons, and Southrons—never ! never !
Shall the foul enemy your city reach !
For souls and hearts are eager with endeavor ;
And God's own sanction on your cause, makes holy
Each arm that strikes for home, however lowly !—
And ye shall conquer by the rolling deep !
And ye shall conquer on the embattled steep !—
And ye shall see Leviathan go down
A hundred fathoms, with a horrible cry
Of drowning wretches, in their agony—
While Slaughter wades in gore along the sands,
And Terror flies with pleading, outstretched hands,
All speechless, but with glassy-staring eyes—
Flying to Fate—and fated as he flies ;
That gives him, when the shark has fed, a grave ɪ

Thus saith the Lord of Battles : " Shall it be,
That this great city, planted by the sea,
With threescore thousand souls—with fanes and spires
Reared by a race of unexampled sires—
That I have watched, now twice a hundred years,
Nursed through long infancy of hopes and fears,
Baptized in blood at seasons, oft in tears ;
Purged with the storm and fire, and bade to grow
To greatness, with a progress firm but slow—
That being the grand condition of duration—
Until it spreads into the mighty nation !

And shall the usurper, insolent of power,
O'erwhelm it with swift ruin in an hour!
And hurl his bolts, and with a dominant will,
Say to its mighty heart—" Crouch, and be still!
My foot is on your neck! I am your Fate!
Can speak your doom, and make you desolate!

" No! He shall know—I am the Lord of war;
And all his mighty hosts but pigmies are!
His hellish engines, wrought for human woe,
His arts and vile inventions, and his power,
My arm shall bring to ruin, swift and low!
Even now my bolts are aimed, my storm-clouds lower,
And I will arm my people with a faith,
Shall make them free of fear, and free of scaith;
And they shall bear from me a smiting sword,
Edged with keen lightning, at whose stroke is poured
A torrent of destruction and swift wrath,
Sweeping the insolent legions from their path!
The usurper shall be taught that none shall take
The right to punish and avenge from me;
And I will guard my City by the Sea,
And save its people for their fathers' sake!"

Selah!—Oh! brothers, sons, and Southrons, rise;
To prayer: and lo! the wonder in the skies!
The sunbow spans your towers, even while the foe
Hurls his fell bolt, and rains his iron blow.
Toss'd by his shafts, the spray above yon height
God's smile hath turned into a golden light;
Orange and purple-golden! In that sign
Find ye fit promise for that voice divine!
Hark! 'tis the thunder! Through the murky air,
The solemn roll goes echoing far and near!
Go forth, and unafraid! His shield is yours!
And the great spirits of your earlier day—

Your fathers, hovering round your sacred shores—
Will guard your bosoms through the unequal fray!
Hark to their voices, issuing through the gloom:
" The cruel hosts that haunt you, march to doom:
Give them the vulture's rites—a naked tomb!
And, while ye bravely smite, with fierce endeavor,
The foe shall reach your city—never! never!"

A FAREWELL TO POPE.

By JOHN R. THOMPSON, of Virginia.

In the " Reminiscences " introducing this volume I have said that some of these poems would be found a little rugged in character, so to speak. The following is a case in point. Let it be remembered that it was in the midst of the strife when harsh things were not only being said, but were being shot from musket and cannon at the very hearts of the two opposing sections. It is all over now. Let us read it, and sympathize with the wild spirit of those times.

" HATS off " in the crowd, " Present arms " in the line!
  Let the standards all bow, and the sabres incline—
Roll, drums, the Rogue's March, while the conqueror goes,
Whose eyes have seen only " the backs of his foes "
Through a thicket of laurel, a whirlwind of cheers,
His vanishing form from our gaze disappears;
Henceforth with the savage Dacotahs to cope,
Abiit, evasit, erupit—John Pope.

He came out of the West, like the young Lochinvar,
Compeller of fate and controller of war,
Videre et vincere, simply to see,
And straightway to conquer Hill, Jackson and Lee;
And old Abe at the White House, like Kilmansegg pere,
With a monkeyish grin and beatified air,
" Seemed washing his hands with invisible soap,"
As with eager attention he listened to Pope.

He came, and the poultry was swept by his sword.
Spoons, liquors, and furniture went by the board ;
He saw—at a distance, the rebels appear,
Pest, pilferer, puppy, pretender, poltroon ;
And "rode to the front," which strangely the rear ;
He conquered—truth, decency, honor full soon,
And was fain from the scene of his triumphs to slope,
Sure there never was fortunate hero like Pope.

He has left us his shining example to note,
And Stuart has captured his uniform coat ;
But 'tis puzzling enough, as his deeds we recall,
To tell on whose shoulders his mantle should fall ;
While many may claim to deserve it, at least,
From Hunter, the Hound, down to Butler, the Beast,
None else, we can say, without risking the trope,
But himself can be parallel ever to Pope.

Like his namesake, the poet, of genius and fire,
He gives new expression and force to the lyre ;
But in one little matter they differ, the two,
And differ, indeed, very widely, 'tis true—
While his verses gave great Alexander his fame,
'Tis our hero's reverses accomplish the same ;
And fate may decree that the end of a rope
Shall award yet his highest position to Pope.

Motto and Emblem of U. D. C.

WAR-WAVES.

By Catherine Gendron Poyas, of Charleston.

What are the war-waves saying,
    As they compass us around?
The dark, ensanguined billows,
    With their deep and dirge-like sound?
Do they murmur of submission;
    Do they call on us to bow
Our necks to the foe triumphant
    Who is riding o'er us now?

        Never!   No sound submissive
            Comes from those waves sublime,
        Or the low, mysterious voices
            Attuned to their solemn chime!
        For the hearts of our noble martyrs
            Are the springs of its rich supply;
        And those deeply mystic murmurs
            Echo their dying cry!

They bid us uplift our banner
Once more in the name of God;
And press to the goal of Freedom
    By the paths our Fathers trod:
They passed o'er their dying brothers;
    From their pale lips caught the sigh—
The *flame* of their hearts heroic,
    From the flash of each closing eye!

        Up! Up! for the time is pressing,
            The red waves close around;—
        They will lift us on their billows
            If our hearts are faithful found!

23

They will lift us high—exultant,
    And the craven world shall see
The Ark of a ransomed people
    Afloat on the crimson sea !

        Afloat, with her glorious banner—
            The cross on its field of red,
        Its stars and its white folds waving
            In triumph at her head ;
        Emblem of all that's sacred
            Heralding Faith to view ;
        Type of unblemished honor ;
            Symbol of all that's true !

Then what can those waves be singing
    But an anthem grand, sublime,
As they bear for our martyred heroes
    A wail to the coast of Time ?
What else as they roll majestic
    To the far-off shadowy shore,
To join the eternal chorus
    When Time shall be no more !

TO A DEJECTED FRIEND.

By Morton Bryan Wharton, D. D.

WHAT though thy way is often dark,
    And billows loudly round thee roar,
Be firm, droop not ; thy gallant bark
    Unharmed shall reach the destined shore.

    There's much in life that's left thee still ;
        The good outweighs the evil here ;
    The less thou dwell'st upon the ill
        The more will happiness appear.

For all there gleams a promise sure;
 Who thinks his lot in misery cast
Should patient wait, in faith endure,
 The blessing rich will come at last.

  And be not overmuch concerned
   When passions wild thy peace annoy;
  I've long ago this lesson learned,
   "No gold's without its base alloy."

Should Slander's voice around thee ring,
 Pass on, stoop not to make reply;
Thus pluck the venom from the sting,
 And leave the crawling worm to die.

  Thy virtues, like the rock-bound coast
   That guards us from the treacherous main,
  Will dash the waves by Envy tossed
   Back on the powerless flood again.

ODE—"SHELL THE OLD CITY! SHELL!"

By W. Gilmore Simms.

Shell the old city! shell!
 Ye myrmidons of Hell,
To serve your master well,
 With hellish arts!
Hurl down, with bolt and fire,
The grand old shrines, the spire;
But know, your demon ire
 Subdues no hearts!

  There, we defy ye still,
  With sworn and resolute will;
  Courage ye cannot kill
   While we have breath!

Stone walls your bolts may break,
But, ere our souls ye shake,
Of the whole land we'll make
    One realm of death!

        Dear are our homes! our eyes
        Weep at their sacrifice;
        And, with each bolt that flies,
            Each roof that falls,
        The pang extorts the tear,
        That things so precious, dear
        To memory, love, and care,
            Sink with our walls.

Trophies of ancient time,
When, with great souls, sublime,
Opposing force and crime,
    Our fathers fought;
Relics of golden hours,
When, for our shrines and bowers,
Genius, with magic powers,
    Her triumphs wrought!

        Each Sabbath-hallowed dome,
        Each ancient family home,
        The dear old southwest room,
            All trellised round;
        Where gay, bright summer vines,
        Linked in fantastic twines
        With the sun's blazing lines,
            Rubied the ground!

Homes, sacred to the past,
Which bore the hostile blast,
Though Spain, France, Britain cast
    Their shot and shell!

MONUMENT TO THE CONFEDERATE DEAD, ATLANTA, GEORGIA

Tombs of the mighty dead,
That in our battles bled,
When on our infant head
    Those furies fell!

        Halls which the foreign guest
        Found of each charm possessed,
        With cheer unstinted blessed,
            And noblest grace ;
        Where, drawing to her side
        The stranger, far and wide,
        Frank courtesy took pride
            To give him place !

The shaded walks—the bowers
Where, through long summer hours,
Young Love first proved his powers
    To win the prize ;
Where every tree has heard
Some vows of love preferred,
And, with his leaves unstirred,
    Watch'd lips and eyes.

        Gardens of tropic blooms,
        That, through the shaded rooms,
        Sent Orient-winged perfumes
            With dusk and dawn ;
        The grand old laurel, tall,
        As sovereign over all,
        And, from the porch and hall,
            The verdant lawn.

Oh ! when we think of these
Old homes, ancestral trees ;
Where, in the sun and breeze,
    At morn and even,

Was to enjoy the play
Of hearts at holiday,
And find, in blooms of May,
    Foretaste ot Heaven!

    Where, as we cast our eyes
    On things of precious prize,
    Trophies of good and wise,
        Grand, noble, brave;
    And think of these, so late
    Sacred to soul and state,
    Doomed, as the wreck of fate,
        By fiend and slave!

The inevitable pain,
Coursing through blood and brain,
Drives forth like winter rain,
    The bitter tear!
We cannot help but weep,
From depth of hearts that keep
The memories, dread and deep,
    To vengeance dear!

    Aye, for each tear we shed,
    There shall be torrents red,
    Not from the eye-founts fed,
        But from the veins!
    Bloody shall be the sweat,
    Fiends, felons, that shall yet
    Pay retribution's debt,
        In torture's pains!

Our tears shall naught abate,
Of what we owe to hate—
To the avenging fate—
    To earth and Heaven!

And, soon or late, the hour
Shall bring th' atoning power,
When, through the clouds that lower,
    The storm-bolt's driven !

    Shell the old city—shell !
    But, with each roof-tree's knell,
    Vows deep of vengeance fell,
        Fire soul and eye !
    With every tear that falls
    Above our stricken walls
    Each heart more fiercely calls,
        " Avenge, or die ! "

THE LINES AROUND PETERSBURG.

By Samuel Davis, of North Carolina.

    " Such a sleep they sleep,
    The men I loved ! "
        —Tennyson.

OH, silence, silence ! now, when night is near,
    And I am left alone,
Thou art so strange, so sad reposing here—
    And all so changed hath grown,
Where all was once exuberant with life
Through day and night, in deep and deadly strife.

    If I must weep, oh, tell me, is there not
    Some plaintive story breathed into mine ear
    By spirit-whispers from the voiceless sphere,
        Haunting this awful spot ?
    To my sad soul, more mutely eloquent
    Than words of fame on sculptured monument
    Outspeaks yon crumbling parapet, where lies

The broken gun, the idly rusting ball,
Mute tokens of an ill-starred enterprise !
Rude altars reared for costly sacrifice !
Vast work of hero-hands left in thy fall !

Where are they now, that fearless brotherhood,
        Who marshalled here,
        That fearful year,
In pain and peril, yet undaunted stood,—
Though Death rode fiercest on the battle-storm
And earth lay strewn with many a glorious form ?
Where are they now, who, when the strife was done,
With kindly greeting 'round the camp-fire met,—
And made an hour of mirth, from triumphs won,
Repay the day's stern toil, where the slow sun had set ?

Where are they ?—
Let the nameless grave declare,—
In strange unwonted hillocks—frequent seen !
Alas ! who knows how much lies buried there !—
What worlds of love, and all that might have been !

The rest are scattered now ; we know not where ;
And Life to each a new employment brings ;
But still they seem to gather round me here,
To whom these places were familiar things !
Wide sundered now, by mountain and by stream,
Once brothers—still a brotherhood they seem ;—
More firm united, since a common woe
Hath brought to common hopes their overthrow !

Brave souls and true ;—in toil and danger tried,—
I see them still as in those glorious years,
When strong, and battling bravely side by side,
All crowned their deeds with praise,—and some with tears !

'Tis done ! the sword is sheathed; the banner furled,
No sound where late the crashing missile whirled—
The dead alone possess the battle-plain ;
The living turn them to life's cares again.

Oh, Silence ! blessed dreams upon thee wait ;
Here Thought and Feeling ope their precious store,
And Memory, gathering from the spoils of Fate
Love's scattered treasures, brings them back once more !
    So let me often dream,
    As up the bright'ning stream
    Of olden Time, thought gently leads me on,
Seeking those better days, lost, lost, alas ! and gone !

"ALL IS GONE."

FADETTE.

SISTER, hark ! Atween the trees cometh naught but summer
    breeze ?
    All is gone—
Summer breezes come and go. Hope doth never wander so—
No, nor evermore doth Woe.

Sister, look ! Adown the lane treadeth only April rain ?
    All is gone—
Through the tangled hedge-rows green glimmer thus the sun-
    beam's sheen,
Dropping from cloud-rifts between.

Sister, hark ! the very air heavy on my heart doth bear—
    All is gone !
E'en the birds that chirped erewhile for the frowning sun to
    smile,
Hush at that drum near the stile.

Sister, pray !—it is the foe !   On thy knees—aye, very low—
      All is gone,
And the proud South on her knees to a mongrel race like these—
But the dead sleep 'neath the trees.

See—they come—their banners flare gayly in our gloomy air—
      All is gone—
Flashed our Southern Cross all night—naught but a meteoric
   light
In a moment lost to sight?

Aye, so gay—the brave array—marching from no battle fray—
      All is gone,—
Yet who vaunteth, of your host, maketh he but little boast
If he thinks on battles most.

On they wind, behind the wood. Dost remember once we stood—
      All is gone—
All but memory, of those days—but we've stood here while the
   haze
Of the battle met the blaze

Of the sun adown yon hill.   Charge on charge—I hear them
   still—
      All is gone !
Yet I hear the echoing crash—see the sabres gleam and flash—
See one gallant headlong dash.

One, amid the battle-wreck, restive plunged his charger black—
      All is gone—
Whirrs the patridge there---didst see where he rode so reck-
   lessly ?
Once he turned and waved to me.

" Ah," thou saidst, " the smoke is dark, scarce can I our banner
   mark "—
      All is gone—
All but memory ; yet I see, darksome howsoe'er it be,
How to death—to death—rode he,

Not a star he proudly bore, but a sword all dripping gore—
    All is gone—
Dashes on our little band like yon billow on the strand—
Like yon strand unmoved they stand.

For their serried ranks are strong : thousands upon thousands
    throng—
    All is gone,
And the handful, true and brave, spent, like yonder dying
    wave,
Fall back slowly from that grave.

Low our banner drooped—and fell.   Back he spurs, mid shot
    and shell—
    All *was* gone,
But he waves it high—and then, on—we sweep them from the
    glen—
But he ne'er rode back again.

Ah, I smiled to see him go.   How my cheek with pride did
    glow !
    All is gone—
All, of pride or hope, for me—but that evening, hopefully
Stood I at the gate with thee,

Sister, when at twilight gray marched our soldiers back this
    way—
    All is gone—
In the woods rang many a cheer—how we smiled !   I did not
    fear
Till—at last was borne a bier.

Sweetest sister, dost thou weep ?   Hush ! he only fell asleep—
    All is gone—
And 'twere better he had died—free, whatever us betide—
Our galling chains untried.

We were leaning on the gate.   Dost remember, it grew late—
          All is gone—
Yet I see the stars so pale—see the shadows down the vale—
Hear the whip-poor-will's far wail,

As if all were in a dream.   Through yon pines the moon did
     gleam—
          All is gone—
On that banner-pall of death—on that red sword without
     sheath—
And I knew who lay beneath.

Did I speak?   I thought I said, let me look upon your dead—
          All is gone—
Was I cold?   I did not weep.   Tears are spray from founts
     not deep—
My heart lies in frozen sleep.

Sister, pray for me.   Thine eyes gleam like God's own mid-
     night skies—
          All is gone—
Tuneless are my spirit's chords.   I but look up, like the birds,
And trust Christ to say the words.

THE FOE AT THE GATES—CHARLESTON.

By J. Dickson Bruns, M. D.

Ring round her! children of her glorious skies,
     Whom she hath nursed to stature proud and great;
Catch one last glance from her imploring eyes,
     Then close your ranks and face the threat'ning fate.

Ring round her! with a wall of horrent steel
     Confront the foe, nor mercy ask nor give;
And in her hour of anguish let her feel
     That ye can die whom she has taught to live.

"LION OF LUCERNE," ATLANTA, GEORGIA

UNKNOWN CONFEDERATE DEAD

Ring round her! swear, by every lifted blade,
　　To shield from wrong the mother who gave you birth,
That never villain hand on her be laid,
　　Nor base foot desecrate her hallowed hearth.

See how she thrills all o'er with noble shame,
　　As through deep sobs she draws the laboring breath,
Her generous brow and bosom all aflame
　　At the bare thought of insult, worse than death.

And stained and rent her snowy garments are ;
　　The big drops gather on her pallid face,
Gashed with great wounds by cowards who strove to mar
　　The beauteous form that spurned their foul embrace.

And still she pleads, oh! how she pleads, with prayers
　　And bitter tears, to every loving child
To stand between her and the doom she fears,
　　To keep her fame untarnished, undefiled!

Curs'd be the dastard who shall halt or doubt!
　　And doubly damned who casts one look behind!
Ye who are men! with unsheathed sword, and shout,
　　Up with her banner! give it to the wind.

Peal your wild slogan, echoing far and wide,
　　Till every ringing avenue repeat
The gathering cry, and Ashley's angry tide
　　Calls to the sea-waves beating round her feet.

Sons, to the rescue! spurred and belted, come!
　　Kneeling, with clasp'd hands, she invokes you now
By the sweet memories of your childhood's home,
　　By every manly hope and filial vow,

To save her proud soul from that loathed thrall
　　Which yet her spirit cannot brook to name ;
Or, if her fate be near, and she must fall,
　　Spare her—she sues—the agony and the shame.

From all her fanes let solemn bells be tolled,
  Heap with kind hands her costly funeral pyre,
And thus, with pæan sung and anthem rolled,
  Give her, unspotted, to the God of Fire.

Gather around her sacred ashes then,
  Sprinkle the cherished dust with crimson rain,
Die! as becomes a race of free-born men,
  Who will not crouch to wear the bondman's chain.

So, dying, ye shall win a high renown,
  If not in life, at least by death, set free—
And send her fame, through endless ages down,
  The last grand holocaust of liberty.

BOWING HER HEAD.

HER head is bowed downwards; so pensive her air,
  As she looks on the ground with her pale solemn face,
It were hard to decide whether faith or despair,
  Whether anguish or trust, in her heart holds a place.

Her hair was all gold in the sun's joyous light,
  Her brow was as smooth as the soft, placid sea;
Bnt the furrows of care came with shadows of night,
  And the gold silvered pale when the light left the lea.

Her lips slightly parted, deep thought in her eye,
  While sorrow cut seams in her forehead so fair:
Her bosom heaves gently, she stifles a sigh,
  And just moistens her lid with the dews of a tear.

Why droops she thus earthward—why bends she?   Oh, see!
  There are gyves on her limbs! see her manacled hand!
She is loaded with chains; but her spirit is free—
  Free to love and to mourn for her desolate land.

Her jailer, though cunning, lacks wit to devise
 How to fetter her thoughts, as her limbs he has done;
The eagle that's snatched from his flight to the skies,
 From the bars of his cage may still gaze at the sun.

No sound does she utter; all voiceless her pains;
 The wounds of her spirit with pride she conceals;
She is dumb to her shearers; the clank of her chains
 And the throbs of her heart only tell what she feels.

She looks sadly around her; how sombre the scene!
 How thick the deep shadows that darken her view!
The black embers of homes where the earth was so green,
 And the smokes of her wreck where the heavens shone
  blue.

Her daughters bereaved of all succor but God,
 Her bravest sons perished—the light of her eyes;
But oppression's sharp heel does not cut 'neath the sod,
 And she knows that the chains cannot bind in the
  skies.

She thinks of the vessel she aided to build,
 Of all argosies richest that floated the seas;
Compacted so strong, framed by architects skilled
 Or to dare the wild storm, or to sail to the breeze

To balmiest winds blowing soft where she steers,
 The favor of Heaven illuming her path—
She might sail as she pleased in the mild summer airs,
 And avoid the dread regions of tempest and wrath.

But the crew quarreled soon o'er the cargo she bore;
 'Twas adjusted unfairly, the cavillers said;
And the anger of men marred the peace that of yore
 Spread a broad path of glory and sunshine ahead.

There were seams in her planks—there were spots on her
      flag—
    So the fanatics said, as they seized on her helm;
And from soft summer seas, turned her prow where the crag
    And the wild breakers rose the good ship to o'erwhelm.

Then the South, though true love to the vessel she bore,
    Since she first laid its keel in the days that were gone—
Saw it plunge madly on to the wild billows' roar,
    And rush to destruction and ruin forlorn.

So she passed from the decks, in the faith of her heart
    That Justice and God her protectors would be;
Not dashed like a frail, fragile spar, without chart,
    In the fury and foam of the wild raging sea.

The life-boat that hung by the stout vessel's side
    She seized and embarked on the wide, trackless main,
In the faith that she'd reach, making virtue her guide,
    The haven the mother-ship failed to attain.

But the crew rose in wrath, and they swore by their might
    They would sink the brave boat that did buffet the sea,
For daring to seek, by her honor and right,
    A new port from the storms, a new home for the free.

So they crushed the brave boat; all forbearance they lost;
    They littered with ruins the ocean so wild—
Till the hulk of the parent ship, beaten and tossed,
    Drifted prone on the flood by the wreck of the child.

And the bold rower, loaded with fetters and chains,
    In the gloom of her heart sings the proud vessel's dirge;
Half forgets, in its wreck, all the pangs of her pains,
    As she sees its stout parts floating loose in the surge.

                               —*Savannah Broadside.*

"IN THE LAND WHERE WE WERE DREAMING."

By D. B. Lucas, Esq., of Jefferson, Virginia.

Fair were our visions! Oh, they were as grand
　　As ever floated out of Faerie land;
　　　　Children were we in single faith,
　　　　But God-like children, whom, nor death,
　　Nor threat, nor danger drove from Honor's path,
　　　　In the land where we were dreaming.

Proud were our men, as pride of birth could render;
As violets, our women pure and tender;
　　　　And when they spoke, their voice did thrill
　　　　Until at eve, the whip-poor-will,
　　At morn the mocking-bird, were mute and still
　　　　In the land where we were dreaming.

And we had graves that covered more of glory
Than ever tracked tradition's ancient story;
　　　　And in our dream we wove the thread
　　　　Of principles for which had bled
　　And suffered long our own immortal dead
　　　　In the land where we were dreaming.

Though in our land we had both bond and free,
Both were content; and so God let them be;
　　　　'Till envy coveted our land
　　　　And those fair fields our valor won:
　　But little recked we, for we still slept on,
　　　　In the land where we were dreaming.

Our sleep grew troubled and our dreams grew wild—
Red meteors flashed across our heaven's field;
　　　　Crimson the moon; between the Twins
　　　　Barbed arrows fly, and then begins
　　Such strife as when disorder's Chaos reigns,
　　　　In the land where we were dreaming.

24

Down from her sun-lit heights smiled Liberty
And waved her cap in sign of Victory—
    The world approved, and everywhere
    Except where growled the Russian bear,
The good, the brave, the just gave us their prayer
    In the land where we were dreaming.

We fancied that a Government was ours—
We challenged place among the world's great powers;
    We talked in sleep of Rank, Commission,
    Until so life-like grew our vision,
That he who dared to doubt met derision
    In the land where we were dreaming.

We looked on high : a banner there was seen,
Whose field was blanched and spotless in its sheen—
    Chivalry's cross its Union bears,
    And vet'rans swearing by their scars
Vowed they would bear it through a hundred wars
    In the land where we were dreaming.

A hero came amongst us as we slept ;
At first he lowly knelt—then rose and wept;
    Then gathering up a thousand spears
    He swept across the field of Mars ;
Then bowed farewell and walked beyond the stars—
    In the land where we were dreaming.

We looked again : another figure still
Gave hope, and nerved each individual will—
    Full of grandeur, clothed with power,
    Self-poised, erect, he ruled the hour
With stern, majestic sway—of strength a tower
    In the land where we were dreaming.

As, while great Jove, in bronze, a warder God,
Gazed eastward from the Forum where he stood,
  Rome felt herself secure and free,
  So, " Richmond's safe," we said, while we
Beheld a bronzed Hero—God-like Lee,
  In the land where we were dreaming.

  As wakes the soldier when the alarum calls—
  As wakes the mother when the infant falls—
   As starts the traveler when around
   His sleeping couch the fire-bells sound—
  So woke our nation with a single bound
   In the land where we were dreaming.

Woe ! woe is me ! the startled mother cried—
While we have slept our noble sons have died !
  Woe ! woe is me ! how strange and sad,
  That all our glorious vision's fled
And left us nothing real but the dead
  In the land where we were dreaming.

  And are they really dead, our martyred slain ?
  No ! dreamers ! morn shall bid them rise again
   From every vale—from every height
   On which they *seemed* to die for right—
  Their gallant spirits shall renew the fight
   In the land where we were dreaming.

SAVANNAH FALLEN.

By Alethea S. Burroughs, of Georgia

Bowing her head to the dust of the earth,
    Smitten and stricken is she,
Light after light gone out from her hearth,
    Son after son from her knee.
Bowing her head to the dust at her feet,
    Weeping her beautiful slain,
Silence! keep silence, for aye in the street,
    See! they are coming again.

    Coming again, oh, glorious ones!
        Wrapped in the flag of the free!
    Queen of the South! bright crowns for the sons,
        Only the cypress for *thee!*
    Laurel, and banner, and music, and drum,
        Marches and requiems sweet;
    Silence! keep silence! alas, how they come,
        Oh! how they move through the street!

Slowly, ah! mournfully, slowly they go,
    Bearing the young and the brave,
Fair as the summer, but white as the snow
    Bearing them down to the grave.
Some in the morning, and some in the noon,
    Some in the hey-day of life;
Bower nor blossom, nor summer, nor June,
    Wooing them back to the strife.

    Some in the billow, afar, oh! afar,
        Staining the waves with their blood;
    One on the vessel's high deck, like a star,
        Sinking in glory's bright flood.*

---

* Captain Thomas Pelot, C. S. N., killed at the capture of the *Water-Witch*.

PRESIDENT JEFFERSON DAVIS
From portrait taken during War Time.

Bowing her head to the dust of the earth,
 Humbled but honored is she,
Lighting the skies with the stars from her hearth,
 Who shall her comforter be ?

  Bring her, oh ! bring her the garments of woe,
   Sackcloth and ashes for aye ;
  Winds of the South ! oh, a requiem blow,
   Sighing and sorrow to-day.
  Sprinkle the showers from heaven's blue eyes
   Wide o'er the green summer lea,
  Rachel is weeping, oh ! Lord of the skies
   Thou shalt her comforter be !

BALLAD—" YES, BUILD YOUR WALLS."

YES, build your walls of stone or sand,
 But know, when all is builded—then,
The proper breastworks of the land
 Are in a race of freeborn men !
The sons of sires, who knew, in life,
 That, of all virtues, manhood first,
Still nursing peace, yet arms for strife,
 And braves, for liberty, the worst !

  What grand examples have been ours !
   Oh ! sons of Moultrie, Marion,—call
  From mansions of the past, the powers,
   That plucked ye from the despot's thrall !
  Do Sumter, Rutledge, Gadsden, live ?
   Oh ! for your City by the Sea,
  They gladly gave, what men could give,
   Blood, life, and toil, and made it free !

The grand inheritance, in trust
    For children of your loins, must know
No taint of shame, no loss by lust,
    Your own, or of the usurping foe !
Let not your sons, in future days,
    The children now that bear your name,
Exulting in a grandsire's praise,
    Droop o'er a father's grave in shame !

DOFFING THE GRAY.

By LIEUTENANT FALLIGANT, of Savannah, Georgia.

OFF with your gray suits, boys—
    Off with your rebel gear—
They smack too much of the cannon's peal,
The lightning flash of your deadly steel,
    The terror of your spear.

Their color is like the smoke
    That curled o'er your battle-line ;
They call to mind the yell that woke
When the dastard columns before you broke,
    And their dead were your fatal sign.

Off with the starry wreath,
    Ye who have led our van,
To you 'twas the pledge of glorious death,
When we followed you o'er the gory heath,
    Where we whipped them man to man.

Down with the cross of stars—
    Too long hath it waved on high ;
'Tis covered all over with battle scars,
But its gleam the Northern banner mars—
    'Tis time to lay it by.

Down with the vows we've made,
Down with each memory—
Down with the thoughts of our noble dead—
Down, down to the dust, where their forms are laid
And down with Liberty.

BULL RUN.—A PARODY.

It is said that in the hasty retreat from Bull Run an Irishman outstripped the rest on his way to Washington. Being met by an officer, he inquired of him why he ran. He answered: "Them as didn't run are there yet."

A T Bull Run when the sun was low,
Each Southern face grew pale as snow,
While loud as jackdaws rose the crow
Of Yankees boasting terribly!

But Bull Run saw another sight,
When at the deepening shades of night,
Towards Fairfax Court-House rose the flight
Of Yankees running rapidly.

Then broke each corps with terror riven.
Then rushed the steeds to battle driven,
The men of battery Number Seven
Forsook their red artillery!

Still on McDowell's farthest left,
The roar of cannon strikes one deaf,
Where furious Abe and fiery Jeff
Contend for death or victory.

The panic thickens—off, ye brave!
Throw down your arms! your bacon save!
Waive, Washington, all scruples waive,
And fly, with all your chivalry!

TO MY CREWEL WIFE.

By Morton Bryan Wharton, D. D.

[These lines were written when among ladies *crocheting* was all the rage. It has been supplanted by silk embroidery, in both of which my wife greatly excels.]—M. B. W.

Kind to my virtues you have been,
  And to my follies blinded,
But though you've not a cruel heart,
  Yet are you crewel-minded.

  For better or for worse, I said,
    When for your charms I thirsted;
  The better part you've ever proved,
    But still have I got worsted.

No crotchets in your heart exist;
  Excuse me, though, for saying,
That ne'er was woman's head more filled
  With fanciful *crocheting*.

  Your ears are deaf to all that's false,
    You ne'er would truth embellish,
  But others' yarns, howe'er retailed,
    You welcome with a relish.

'Tis said the west wind can't be chained,
  That in it blows forever,
But well I know your fingers trained
  Have caught and trained the zephyr.

  A consolation 'tis to feel,
    As down life's road we travel,
  That all the tangled webs I weave
    Your fingers can unravel.

The rainbow's splendid hues that glow
    When o'er the heavens bended,
Can ne'er in radiant beauty match
    The colors you have blended,—

    Yes, blended in your eyes and hair,
        And in your fair complexion,
    Your teeth of pearl, your pure white soul,
        That won my heart's affection.

" WHEN THIS CRUEL WAR IS OVER."

Dearest one, do you remember
    When we last did meet;
When you told me how you loved me
    Kneeling at my feet?
Oh! how proud you stood before me
    In your suit of gray,
When you vowed for me and country
    Ne'er to go astray.

            Chorus :

    Weeping sad and lonely
        Sighs and tears how vain,
    When this cruel war is over,
        Pray that we meet again.

When the summer breeze is sighing
    Mournfully along,
Or when autumn leaves are falling,
    Sadly breathes the song.
Oft in dreams I see you lying
    On the battle plain,
Lonely, wounded, even dying,
    Calling, but in vain.—*Chorus.*

If amid the din of battle
    Nobly you should fall,
Far away from those who love you—
    None to hear your call—
Who would whisper words of comfort?
    Who would soothe your pain?
Ah, the many cruel fancies
    Ever in my brain!—*Chorus.*

        But our country called you, loved one—
            Angels guide your way;
        While our "Southern boys" are fighting,
            We can only pray.
        When you strike for God and freedom,
            Let all nations see
        How you love our Southern banner—
            Emblem of the free.—*Chorus.*

FAREWELL TO THE STAR-SPANGLED BANNER.

LET tyrants and slaves submissively tremble
    And bow down their necks 'neath the Juggernaut car;
But brave men will rise in the strength of a nation
    And cry " Give me freedom, or else give me war."

           CHORUS:
Farewell, forever!   The Star-Spangled Banner,
    No longer shall wave o'er the land of the free!
But we'll unfurl to the broad breeze of heaven
    Thirteen bright stars around the Palmetto Tree.

We honor, yes, honor, bold South Carolina!
    Though small she may be, she's as brave as the best.
With flagship of States, she's out on the ocean
    Buffeting the waves of a dark billow's crest.—*Chorus.*

We honor, yes, honor, our seceding sisters,
　　Who launched this brave bark alone on the sea;
Though storms may howl, and thunder distraction
　　We'll hurl to the blast the proud Palmetto tree.—*Chorus.*

And when to the conflict the others cry " Onward ! "
　　Virginia will be first to rush to the fight.
She'll break down the iceberg of Northern coërcion
　　And rise in her glory of freedom and right.—*Chorus.*

When the thirteen sisters in bright constellation
　　Shall dazzling shine in a nation's emblem sky,
With no hands to oppose nor foes to oppress them,
　　They will shine there forever, a light to every eye.
　　　　　　　　　　　　　　　　—*Chorus.*

"LET ME KISS HIM FOR HIS MOTHER."

Let me kiss him for his mother,
　　Let me kiss his dear, youthful brow;
I will love him for his mother,
　　And seek her blessing now.
Kind friends have soothed his pillow,
　　Have watched his every care,
Beneath the weeping willow,
　　O lay him gently there.

Chorus:

　　Sleep, dearest, sleep;
　　　　I loved you as a brother,
　　Kind friends around you weep;
　　　　I've kissed you for your mother.

Let me kiss him for his mother;
　　What though left a lone stranger here;
She has loved him as none other;
　　I feel her blessing near.

Though cold that form lies sleeping,
  Sweet angels watch around.
Dear friends are near thee weeping;
  O, lay him gently down.—*Chorus.*

> Let me kiss him for his mother;
>   Or, perchance, fond sister dear.
> If a father or a brother,
>   I know their blessing's here.
> Then kiss him for his mother;
>   'Twill soothe her after years.
> Farewell, dear stranger, brother;
>   Our requiem, our tears.—*Chorus.*

"I GIVE MY SOLDIER BOY A BLADE."

By H. M. L....

I GIVE my soldier boy a blade,
  In fair Damascus fashioned well:
Who first the glittering falchion swayed,
  Who first beneath its fury fell,
I know not; but I hope to know,
  That, for no mean or hireling trade,
To guard no feeling base or low—
  I give my soldier boy the blade!

Cool, calm and clear—the lucid flood
  In which its tempering work was done;—
As calm, as clear, in wind and wood,
  Be thou where'er it sees the sun!
For country's claim, at honor's call,
  For outraged friend, insulted maid,
At mercy's voice to bid it fall—
  I give my soldier boy the blade!

THE CAPITOL AT RICHMOND, VIRGINIA

The Congress of the Confederate States of America came here in 1862 from Montgomery, Alabama, and sat until the day in April, 1865, when Lee was turned back at Petersburg and "all was lost save honor."

The eye which marked its peerless edge,
    The hand that weighed its balanced poise,
Anvil and pincers, forge and wedge,
    Are gone, with all their flame and noise;
Yet still the gleaming sword remains!
    So, when in dust I low am laid,
Remember, by these heart-felt strains,
    I give my soldier boy the blade!

TO HON. JEFFERSON DAVIS.
By M. B. Wharton.
In answer to the following letter.

My dear sir,

Your beautiful poem to the city of Montgomery and the memories of the struggle then initiated to defend the rights our fathers left us, and to maintain constitutional liberty have been read with grateful admiration.

Respectfully and truly yours,

Jefferson Davis.

Such was the joy thy greeting gave,
    High leap'd my heart beyond control;
Thy kindly wish, like ocean's wave
Singing amid the storms that rave,
    Bright o'er my flood of years shall roll,
    And waft soft music to my soul.

Fair leaf from the majestic tree
  From whence our Southland glory springs,
Thy letter e'er shall treasured be,—
Pressed in the book of memory,
  And shrined among the sacred things,
  More prized than autographs of kings.

He who the world's applause has won,
  Whose fame shall gild remotest days,
Is thankful for my service done,
Oh, 'tis as if the lustrous sun,
  That floods our fields with kindly rays,
  Had thanked some plant that drank his rays!

And to thy quiet seaside home,
  Where tall magnolias wave their crowns,
And skies cerulean lift their dome,
With generous quest thou bidst me come.
  Oh, sweet to tread those flowery downs,
  And catch the inspiring ocean sounds!

But sweeter far to see again
  The noble form that first I viewed
Careering to Manassa's plain,
'Mid wilder sounds than sweep the main,—
  Where threes stood bare and bullet-hewed,
  And skies wept o'er the battle-strewed.

I saw thee oft with rank and file,
  Gazed on thee in thy chair of state,
Thy great Inaugural heard, the while,
Thou stood'st upon the sacred pile
  Upreared to Washington the Great,
  And deemed thee linked with him in Fate.

Shone, through the dark and bitter gale,
  Thy martial form, thy eagle eye,
One hand sure guiding at the wheel

And one directed to the steel
    That flashed above the battle's cry
    And nerved thy hosts to do or die.

    But Fate thy dauntless spirit mocks,
        The hopes of millions quick are fled ;
    Our ship succumbs to ruthless shocks
    And sinks dismantled on the rocks,
        While grim Monroe with menace dread
        Frowns o'er our prisoned chieftain's head.

Brave victors e'er must generous be
    Unto a brave and fallen foe ;
The hand that plucked the sword from Lee
Is raised to set the captive free,
    Who ne'er recoiled from martial blow
    Nor triumph'd in a brother's woe.

        Nor can the spangled flag disdain
        The star that flamed at Monterey ;
    Its crimson stripe must speak the vein
    That streamed on Buena Vista's plain,—
        Those memories bright can ne'er decay
        While breezes round that banner play.

The world, full conscious of thy worth,
    Rejoiced then at thy just release.
Untrammeled by a cruel oath,
Thou from thy cell didst wander forth,
    To seek in quiet walks of peace
    From patriot woes a calm surcease.

    Majestic silence sat enthroned
        Upon thy great and lofty brow,
    And while the past was sore bemoaned,
    The conquering Power was loyal owned ;
        The bright peace Angel sealed the vow—
        Defeat grander than victory now !

But stars are never long concealed;
    The darksome clouds that hang before,
Soon drifting from the nightly field,
Unwonted splendors are revealed.
    Lo! thus our days of darkness o'er,
    Thou loom'st thy country's cynosure!

THE LITTLE SOLDIER.

By J. L. Molloy.

"When I'm big I'll be a soldier—
    That's what I'll be;
Fight for father, fight for mother,
    Over land and sea!"
And before him on the table
    Stood in bright array
All his little wooden soldiers,
    Ready for the fray.
Then he charged his little cannon,
    Singing out in glee,
"When I'm big I'll be a soldier—
    That's what I will be!"

    By the firelight sat the mother;
        Tears were in her heart,
    Thinking of the swift time coming
        When they two must part.

   *   *   *   *   *

Soon the shadow fell between them—
    Soon the years flew by;
He has left his little mother—
    Left her, perhaps to die.

All the laughter gone forever,
  All the sunshine fled ;
Only little mother praying
  By his empty bed.

    Then there came a dreadful battle,
      And upon the plain
    Crept the little mother, seeking
      Some one 'mid the slain ;
    But she never found her darling
      In the white moon gleam,

For the little cannon firing
  Woke her from her dream.
All a dream ! He stood beside her,
  Singing out with glee,
" When I'm big I'll be a soldier—
  That's what I will be ! "

THE COUNTERSIGN.

A LAS ! the rolling hours pass slow—
    The night is very dark and still—
And in the marshes far below
    Is heard the lonely whippoorwill ;
I scarce can see a foot ahead—
    My ears are strained to catch each sound,
I feel the dead leaves beneath me spread
    And the springs bubbling thro' the ground.

    Along the beaten path I pace,
      Where white rays mark my sentry's track ;
    In formless things I seem to trace ;
      The foeman's form, with bended back.

25

I think I see him crouching low !
　　I stop and list—I stop and peer—
Until the neighboring hillocks grow
　　To groups of soldiers, far and near.

　　　　With ready piece I wait and watch
　　　　　　Until my eyes familiar grown—
　　　　Detect each harmless earthen notch,
　　　　　　And turn "guerrillas" into stone ;
　　　　And then amid the lonely gloom,
　　　　　　Beneath tall magnolia trees,
　　　　My silent marches I resume
　　　　　　And think of other times than these.

" Halt ! who goes there ? " my challenge cry—
　　It rings along the watchful line—
" Relief ! " I hear a voice reply.
　　　" Advance and give the countersign ! "
With bayonet at the charge I wait—
　　The corporal gives the mystic spell—
With " arms aport " I charge my mate
　　Then onward pass, and all is well !

　　　　But in my tent, that night awake,
　　　　　　I ask, " if in the fray I fall,
　　　　Can I the mystic answer make
　　　　　　When the angelic sentries call ? "
　　　　And pray that Heaven so ordain,
　　　　　　Where'er I go, what fate be mine,
　　　　Whether in pleasure or in pain
　　　　　　I still may have the " countersign ! "

"POP GOES THE WEASEL."

KING ABRAHAM is very sick,
  Old Scott has got the measles,
Manassas we have now at last—
  Pop goes the weasel!

      All around the cobbler's house
      The monkey chased the people,
      And after them in double haste
        Pop goes the weasel!

When the night walks in as black as a sheep,
And the hen on her eggs was fast asleep,
When into her nest with a serpent's creep
  Pop goes the weasel!

      Of all the dance that ever was planned
      To galvanize the heel and the hand,
      There's none that moves so gay and grand
        As pop goes the weasel!

TO MY SOLDIER BROTHER.

BY SALLIE M. BALLARD, of Texas.

WHEN softly gathering shades of ev'n
  Creep o'er the prairies broad and green,
And countless stars bespangle heav'n,
  And fringe the clouds with silv'ry sheen,
My fondest sigh to thee is giv'n,
My lonely wand'ring soldier boy;
    And thoughts of thee
    Steal over me
Like ev'ning shade, my soldier boy.

My brother, though thou'rt far away,
    And dangers hurtle round thy path,
And battle lightning's o'er thee play,
    And thunders peal in awful wrath,
Think, whilst thou'rt in the hot affray,
Thy sister prays for thee, my boy.
        If fondest prayer
        Can shield thee there
Sweet angels guard my soldier boy.

        Thy proud young heart is beating high
            To clash of arms and cannon's roar ;
        That firm-set lip and flashing eye
            Tell how thy heart is brimming o'er.
        Be free and live, be free or die ;
        Be that thy motto now, my boy ;
                And though thy name's
                Unknown to fame,
        'Tis graven on my heart, my boy.

———————

THE SOLDIER'S AMEN.

As a couple of good soldiers were walking one day,
    Said one to the other : " Let's kneel down and pray ;
I'll pray for the war, and good of all men,
And whatever I pray for, do you say—" Amen ! "

" We'll pray for the generals and all of their crew,
Likewise for the captains and lieutenants, too ;
May good luck and good fortune them always attend;
And return safely home ! "   Said the soldier—" Amen ! "

" We'll pray for the privates, the noblest of all ;
They do all the work and get no glory at all ;
May good luck and good fortune them always attend,
And return crowned with laurels!" Said the soldier—"Amen !'

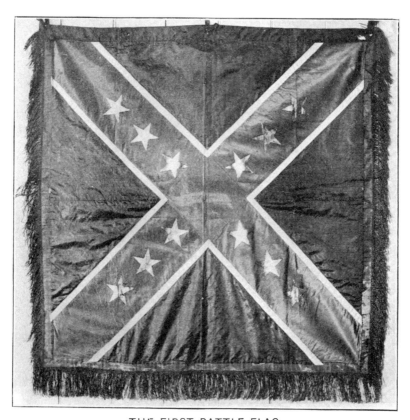

THE FIRST BATTLE FLAG
DESCRIPTION:—Red Ground, Blue Cross, Gold Stars, Gold Fringe

In 1861, after the first battle of Manassas, the flag with the St. Andrews Cross was adopted as the Battle Flag of the Confederate States Army, and the Misses Carey (Hettie and Constance) made three and presented them to Generals Johnston, Van Dorn and Beauregard. The latter's flag was sent by him to New Orleans, and upon the fall of the city, to Havana, then returned to New Orleans, and placed in custody of the Washington Artillery, where it is at present. The other two seem to have been lost.

" We'll pray for the pretty boys who want themselves wives,
And have not the courage to strike for their lives;
May bad luck and bad fortune them always attend;
And go down to Old Harry;" Said the soldier—"Amen!"

" We'll pray for the pretty girls, who make us good wives,
And always look at a soldier with tears in their eyes;
May good luck and good fortune them always attend,
And brave gallants for sweethearts!" Said the soldier—
    " Amen!"

" We'll pray for the conscript, with frown on his brow,
To fight for his couutry he won't take the vow:
May bad luck and bad fortune him always attend,
And die with dishonor!" Said the soldier—" Amen!"

MY WARRIOR BOY.

Thou hast gone forth, my darling one,
    To battle with the brave,
To strike in Freedom's sacred cause,
    Or win an early grave;
With vet'rans grim, and stalwart men,
    Thy pathway lieth now,
Though fifteen summers scarce have shed
    Their blossoms on thy brow.

My babe in years, my warrior boy!
    Oh, if a mother's tears
Could call thee back to be my joy
    And still these anxious fears,
I'd dash the traitor drops away,
    That would unnerve thy hand,
Now raised to strike in Freedom's cause
    For thy dear native land.

God speed thee on thy course, my boy,
  Where'er thy pathway lie,
And guard thee when the leaden hail
  Shall thick around thee fly ;
But when our sacred cause is won,
  And peace again shall reign,
Come back to me, my darling son,
  And light my life again.

THE SOUTHERN DEAD.

By Morton Bryan Wharton, D. D.

WHERE are the men who at the call
    Of duty battled for the right,
Who to their country gave their all
    And bore our banner in the fight?
Ye winged winds that round them play,
    Where are these noble men to-day?

" Each one a soldier's coffin fills,"
  The answer comes in plaintive moan ;
" They rest upon a hundred hills
  Unmarked, unhonored and unknown,"
Or else their bones uncoffined lie
  Beneath Virginia's weeping sky.

    The flower of old Virginia's pride
        With bounding heart sped to the foe,
    And grappling bravely hand to hand,
        For Southern honor struck the blow,
    Resolved to free their homes opprest
    Or on their broken shields to rest.

And there they fell, perchance 'twas meet
    (They knew not then their country's fall),
The stars and bars their winding-sheet,
    The blood-laved earth their funeral pall,
While trysting nature o'er their graves
In vernal beauty blooms and waves.

    And shall they unremembered lie
        Save by the flowers and grasses wild?
    What says the State?   Does she reply,
        I care not for my soldier child?
    Avaunt the thought!   Oh, mother, turn,
    And deck the son's neglected urn.

Who doubts that had our guardian star
    Rained fortune on our struggling band,
The bright memorials of the war
    Had crowned each hill-top in the land,
And angels waked from Parian bed
Their white wings o'er the sleepers spread?

    Oh, who can paint the pageant bright
        When (five-and-twenty years sped by)
    Thou pressed again the historic site
    On yonder Capitolian height,
        Where Dixie's flag first leap'd on high,
        Amid the new-born nation's cry!

Sun never graced a scene more grand!
    Nor wilder shouts could mortals raise,
When Pettus stood with veteran band
And scar-marked Gordon took the stand,
    Flashing the light of other days,—
    Speaking the Southern leader's praise!

And thus t'will be till time shall end,—
    The world shall with thy plaudits ring,
Great hist'ry shall thy name defend,
Sculpture its guardian graces lend,
        And future bards shall joy to sing
        The glories of our uncrowned king.

" Peace hath its victories great as war,"
        Oh, bright example here we find !
While Englaud boasts her Trafalgar,
We point with pleasure to Beauvoir,
            Where stainless Honor sits enshrined
            Within a true and constant mind.

Enjoy then, sire, thy cherished rest
        From care and strife and sorrow free ;
And when thy sun shall seek the west,
Thy Mother take thee to her breast,
        The music of the sounding sea
        Shall thy perpetual requiem be !

Till then, bloom on, ye roses sweet,
        Ye forests waft your fragrant gales,
Sweet birds your loveliest lays repeat.
Join in, O sea, with chorus meet,—
        Oh, Thou, whose mercy never fails,
        Spare him who treads these smiling vales !

Yet not in old Westminster's aisle,
        Where sculptured glory lifts its charms,
Can there be viewed a holier pile
        Than that we build to Southern arms ?
Could heroes serve a cause more just,
Or crypts enshrine more sacred dust ?

We've waited long the shaft to rear,
   'Tis well our braves unconscious sleep,
Or eyes that cannot know a tear
   O'er man's ingratitude would weep.
Ah! but for woman, brave and pure,
How long would Southern fame endure?

     Then let our column pierce the sky,
        Rise tall and graceful from the square,
     And then should glorious Freedom die,
        Her spirit still may linger there,
     And sweet communion hold with those
     Who never quailed before their foes.

"IF YOU LOVE ME."

By Augustine Signaigo.

You have told me that you love me,
   That you worship at my shrine;
That no purity above me
   Can on earth be more divine.
Though the kind words you have spoken,
   Sound to me most sweetly strange,
Will your pledges ne'er be broken?
   Will there be in you no change?

     If you love me half so wildly—
        Half so madly as you say,
     Listen to me, darling, mildly—
        Would you do aught I would pray?
     If you would, then hear the thunder
        Of our country's cannon speak!
     While by war she's rent asunder,
        Do not come my love to seek.

If you love me, do not ponder,
  Do not breathe what you would say,
Do not look at me with wonder,
  Join your country in the fray.
Go! your aid and right hand lend her
  Breast the tyrant's angry blast;
Be her own and my defender—
  Strike for freedom to the last.

        Then I'll vow to love none other,
          While you nobly dare and do ;
        As you're faithful to our mother,
          So I'll faithful prove to you.
        But return not while the thunder
          Lives in one invading sword ;
        Strike the despot's hirelings under—
          Own no master but the Lord.

"THE CONTRABAND."

(A song of Mississippi negroes in the Vicksburg campaign.)

Among the most faithful of all the Southerners we must not forget the negro slaves. They were true to their masters, and to their families, and oftentimes our unprotected women found in them perfect safety. When the war closed, my father called up his slaves, and said to them, "You are free now; you can go wherever you please, and do whatever you wish to do." Old Uncle Alec, the foreman of the plantation, turned to my father, and said, "Marster, you have always been good to me, and I don't care what the others do, I am going to stay with you." He returned to his cabin, and so did the others to theirs. For years they remained with my father, and only drifted away by marriage, and with changes that followed in our family. I cannot express the tender love that is in my heart for those dear, true-hearted friends who never knew what want was, and were as happy as children under my father's care.

Say, darkies, has you seed my massa,
    Wid de mustache on his face ?
He came along some time dis morning
    As dough he'd leave de place.

He seed de smoke away up de river,
    Where de Lincum gunboats lay;
He took his hat and lef' bery sudden,
    I speck he's runned away.

CHORUS:

    Massa run away,
    Darkie stay at home ;
    It must be now dat de kingdom's comin'
    In de year of Jubilum !

He's six feet one way, four feet t'other,
    And weighs three hundred pounds;
His coat's so big he can't pay the tailor,
    And it won't go half around.
He drills so much dey call him cap'n,
    And he am so very tan,
Speck he'll to fool dem Yankees
    And pass for a contraban'—*Chorus.*

    Dis darky gets so very lonesome,
        In de cabin on de lawn.
    He moves his things to massa's parlor
        To keep 'em while he's gone.
    There's wine and cider in de cellar,
    And de darkies dey'll have some ;
    I speck it will be confiscated
        When de Lincum soldiers come.—*Chorus.*

De overseer will give us trouble,
    And run us round a spell ;
We'll lock him up in de smokehouse cellar,
    Wid de key thrown in de well.
De whip is lost and de handcuffs broken,
And massa'll lose his ; ay,
He's big enough and old enough
    Dan to gone and runned away.—*Chorus.*

IS THIS A TIME TO DANCE?

THE breath of evening sweeps the plain,
    And sheds its perfume in the dell,
But on its wings are sounds of pain,
    Sad tones that drown the echo's swell;
And yet we hear a mirthful call,
    Fair pleasure smiles with beaming glance,
Gay music sounds in the joyous hall;
    Oh, God! is this a time to dance?

    Sad notes, as if a spirit sighed,
        Float from the crimson battle-plain,
    As if a mighty spirit cried
        In awful agony and pain;
    Our friends we know there suffering lay,
        Our brothers, too, perchance,
    And in reproachful accents say,
        Loved ones, is this a time to dance?

Oh, lift your festal robes on high!
    The human gore that flows around
Will stain their hues with crimson dye;
    And louder let your music sound
To drown the dying warrior's cry!
    Let sparkling wine your joy enhance,
Forget that blood has tinged its dye,
    And quicker urge the maniac dance.

    But stop! the floor beneath your feet
        Gives back a coffin's hollow moan,
    And every strain of music sweet,
        Wafts forth a dying soldier's groan.
    Oh, sisters! who have brothers dear
        Exposed to every battle's chance,
    Brings dark remorse no forms of fear,
        To fright you from the heartless dance?

MAJOR-GENERAL DABNEY H. MAURY

GENERAL ALBERT SIDNEY JOHNSTON

Go, fling your festal robes away!
    Go, don the mourner's sable veil!
Go, bow before your God, and pray!
    If yet your prayers may aught avail.
Go, face the fearful form of Death!
    And trembling meet his chilling glance,
And then, for once, with truthful breath,
    Answer, Is this a time to dance?

ONLY A PRIVATE.

By F. W. D.

ONLY a private! his jacket of gray
    Is stained by the smoke and the dust;
As Bayard he's brave, as Rupert he's gay,
Reckless as Murat in heat of the fray,
    But in God is his only trust!

Only a private! to march and to fight,
    Suffers and starve and be strong;
With knowledge enough to know that the might
Of justice and truth, and freedom and right
    In the end must crush out the wrong!

Only a private! no ribbon or star
    Shall gild with false glory his name!
No honors for him in braid or in bar,
His Legion of Honor is only a scar,
    And his wounds are his roll of fame!

Only a private! one more hero slain
    On the field lies silent and chill!
And in the far South a wife prays in vain—
One clasp of the hands she may ne'er clasp again,
    One kiss from the lips that are still!

Only a private! there let him sleep,
   He will need no tablet nor stone;
For the mosses and vines o'er his grave will creep,
And at night the stars through the clouds will peep
   And watch him who lies there alone!

    Only a martyr! who fought and who fell,
       Unknown and ·unmarked in the strife;
    But still as he lies in his lonely cell,
    Angel and seraph the legend shall tell—
       Such a death is eternal life

ODE—" DO YE QUAIL? "

By W. Gilmore Simm.

Do ye quail but to hear, Carolinians,
   The first foot-tramp of Tyranny's minions?
Have ye buckled on armor, and brandished the spear,
But to shrink with the trumpet's first peal on the ear?
Why your forts now embattled on headland and height,
Your sons all in armor, unless for the fight?
Did ye think the mere show of your guns on the wall,
And your shouts, would the souls of the heathen appall?
That his lusts and his appetites, greedy as Hell,
Led by Mammon and Moloch, would sink at a spell;—
Nor strive, with the tiger's own thirst, lest the flesh
Should be torn from his jaws, while yet bleeding afresh.

For shame! To the breech, Carolinians!—
To the death for your sacred dominions!
Homes, shrines, and your cities all reeking in flame,
Cry aloud to your souls, in their sorrow and shame;
Your graybeards, with necks in the halter—
Your virgins, defiled at the altar,—
In the loathsome embrace of the felon and slave,
Touch loathsomer far than the worm of the grave!

Ah! God! if you fail in this moment of gloom!
How base were the weakness, how horrid the doom!
With the fiends in your streets howling pæans,
And the Beast o'er another Orleans!

Do you quail, as on yon little islet
They have planted the feet that defile it?
Make its sands pure of taint, by the stroke of the sword,
And by torrents of blood in red sacrifice pour'd!
Doubts are traitors, if once they persuade you to fear,
That the foe, in his foothold, is safe from your spear!
When the foot of pollution is set on your shores,
What sinew and soul should be stronger than yours?
By the fame—by the shame—of your sires,
Set on, though each freeman expires;
Better fall, grappling fast with the foe, to their graves,
Than groan in your fetters, the slaves of your slaves.

The voice of your loud exultation
Hath rung, like a trump, through the nation,
How loudly, how proudly, of deeds to be done,
The blood of the sire in the veins of the son!
Old Moultrie and Sumter still keep at your gates,
And the foe in his foothold as patiently waits.
He asks, with a taunt, by your patience made bold,
If the hot spur of Percy grows suddenly cold—
Makes merry with boasts of your city his own,
And the Chivalry fled, ere his trumpet is blown;
Upon them, O sons of the mighty of yore,
And fatten the sands with their Sodomite gore!

Where's the dastard that cowers and falters
In the sight of his hearthstones and altars?
With the faith of the free in the God of the brave,
Go forth; ye are mighty to conquer and save!
By the blue heaven shining above ye,
By the pure-hearted thousands that love ye,

Ye are armed with a might to prevail in the fight,
And an ægis to shield and a weapon to smite !
Then fail not, and quail not ; the foe shall prevail not ;
With the faith and the will, ye shall conquer him still.
To the knife—with the knife, Carolinians,
For your homes, and your sacred dominions!

GENERAL DABNEY H. MAURY.

By Rosewell Page.

He sleeps, the " little general " sleeps,
    With all the great before him ;
Another son Virginia weeps,
    Proud that 'twas she who bore him.

Away from home, far, far away,
    He crossed life's utmost barrier;
Subdued, but still without dismay
    He comes, our gentle warrior.

He fell not, 'twas his cause that fell,
    Upon the field of glory.
He lived, that living he might tell
    His country's gallant story.

With heroes he was wont to share
    The trial and the peril ;
With them to do, with them to dare,
    With them shall be his burial.

He rests, the tired soldier rests,
    Upon the field of battle,
Recalling deeds of dauntles breasts
    And scenes of boyish prattle.

He sleeps, the " little general " sleeps,
    With all the great before him ;
Virginia now her vigil keeps,
    Proud that 'twas she who bore him

THE SOUTHERN SOLDIER BOY.

By Father Ryan.

Young as the youngest who donned the gray,
  True as the truest who wore it,
Brave as the bravest he marched away,
(Hot tears on the cheeks of his mother lay);
Triumphant waved our flag one day,
  He fell in front before it.

Chorus.

A grave in the wood with the grass o'er grown,
  A grave in the heart of his mother,
His clay in the one lifeless and lone,
  But his memory lives in the other.

Firm as the firmest where duty led,
  He hurried without a falter;
Bold as the boldest he fought and bled,
And the day was won but the field was red;
And the blood of his fresh young heart was shed,
  On his country's hallowed altar.—*Chorus*.

On the trampled breast of the battle plain,
  Where the foremost ranks had wrestled,
The fairest form 'mid all the slain
  Like a child asleep he nestled.
In the solemn of the woods that swept
  The field where his comrades found him,
They buried him there, and strong men wept,
  As in silence they gathered 'round him.—*Chorus*.

26

THE CONQUERED BANNER.

BY FATHER ABRAM J. RYAN, THE POET PRIEST OF THE SOUTH.

Perhaps the most gifted of all the Southern poets during the War of the Confederacy was Father Abram J. Ryan: of New Orleans, and one of his very best poems is "The Conquered Banner." It not only does credit to the author, but is a splendid tribute to the Flag which went down at last all covered with glory.

FURL that banner! for 'tis weary,
 Round its staff 'tis drooping dreary;
Furl it, fold it, it is best :
For there's not a man to wave it,
And there's not a sword to save it,
And there's not one left to lave it,
In the blood which heroes gave it.
And its foes now scorn and brave it,
 Furl it, hide it, let it rest.

   Take that banner down ! 'tis tattered,
   Broken is its staff and shattered,
   And the valiant hosts are scattered
    Over whom it floated high.
   Oh ! 'tis hard for us to fold it,
   Hard to think there's none to hold it,
   Hard that those who once unrolled it
    Now must furl it with a sigh.

Furl that banner !   Furl it sadly—
Once ten thousands hailed it gladly,
And ten thousands wildly, madly,
 Swore it should forever wave ;
Swore that foeman's sword could never
Hearts like theirs entwined dissever
Till that flag would float forever
 O'er their freedom or their grave.

Furl it! for the hands that grasped itf
And the hearts that fondly clasped it,
    Cold and dead are lying low.
And the banner, it is trailing,
While around it sounds the wailing
    Of its people in their woe.
For, though conquered, they adore it,
Love the cold, dead hands that bore it,
Weep for those who fell before it,
Pardon those who trailed and tore it,
And—oh! wildly they deplore it—
    Now to furl and fold it so.

    Furl that banner! true, 'tis gory,
    Yet 'tis wreathed around with glory,
    And 'twill live in song and story,
        Though its folds are in the dust;
    For its fame on brightest pages,
    Penned by poets and by sages,
    Shall go sounding down the ages,
        Furl its folds though now we must.
    Furl that banner! softly, slowly,
    Treat it gently—it is holy—
        For it droops above the dead;
    Touch it not, unfold it never,
    Let it drape there, *furled* forever,
        For its people's *hopes* are dead.

A REPLY TO THE CONQUERED BANNER.

By Sir Henry Houghton, Bart., England.

It will be seen by this that the sympathy of people of other lands, and especially our Mother Country, was not altogether on one side. To this day great respect is shown those who fought on the Southern side, and far more of consideration expressed now that we have gone so far away from the prejudice and passion of those days. Recently, while in London, I had the privilege of being the guest of Lord Kinnaird, a man as well distinguished for his Christianity as for his splendid success in business life. Another gentleman present, speaking of the war, turned to me and said, "Give me the history of that war;" to which I replied that it might be done in one sentence: "The people of New England brought slaves from Africa, and traded them to us in the South for molasses, and sugar and cotton, and then came and fought us and took them away from us." This seemed to satisfy my questioner, and I hope it will not be denied or severely criticised by my reader. Amen.

Gallant nation, foiled by numbers!
    Say not that your hopes are fled;
Keep that glorious flag which slumbers,
    One day to avenge your dead.
Keep it, widowed, sonless mothers!
Keep it, sisters, mourning brothers!
Furl it with an iron will;
Furl it now but keep it still—
    Think not that its work is done.
Keep it till your children take it,
Once again to hall and make it,
All their sires have bled and fought for;
All their noble hearts have sought for—
    Bled and fought for all alone.
All alone! ay, shame the story!
    Millions here deplore the stain;
Shame, alas! for England's glory,
    Freedom called, and called in vain!
Furl that banner sadly, slowly,
Treat it gently, for 'tis holy;
Till that day—yes, furl it sadly;
Then once more unfurl it gladly—
    Conquered banner! keep it still!

THE
ROLL OF CONFEDERATE STATES
THE DISTINGUISHED MEN AND
EVENTS OF FOUR YEARS

SOUTH CAROLINA.
Seceded December 20, 1860

Bombardment of Fort Sumter, April 12-14, 1861. Engagement between United States Monitors and Sullivan's Island Batteries, November 16, 1863. Battle of Port Royal, November 7, 1861. Repulse of the Federal Iron-Clad Squadron in Charleston Harbor, April 7, 1863. Capture and Burning of Columbia, February 15, 1865.

MISSISSIPPI.
Seceded January 9, 1861.

Siege of Corinth, April 29 to June 10, 1862. Siege of Vicksburg, May 18 to July 4, 1863. Surrender of Vicksburg, July 4, 1863. Attack on Union gunboats near Greenwood, May 27, 1863. Engagement of the Confederate Ram, "Arkansas," June, 1862, one of the most brilliant naval fights on record.

FLORIDA.
Seceded January 10, 1861.

February 20, 1865, Battle of Fort Myers. Battle of Fort Taylor, August 21, 1864. General E. Kirby Smith, born in St. Augustine, May 16, 1824. Total number of engagements during the war, 32. General James McIntosh, killed at Battle of Pen Ridge, Arkansas, March 7, 1862. November 10, 1876, Florida redeemed from carpet-bag rule. Florida, the first State to make Mr. Davis' birthday a legal holiday, June 3, 1893.

ALABAMA.

Seceded January 11, 1861.

The election of President Jefferson Davis and Vice-President A. H. Stephens, February 9, and their inauguration, February 18, 1861.   Forrest's pursuit and capture of Colonel A. D. Streight, May 3, 1863.   Evacuation of Mobile, by General D. H. Maury, April 12, 1865.   Battle of Mobile Bay, August 5, 1864.

GEORGIA.

Seceded January 19, 1861.

Lieutenant-General Leonidas Polk, killed at Battle of Pine Mountain, June 14, 1864.   Battle of Chickamauga, September 19-20, 1863.   Siege of Atlanta, July 28 to September 2, 1864.   May 10, 1865, Jefferson Davis captured.   Naval Attack on Forts Rosedew and Beaulieu, Vernon River, December 14-21, 1864.

LOUISIANA.

Seceded January 26, 1861.

Siege of Port Hudson, May 12 to July 9, 1863.   New Orleans Captured, April 25, 1862.   General Beauregard born near New Orleans, May 28, 1818.   Total number of engagements during the war, 118.   Bombardment of Fort Barrancas, January 1, 1862.

TEXAS.

Seceded February 1, 1861.

United States Senators expelled from the Senate, July 11, 1861.   Capture of Steamer "Harriet Lane," January 1, 1863. Last action of war at Palmetto Ranch, near Brownsville, May 13, 1865.   Repulse of Franklin's expedition, Sabine Pass, September 7, 1863.   General Albert Sidney Johnston, of Texas, killed April 6, 1862, at Battle of Shiloh, Tenn,

VIRGINIA.

Seceded April 17, 1861

Capitol moved from Montgomery, Alabama, to Richmond, May 6, 1861. General J. E. B. Stuart wounded at Yellow Tavern, May 12, 1864. General R. E. Lee, born January 19, 1807. General R. E. Lee, died October 12, 1870, at Lexington, Va. April 9, 1865, Lee surrenders at Appomattox Courthouse. "Stonewall" Jackson died May 10, 1863.

ARKANSAS.

Seceded May 6, 1861.

United States Senators expelled from the Senate, July 11, 1861. Engagement with United States Steamer "Curlew," May 25, 1864. General James McIntosh killed at the Battle of Pea Ridge, March 7, 1862. General Benjamin McCulloch killed at Pea Ridge, March 7, 1862. Engagement at St. Charles, between the Confederate forces and Federal gunboats, June 17, 1862. Engagement at Helena, August 11-14, 1862.

NORTH CAROLINA.

Seceded May 20, 1861.

General Leonidas Polk, born in Raleigh, April 10, 1806. Bombardment by naval fleet off Fort Fisher, December 25, 1864. Battle of New Berne, March 14, 1862. Siege of Fort Macon, March 23 to April 26, 1862. Surrender of the Confederate army in North Carolina, at Bennett's House, near Durham Station, April 26, 1865.

TENNESSEE.

Seceded June 24, 1861.

General Albert Sidney Johnston, killed April 6, 1862, at Battle of Shiloh. February 14-15, 1862, Fort Donelson taken. Naval engagement at Memphis, June 6, 1862; the city was then occupied by the Federals. Battle of Missionary

Ridge, November 23-25, 1863. Second Battle of Fort Donelson, February 3, 1863. Forrest's Raid into Memphis, August 20. 1864. Battle of Lookout Mountain, November 24, 1863. Battle of Murfreesboro, December 31, 1862, General N. B. Forrest, born July 13, 1821, in Bedford County. General N. B. Forrest, died October 29, 1877, in Memphis. Total Number of engagements in State, 298. Sam Davis, noted Confederate scout, hanged by United States troops, November 27, 1863.

MISSOURI.
Seceded October 31, 1861.

Meeting of the State Convention, February 28, 1861. Surrender of Camp Jackson, May 10, 1861. Battle of Boonville, June 16, 1861. Battle of Carthage, July 5, 1861. Battle of Lexington, September 13-20, 1861. Battle of Franklin, November 30, 1864.

KENTUCKY.
Seceded November 20, 1861.

General Albert Sidney Johnston, born February 3, 1803. Jefferson Davis, President of the Confederacy, born in Christian County, June 3, 1808. General John C. Breckinridge, born January 21, 1821, at Lexington. Battles of Lebanon, July 12, 1862, July 5, 1863, and July 30, 1864. Battles of Lexington, October 17, 1862, July 28, 1863, and June 10, 1864. General John Bell Hood, born at Owingsville, June 20, 1831.

NOTES ON THE ILLUSTRATIONS.

"JEFFERSON DAVIS AND HIS CABINET"

This rare picture is reproduced in this work from an engraving in the possession of Mrs. James T. Halsey, the President of the Philadelphia Branch of the " Daughters of the Confederacy,'' through whose courtesy the use of the picture is permitted. In speaking of it she says :

" It is believed that the engraving in my possession, 'Jefferson Davis and His Cabinet,' is the only one in existence, the plate from which this picture was taken having been ordered to be destroyed by the Northern Government during the war. Some months ago I talked with Mrs. Jefferson Davis regarding the picture. She told me that when Mr. Davis was captured and taken a prisoner to Fortress Monroe, she took from its frame this picture, carefully rolled it, and placed it in her trunk. Some time afterwards, when allowed access to her trunks, she found that the picture had been stolen. This picture, now in my possession, Mrs. Davis believes, in all probability, is hers, and the appearance of the picture, both in creases and evident age, bears out this story.''

"MUTE MEMENTOES OF THE RAVAGES OF WAR"

These Goblets, and Candlestick, are the property of Mrs. James T. Halsey, President of the Philadelphia Branch of the " Daughters of the Confederacy.'' Through her courtesy to the author, the photograph was taken, and has been reproduced for this work. Speaking of the objects in the picture, she says :

" During Sherman's march, in one of the many churches burned, or desecrated, by his soldiers, was a church in Georgia. After the soldiers had left, an old negro and his wife found these Goblets battered and broken. They buried them, and feared to reveal their hiding place. Some years ago, they came to Philadelphia to live, and brought their treasures and sold them to a Collector of Antiques, from whom I bought them. On one is a picture of Mount Vernon and Washington's Tomb ; on the other,

Monticello and Jefferson's Old Mill. The Brass Candlestick was given me by a Confederate Soldier. It was picked up on the battlefield near the "Bloody Angle" not far from Fredericksburg, Virginia, where it had been used in looking for the dead and caring for the wounded."

"THE BURIAL OF LATANE"

This beautiful picture is a reproduction of an engraving now in the possession of Mrs. James T. Halsey, of Philadelphia, through whose courtesy it has been reproduced for this work. The picture is not a common one, but presents, in a most vivid way, the pathetic story of the soldier boy who was buried by stranger hands. The interesting poem describing this scene will be found in another part of this work.

"A MEMORIAL OF MARYLAND VALOR"

The monument in Baltimore to Maryland soldiers and sailors who fought for the Confederacy was unveiled May 2, 1903, with impressive ceremonies. This memorial of Confederate valor is the tribute of the Maryland Daughters of the Confederacy to the brave men from this State who, from a sense of patriotic duty, as they understood their duty, upheld the cause of the South in the war between the States. Thirty-eight years have passed since the end of that mighty conflict. The issues which were submitted to the arbitrament of the sword have been settled finally. The South has loyally accepted the verdict, and sectional bitterness is now almost entirely a thing of the past. The Maryland soldiers and sailors in the Confederate service distinguished themselves by courage and devotion. They upheld the best traditions of the State, and were worthy in every way of the beautiful memorial which the Daughters of the Confederacy have reared in their honor. The sculptor embodies in this memorial an admirable idea, namely, that " the South had as good a right as the North to be proud of the valor, fidelity and patience of its soldiers, and that the day would come when the nation as a whole would regard the heroic deeds done by both the Blue and the Gray as a national heritage." That day has already come, as far as broad-minded-men are concerned.—*The Baltimore Sun.*

"THE CAPITOL AT RICHMOND, VIRGINIA"

No point in Richmond is more interesting than the beautiful Capitol Square, on whose grounds are the State Capitol, new State Library Building, Governor's Mansion, Old Bell Tower, the equestrian statue of Washington, and the statues of Clay and "Stonewall" Jackson. Tame squirrels frolic in the trees and on the grass in this Square, and come to the visitor in perfect fearlessness. The railing enclosing the Square is of wrought iron, representing Roman spears.

Mr. Jefferson chose the model for the new Capitol when in Paris, in 1785, selecting an ancient Roman temple, the Maison Caree, at Nismes, France. Its cornerstone was laid August 18, 1785, and the Legislature met in it October 19, 1789, the anniversary of Cornwallis' surrender at Yorktown, eight years previously. This grand old edifice is filled with memories and relics of the past. Here met the Convention of 1788, and the resolutions of 1798-99, by James Madison, truly interpreted the Federal compact. The Convention of 1829-30, including Madison, Monroe, Marshall, and John Randolph, of Roanoke, sat here, and the Universal Suffrage Convention of 1851, and the Secession Convention of 1861 also met here.

The Congress of the Confederate States came here in 1862 from Montgomery, Alabama, and sat until the day in April, 1865, when Lee was turned back at Petersburg, and "all was lost save honor."

"THE WHITE HOUSE OF THE CONFEDERACY"

President Jefferson Davis, of the late Confederate States of America, lived in the imposing building at Clay and Twelfth Streets during the war. The large grounds attached to the house were beautifully laid out and adorned with statuary, flowers and fountains.

Mr. Davis, to whom it had been presented by the city of Richmond on the removal of the seat of government here from Montgomery, Alabama, would only occupy it on the condition of its remaining the property of the city. After Richmond's evacuation, it was taken by the Federal troops for use as a residence and headquarters for the military commanders of Virginia until the army was withdrawn, and the State's representation in the Union restored ; the city then received it back, and it was used a long time as a public school. Lately it has been renovated and restored to its former condition, to be henceforth devoted to the purposes of a Confederate Museum, without any material change from its appearance during its occupancy by President Davis.

"MONUMENT TO THE CONFEDERATE DEAD IN HOLLYWOOD CEMETERY, RICHMOND, VIRGINIA "

A beautiful spot naturally, and made more beautiful by careful attention, is Hollywood Cemetery, in the western part of the city. " Hollywood,'' as it is generally called, was laid off in 1848, and dedicated June 26, 1849, the first interment, however, being made in July, 1848. More than one hundred acres in extent, it is shaded with trees of original forest growth ; and by the hills and valleys, with the streams that ripple through them, we are brought to feel that here, indeed, nature makes beautiful even the sad surroundings of the dead.

In the Soldiers' Section there lie 20,000 of Confederate dead waiting the last trump, and to their memory there has been erected by the efforts of Virginia's noble women, a monument of rough Virginia granite, nearly one hundred feet tall, in the shape of a pyramid, covered with Virginia creeper and ivy. There are appropriate inscriptions on it, and once a year, in May, on " Memorial Day,'' the graves of the soldiers are covered with flowers by loving hands.

"ALABAMA STATE CAPITOL, MONTGOMERY "

Montgomery is rightly called the " Cradle of the Confederacy.'' Here was enacted the stirring scenes which culminated in the formation of the Southern Confederacy. In the Capitol assembled the Convention, January 7, 1861, of which Mr. Yancey was Chairman, when the ordinance of secession was passed by a vote of 61 to 39. In this building Jefferson Davis was inaugurated as the President of the Southern Confederacy, February 8, 1861, when Mr. Yancey uttered the famous words, " The Man and the Hour Have Met.''

Note.—There are 96 pages given to illustrations in this volume which are not included in this folio number. They make a total of 508 pages.

Kind Words of Approval and Endorsement
Selected from the Many
Received from Comrades and Friends

Letter from GENERAL STEPHEN D. LEE
Commander-in-Chief of United Confederate Veterans.

COMMANDING GENERAL'S OFFICE,

COLUMBUS, MISS., FEB. 4, 1904.

REV. H. M. WHARTON, D.D.,

My Dear Comrade:

I desire to commend your effort of saving to us, and to generations yet to come, those old poems and war songs of the Confederacy, and that you will bring out a handsome book, published in the best style, for the sons and daughters of the South, and also of the North. I wish you God speed and success in your effort.

With kind wishes,

Yours truly
Stephen D. Lee
Gen. Comdg. U. C. Veterans

From H. H. CABANISS,
The Well-known Editor of The Augusta Chronicle.

AUGUSTA, GA., FEB. 2, 1904.

Dear Doctor:

Yours of the 27th of Feb. at hand.

I congratulate you on the practical completion of your patriotic work, and trust that it will meet with a generous reception, not only in the South, but in the (late) "enemy's country."

You are to be highly commended for your labor of love in reproducing enduringly the dear old songs of the Confederacy, some of which may otherwise have perished. It was noble in the men and women who wrote them, but not less is the man who preserves them entitled to honor. I remain,

Your sincere friend,

(signature)

Letter from GENERAL CLEMENT A. EVANS,
The Distinguished Commander who Succeeded the Lamented
Stonewall Jackson. General Evans is Himself an Author
of Distinction.

ATLANTA, GA., JAN. 29, 1904.

My Dear Doctor:

Your efforts to give to our Countrymen now living, and to those hereafter born, a permanent book of War Songs and Poems of the Confederacy excites my own interest in a high degree, and not mine only but that of all who have taken thought of the immense value for all time such a collection will be. Productions of that kind brought into being during an era of intense feeling, and during the period following the last Confederate throes, will illustrate the times of the great struggle.

I earnestly trust you will have all the assistance you require to enable you to compile your work in a completeness not heretofore attained. I will gladly comply with your request, and wish you abundant success.

Your friend

Clement A Evans

I am glad to learn from your letter that you contemplate, and are preparing, a work on Confederate War Songs. The trials and troubles, the sorrows and sufferings of the Southern soldier from 1861 to 1865 were great, and so was his splendid courage on many hard-fought fields. It is well to recall those heroic days in song and story, " lest we forget, lest we forget."

From the Honorable W. S. JENNINGS,
Governor of Florida.

STATE OF FLORIDA.

EXECUTIVE DEPARTMENT.

TALLAHASSEE, JANUARY 30, 1904.

My Dear Doctor Wharton :

I have just learned with the keenest pleasure that you are about to publish a compilation of the poems and war songs of the Southern Confederacy. In my mind, this is an undertaking for which there is a real necessity and demand, and which is entered upon none too soon. There can scarcely be a doubt that your work will commend itself strongly to the reading public, and throughout the Sunny South it should receive a general welcome, since from its pages, generations yet to come, will learn to sing and to repeat the war songs and the poetry of the great four years' struggle.

Sincerely yours,

W. S. Jennings

From Mrs. JAMES T. HALSEY,
Honorary President General Dabney H. Maury Chapter U. D. C.,
Philadelphia, and Member of Historical Committee,
Grand Division of Virginia.

PHILADELPHIA, JUNE 4, 1904.

I have read with much pleasure and interest Dr. H. M. Wharton's book, "War Songs and Poems of the Southern Confederacy," and heartily commend it to every Southern home and library. It contains an unusual number of rare and choice poems not to be found in other collections, and Dr. Wharton has done a great service to the Nation as well as to the Southern people in perpetuating them in this form.

Sue Mason Maury Halsey